FINDING MY PEACE

HEALING FROM A DEEPLY UNSTABLE
CHILDHOOD AND A CHAOTIC LIFE

HEIDI HAYDEN

ADVANCE PRAISE

Heidi Hayden's memoir is, by turns, playful, painful and profound. Fittingly, her memories are, in the familiar Marine motto, always faithful — to her truth, her trek, her trials, and her triumphs. This special book illustrates the fundamental truth that the journey forward often best starts by looking back.

— **Jim Flynn**, *Managing Director, Epstein Becker Green*

Finding My Peace is a dig deep story filled with audacious honesty. Embracing the power of truth-telling, Heidi Hayden beautifully shows us that we can overcome incredible suffering by facing our past and shedding the protective cloak that conceals our fears and negative beliefs. This memoir will undoubtedly act as a beacon for the broken, exhausted, and worn-out — those who yearn to turn hopeless, unhappy living into real contented aliveness.

— **Aoifa O'Donnell**, *LCSW, President & CEO of National EAP, Inc.*

For anyone stuck in a place of unhappiness and self-doubt, Finding My Peace will provide inspiration and understanding that meaningful change is possible. Heidi Hayden's deeply personal and unflinchingly honest story is a revelation. It is the brave, beautifully written, and intimate story of one woman's journey that will resonate with others.

— **Lisa Smith**, *author of Girl Walks Out of a Bar*

Heidi Hayden's book is an inspirational account of how seemingly impossible challenges in life are the very lessons we need as we move forward on our path. Always fighting her way forward when most would have given up, Heidi triumphantly transforms her hurt and pain into a peaceful spiritual awakening.

— **Anthony Torres**, *NYPD Detective (ret.), USAF Veteran (ret.), and Non-Violent Communication (NVC) proponent*

*"We can never obtain peace in the outer world
until we make peace with ourselves."*

—— *Dalai Lama*

DEDICATION

To Dad

I love you. While I miss your physical presence, I am so amazed and will always be in awe of the wonderful connection we have now that you are in Spirit. Thank you for giving me your blessing to write this book and guiding and protecting me every step of the way.

To Mighty Heidi

I sincerely thank you for finding the courage to finally move away from the past. You have come to learn and experience that you have never been alone. You truly are one with the Universe. How joyful it is to now exist in this knowledge and in the peace you finally found for yourself!

A THREE PART STORY

CONTENTS

PART THREE
GETTING TO NOW

ACKNOWLEDGMENTS

Writing and publishing this book was not a simple or easy undertaking, and I could not have completed it without the support and guidance of so many.

A huge thank you to my brothers, Keith and Robin, for setting aside their desire to keep the past in the past and willingly reliving difficult memories to help me gain context. Your love and support mean the world!

Thank you to my writing coach, Victoria Fann, for providing a safe space to write and share my stories. Her perceptive feedback and sincere desire to share her extensive knowledge on the craft of writing were essential.

Thank you to Kathy Williams for all she provided both to me and to the final product. Her support, positive energy, sound reasoning, and profound insights were invaluable.

Thank you to David Poppick. I have so much appreciation for him and his enthusiastic and exhaustive review of the final draft, which brought correctness and needed clarity to the book.

Thank you to Mimi for being a sounding board and, at times, my contrarian. I will be eternally grateful for the strength provided and the insistence that this book was important and it needed to be out in the world.

Thank you to Greg Duddy for believing in me, always being there with a listening ear, and for his 'value-added' feedback on the first draft.

Thank you to Jade Weiner for highlighting the potential value of this book and for her thought-provoking and judicious feedback on the first draft.

Thank you to Jim Flynn, Aoifa O'Donnell, Lisa Smith, and Anthony Torres for their unquestioning support and expressive advance praise.

Thank you to those who helped hold me together through the difficult and, at times, painful writing process. But for their support and encouragement, I might have broken. This includes Colleen Wyman, Cindy Batcher, John Nobles, Emi Maresole, Andy Owensby, Lenore Corazza Harrison, Diane Edwards Pirzada, Janine Reithel, and Noreen Heyer.

Much appreciation for those in the various writing critique groups I participated in, including Andy Owensby, Glenna Sears-Brinker, Jewel Ramos, and Marilyn Martin.

Thank you to Andy Owensby for so beautifully capturing 'me' in my author photograph.

Thank you to Regina Lifrieri for her beautiful editing, detailed proof-reading, and enthusiastic feedback.

Thank you to Kate Seger for the gorgeous formatting and her invaluable guidance on self-publishing.

And lastly, a nod to the many others who kept me energized by reaching out to inquire about the book or to express interest in reading it.

INTRODUCTION

Hello and Welcome to *Finding My Peace*!

I did not set out to write a book about my life, yet here it is. It all started with an idea for a small book I referred to as a 'business' book, and then I saw an ad for a class at the local college on how to write your memoir. As the book I had anticipated writing would include stories from my professional career, I thought the course would be helpful. I had never considered myself a writer, and the only things I had written previously had been required assignments for school or work. I was excited to begin the book and was looking forward to the class.

The class began in September 2019, and I quickly found myself writing what I came to call 'healing' stories instead of business content. While some were about happier times, most were based on negative and chaotic periods in my life. As I had done a good deal of work to move away from my past to a place where life felt easy and comfortable, I was a bit surprised. The writing process, as it turned out, led me to more closely examine things I thought I had left in the past, as well as to unearth memories that I had not realized I was holding onto. It felt really good to get these stories out of me as, for the most part, the difficulties associated with them no longer existed inside me once I put them on paper.

While I did write some business stories, after participating in the class and subsequent writing critique groups for about a year, I discovered that I had many more healing stories than those written for the business book. Feeling a nudge from the Universe, I embraced the idea of putting the stories into a book to help me further heal from my past and perhaps help others by providing them hope that finding a path to a peaceful life is possible. I spent many more months working on additional stories that I felt compelled to write, and, in the end, I had 400 pages of text and 66 individual stories, which I then fashioned into the book that awaits you.

This unexpected journey was not easy. In fact, it was excruciating at times. Reliving a painful memory can make it feel like an event is happening all over again. I knew it was important so, even when I sat for hours in front of my computer, having written only a few words, I found a way to stay with it. Having written the stories I felt compelled to release, my insides feel void of the gunk and heaviness that had been lodged inside of me. While I am sure that there is more healing that I need to do, I feel incredibly free from my past now.

* * *

This book is not about everything that has happened in my life but includes stories from early childhood to the present. It does contain some difficult topics, such as sexual abuse. Some names have been changed and, to the best of my ability, I present memories and situations as I recall them. It is possible that as you read, you may find yourself wanting more information or insights on certain people. This could not be helped as it was my wish to keep the focus on me, telling my story, and to do my best not to tell someone else's.

* * *

While each of our lives is unique, we are absolutely the same in that we all face struggles, fears, and difficulties as we navigate our way through life. I hope that the reader takes something from my story that positively impacts their life and — perhaps — assists them in finding their own peace. This is my wish for you.

PART ONE
HOW LIFE WAS

*"Loneliness and the feeling of being unwanted
is the most terrible poverty."*

—— *Mother Teresa*

1

IT DIDN'T HAPPEN

DESPITE THE INTENSE HURT I WAS FEELING FROM BEING betrayed by an internal hiding place revealing one of my secrets, I felt safe in David's arms. The words that tumbled out of my mouth came up from the place where no one, including myself, ever thought they could escape. As they poured out, my brain was having a difficult time processing them. I was sobbing, and my words were garbled as I tried to keep up with how quickly they were coming. David kept asking me to slow down and to repeat what I was saying, but I just couldn't. At some point, resigned to the fact that he was just going to have to let this play out, he sat down next to me. He put his arm around my shoulders, pulled me into his chest, and held me as he continued to listen to the incomprehensible words through my uncontrollable sobbing.

I did not know that this particular memory was inside me, and I also wasn't sure why it chose this particular moment to reveal itself. The words were slowly beginning to take shape in my mind, then somehow made it out of my mouth — and what I was hearing myself say brought back images from long ago as I relived this forgotten and hidden memory.

It was early 1985. I was 19 years old and had been in the U.S. Marine Corps for about a year and a half. I was stationed at Henderson Hall, a small base just outside of Washington, D.C. in Alexandria, Virginia. David and I had been dating for a few months. We had just arrived back at the barracks after a fun night out in Georgetown. As usual, we were out with a group of fellow Marines. There was drinking and much laughter. David and I had a good night. We had not been arguing, not that we ever did, and

I wasn't particularly sad or upset about anything. As we arrived in his room, however, I began to get very emotional. I soon found myself sitting on the narrow, white-tiled shelf-like lip that separated the shower from the toilet in the small, cold, cramped bathroom.

Gradually my sobbing stopped, and the words I had just spoken evaporated into the stuffy feeling of the room. I was numb inside and what had just been revealed exhausted me mentally, physically, and emotionally. When he sensed my body quieting, David gently asked, "Can you repeat what you said? I couldn't understand all that you were saying but, what I do know," he continued, "is that you were saying something about being sexually abused. I want to hear it. It's important."

With fresh tears streaming down my face as both my heart and brain began to comprehend the story more fully, and I also began to realize the weight of it, I took a deep breath and slowly repeated what had just come up from my inner depths. I began to relive, again, that horrible long-lost memory.

I was no more than five-years-old. I was at the little white church down the block from our house on Long Island, New York. Across the four-lane road, within walking distance from the church, was the small local bar where my mother worked as a cocktail waitress. The church is tall and thin across the front, with a long left side enveloped by a row of tall green hedges that have been growing there for years. Four concrete steps lead up to the red door, above which is a steeple holding the bell which rang every day at noon and again at 6 p.m. Behind the church, on the same property, is a one-story ranch-style house. It has a basement and, on the main floor, a kitchen, bathrooms, and a large open area used for church gatherings and other types of meetings.

I don't know how I got there and I am not sure why I was there. It wasn't a Sunday, not that we ever went to Church, and I wasn't with anyone in my family. It was just me and the man who was the caretaker of the church. He had keys to all the doors and buildings. Tall, with a stocky build, he had greasy brown thinning hair. He was someone I knew. He also knew my mother. On this particular day, as I sometimes was, had I been at work with my mother? Had he asked her, or did she suggest that he take me across to the church to show it to me?

As we entered the house behind the church, it was dark, with the only light coming from the brightness of the sun streaming through the front windows. He did not turn on any lights and he didn't say anything. He took me by my hand. I didn't know where we were going. The open kitchen was on the left, and he led me down the hall to a bathroom door just in front of us. He opened the door and led me inside. It was a small bathroom, with familiar one-inch by one-inch ceramic tiles. There were two bathroom stalls straight ahead and two sinks set against the right-hand wall. Continuing to hold my hand, he walked over toward the sinks. He was very tall and wore dark pants, a tan long-sleeve button-down shirt, and a belt. I didn't like being with him. He wasn't very friendly, and he did not smell good. He smelled of cigarette smoke and something else I just couldn't place.

Without saying a word, he undid his belt, and his pants fell past his knees. He pulled down his underwear, exposing his private parts to me, and told me to touch his thing. I didn't want to. It wasn't like I hadn't seen one before. I have older brothers, but his looked gross — and he smelled worse now that his pants were down. It was a stale-like stench. Touching the side of my arm, he again told me to touch him. I did what I was told and, when I did, he placed his right hand on top of my head. I was frightened and wanted to run away, but I couldn't. I didn't know what to do, so I just held onto his thing. It felt weird, and I didn't like touching it. I didn't want to be doing this, but before I could take my hand away, he reached down and put his left hand over mine. He then started to move my hand back and forth. His hand was large and heavy, and it felt clammy and hot as it fully engulfed mine. I felt completely trapped. His right hand was still on top of my head, and, every once in a while, he would pat my head and say, "good girl." I didn't like when he said this. I didn't feel like a good girl.

I began to feel his thing twitching, and then it went from being squishy to hard and grew much bigger. I was so confused by what was happening and more than a little frightened. I wanted desperately to get away and must have made a sudden move because he tightened the hand that was around mine. The hand he had on my head had already begun to feel heavy and, as he shifted it to the back of my head, he forced his thing into my mouth. I tried to move away from him, but he wouldn't let me. His smell was awful, but the taste was much worse — a mixture of smoke and urine. I wanted to throw up. I found myself choking. It was hard to breathe, and even though I wanted to scream, I couldn't. I do not know if I cried. I just wanted it to be over, but he continued to rock me back and forth for a few minutes. It was then that the feeling of choking became my reality, and I thought I was going to die. Liquid filled my mouth and, by then, my jaw hurt so much that I thought maybe it was blood — although, somehow, I knew it wasn't. At the same time, I was choking while my body convulsed, trying to vomit. Whatever was in my mouth needed to come out. His thing finally became softer, and his grip on my head eased.

It was only then that I was able to back away from him while I threw up at his feet.

From the moment he first moved his hand to the back of my head to the moment I finally stepped away from him, I was not in my body. I had ascended upward, becoming a witness to what was happening to me. I was above the bathroom door, in the corner where the ceiling and the two side walls converged. It was from this vantage point, high above the horrifying event, that I watched my abuser commit these acts against me. I knew that it was happening to me, but it somehow felt like it wasn't as bad watching it from up here. It felt like I was watching a movie. The moment I was able to get away was the moment when the essence of me merged back into my physical body. Perhaps this was also the moment that the memory buried itself deep down in my innermost hiding place.

Until the evening it finally came up and out of me, my conscious brain had no recollection of this event. When it did finally surface, however, I did not doubt that it had happened. The memory and the feelings were too vivid, and the feelings in my body as I recalled what had happened brought me right back there. I was again experiencing all that I had endured so long ago, including the thought that I was going to die. If it hadn't happened to me, I would never have believed that one could repress such a significant and horrific memory. I would also not have thought that an out-of-body experience was possible, but it was. These things happened to me.

When I finished telling David the story again, I knew that what had just bubbled up from inside of me was huge, and, as time went on, it lingered in my mind disrupting my thoughts with questions and the desire to understand. I spoke with David about what I was thinking on a few occasions, and he encouraged me to go speak with someone that could help me.

* * *

I WASN'T GOOD AT CONFIDING IN OR TRUSTING PEOPLE, SO IT took more than a year before I finally sought the assistance of the Base Chaplain. The Chaplain and I worked in the same building, and I knew him to be a kind and caring individual. Had I not already known him, I am sure I would not have gone to see him. When I did go to speak with him, I told him the story. He was so compassionate and comforting. He made me feel safe and like I had made the right decision in seeking his help. He said he wanted to assist me, and while there was no one on the base where I was currently stationed that could assist with this particular issue, he had the authority to find me an off-base counseling resource. I left his office feeling a bit better for having trusted him and hoped that I would get whatever assistance I needed.

The Chaplain came back to me a few days later and told me that he had found someone. He explained that the man was a doctor of psychiatry and that, if I wanted to, he could arrange a meeting with him. While I had agreed to have him find me this resource, I was now second-guessing it. I wasn't sure I wanted to revisit the story, let alone tell it to someone I didn't know. In talking through my apprehension with him, the Chaplain helped me understand that it would be best for me to have the meeting. He said it would help me find answers and to begin the process of putting this behind me. He helped me find the courage to say yes, especially after telling me that he would be with me if I wanted him there. Once I knew that he was willing to be there, I agreed and thanked him for his help.

I was nervous on the day of the meeting, but glad that I had let the Chaplain convince me to have it. I had never asked for this type of help before, and it had taken a lot for me to do so. As the memory and feelings were persisting, I knew I had no choice.

The meeting was held in the Chaplain's office, which was warm and inviting with its comfortable chairs and dark wood paneling. The therapist was already there when I arrived. The Chaplain invited me to sit down in a chair across from them and to share my story. I did as I was asked and did so willingly. I told this man, a doctor but still a stranger, the entire story. I told him about it being a repressed memory. I told him that I had watched much of the event as I was floating up in the corner. I told him how the man smelled. I told him what the man had done to me.

The therapist sat there quietly, listening to all I had to say, never interrupting, seeming to take what I said as the truth. Once I finished, he began to speak. He told me about his expertise and his background, speaking in a soft, informed, informative, and authoritative way. He thanked me for sharing my story with him but went on to say that while people do repress memories, it is exceedingly rare. He also told me that when people recall memories, they don't experience them from an out-of-body perspective, which indicated that this event had not occurred. This, he wanted me to know, was good news as it would be just like getting over a bad dream.

I sat there stunned. I could not believe what I was hearing. He was telling me that it didn't happen. I started crying and pleaded with him to understand, repeatedly, that I knew it had happened. No, he said calmly, it didn't. I looked to the Chaplain for support, but realized he was no longer on my side. He had sided with the therapist. Once I understood this, I went from being upset and crying to extremely angry and defensive. It was so rare for me to trust anyone in authority, and now I knew why ... people couldn't be trusted.

After the Chaplain dismissed the therapist, he said he had done what he could to help me and was glad to find out that it was just a bad dream. "Would you like to schedule time for us to meet and talk through why you might think that something like what you described had happened to you?" the Chaplain asked. I got up out of my chair, not answering his question, and, without saying a word, walked out of his office. I knew I was expected to answer his question and wait to be dismissed as he was the Chaplain and a military officer. I also knew I was being disrespectful and that I could be disciplined. I didn't care. I couldn't help myself.

I was so confused and immediately started questioning myself. I had been so certain that this event had happened, but did I make it up? I must have. I was brought up to not question authority. I was now in the military, and one certainly didn't question authority here. I had found my voice to speak up when I looked to get myself some help, but the entire experience was just reinforcing that I should have kept quiet.

I thought about that meeting over and over for many weeks, and after much internal debate, I decided that I must have been wrong, and they must be right given their experience and authority. I again did what I had repeatedly learned to do throughout my life; I stuffed the feelings and difficulties I was having deep down inside myself and ignored them from that moment on.

Sadly, I did not get the help or support that I so needed. It would take me several decades to learn that people do repress memories and have out-of-body experiences. It happens during events that are particularly traumatic or stressful, and it is caused by fear and the need to disassociate from what is happening to survive it.

2

PREDICTABLY
UNPREDICTABLE

DURING HIGH SCHOOL, I DIDN'T HAVE A SPECIFIC DIRECTION
or goal for after graduation. But, unbeknownst to me at the time, my path
to joining the military started one morning in the fall of my senior year. As
I sat in my homeroom class, watching the morning announcements given
by the audio-visual students on the closed-circuit TV, one announcement
caught my attention. It was about an opportunity to take a special test that
was not mandatory but designed to tell you what career you might be good
at. That was not what interested me, though, as I expected the results
would tell me what I already knew — which was that I would spend my
working years doing clerical or secretarial type work. What interested me
about taking the test was getting out of class for two and a half hours.
Count me in. Anything to get out of class.

I took the exam, and a few weeks later, I was invited to the library to
review the results. This was when I received a huge surprise. In the library,
waiting for all of us to arrive, was a small group of individuals. They were
all dressed in military uniforms. They were military recruiters. "What is this
about?" I inquired of the teacher standing at the library door welcoming us.

As it turned out, I did not listen very well when the test was
announced. I had taken the test that one is required to take if one wants to
join the military. It is an aptitude test that helps place an individual into an
appropriate military field that aligns with their skills and aptitude. This was
not the first time I had not fully listened to the details of something, and it
got me in over my head, but what could I do? The military was not on my
list of career possibilities ... not that I had any such list. The recruiters

expected to meet with each of us and, while I did not want to meet with them, as usual, I did what I was expected to do.

As I left the library, I was shaking my head, saying to myself, "Me, join the military? No way am I going to do that!"

I had a few family members who had served. My dad and my oldest brother, Ronnie Bill, had served in the Navy, and Chris, my youngest brother, was currently serving. My dad's second wife, Joan, the woman who raised me and was the closest thing I ever had to a mother, had been a reserve officer in the Marine Corps. But me? This was not something I could do. I was sure I would not be able to do it. I would get yelled at. It would be hard. I wouldn't be able to meet their high standards. The military was for people who were better than me. On and on, my thoughts went about how I would not and could not join the military. It was hard to put them out of my head as the recruiters were relentless. They kept in constant contact, including regularly stopping by the school to touch base.

One day I was walking along the fence by the school parking lot and thought, that fence makes this place look like a prison. Then, I thought of the military and said to myself, "Yup, that is what it would feel like in the military. It would feel like prison. Nope. Not going to join. That is just not for me."

My decision to join the military was gradual and only developed into a yes as the realization settled in that there weren't many other viable or appealing options. College was out, as there was no money to send me, and staying at home and getting a job didn't seem right as I wasn't comfortable there. One positive was that I grew up in a very organized and regimented household and was used to structure and process. This would certainly help with adapting to military life, I thought.

What eventually turned me was when I said to myself, "Well, how bad could it be? It will get me away from home. They will feed and clothe me, and how much trouble could I possibly get into in the military?" That was it. I was going to join.

I still needed to decide which branch. Although I figured it was probably the easiest, the Army was out. I had no interest in joining the Air Force or the Coast Guard, as their focus was narrower than others. Maybe the Navy, I thought? No, I don't like their white bell-bottom pants with the crisply ironed inward seam. That leaves the Marines. What am I, crazy? That's the hardest one! Why would I even consider doing that? I was five feet two inches and 95 pounds soaking wet. How could I even make it through Bootcamp?

Given my lack of confidence in myself, I am not sure where I found the courage to call the Marine recruiter and tell him that I wanted to join, but I did. As I was not yet eighteen, I would need a parent's signature. This would be the hard part; telling my dad about my decision to join up and asking him if he would sign the papers. I had not even told him that I was considering this option, but there I was, in January 1983 — a few months before my high school graduation — calling my dad at work to tell him that there was something I needed to speak with him about when he arrived home. I did not tell him what it was. Had I not agreed when the persistent recruiter said he could come to my house that night at 7 p.m., I am sure I would have procrastinated and pushed off the conversation.

After serving four years in the Navy following college, my dad earned a master's degree by going to night school, then spent his career teaching math to junior high school students. He never missed a day of work. Dad was smart, regimented, very opinionated, and set in his thoughts and ways. With his background, one might have expected that he would have been talking with me about going to college, but he had not been. It was never discussed, and I don't recall any discussions about the future. What my father did say, on many occasions, was that I could be anything I wanted to be. As I had just this statement to go on, I was going into this conversation with no guidance, which, for me, meant no reassurance as to how he would react.

* * *

I WAITED NERVOUSLY FOR MY DAD TO ARRIVE HOME TO TELL him that his baby girl, his only girl and youngest child, wanted to join the U.S. Marine Corps. When he arrived, we sat down in the small living room of our two-bedroom one-story house. That is where all the serious conversations took place. I was on the couch, with its big white flowers on a muted orange background and heavy dark wood arms, which sat underneath the front window. Dad sat in his chair to the left of me, and his girlfriend, Ann, sat across the way from both of us.

I was unsure how to start the conversation, but I opened my mouth and began my short statement. I had learned during my childhood that it was best to initially provide as little information as possible and just allow questions to be asked. As I spoke, my dad sat there calmly, listening to everything I said. He did not interrupt. He did not say a word, and his face did not provide any clues about what he was thinking. He didn't look mad, nor did he look happy, but, as always, he appeared interested in what I was saying. The last thing I said was, "Oh, and dad, the recruiter is coming here at 7 p.m. to have you sign the papers." I ended there. I didn't even ask him if he was okay with all I said. I just stopped talking.

I could never predict what my father would say on any given day about any given subject, so it was hard for me to anticipate his response to this. I did, however, expect a yes or no answer. That is not what I got. My father did not disappoint in his unpredictability.

The first words he said were, "Why don't you become a shrimper?" I might have thought this a bizarre and random thing to say had the man who lived across the canal from us not earned his living catching and selling shrimp. My dad had commented in the past about this, admiring the fact that he left around 5:00 a.m., was back by 10:00 a.m., and that he seemed to make a decent wage. I guess my dad thought this would be an easier way for me to make a living versus the more difficult route of going into the military.

"Ummmm ..." I said, "no thanks."

My dad proceeded to ask me a few additional questions like, "Why don't you go to college? Why don't you work as a waitress? Why don't you take a year off? Why don't you go to a trade school?"

This went on for only three or four minutes. He wasn't angry, and he didn't look or sound disappointed. He just asked these questions in a very straightforward quizzical way. To each suggested alternative, I responded no, and after those few short minutes, he simply said, "Okay, if you want to join the Marine Corps, I'll sign the papers." That was it. No big discussion. No talking me out of it. No asking me why not the other branches. There was not even a discussion about if I understood what it would be like in the military.

I think that a part of me was counting on my dad to convince me not to join or to maybe refuse to sign the papers until I could sign them myself at age eighteen. Even while watching him sign the papers, I found myself thinking that my dad was unpredictable, even though he was being true to his word. Dad had always told me I could do anything I wanted — and when I told him what I wanted to do, that was good enough for him.

* * *

WHILE MY DAD COULD BE UNPREDICTABLE, HE WAS ALSO "predictably predictable" in certain instances, especially when it related to personal responsibility or fulfilling a commitment. Early in my childhood, dad had instilled in me that if you said you were going to do something, you were expected to do it, as was the case when a college reached out to offer me a music scholarship.

While I had started playing an instrument in the fall of second grade, when all students were provided an opportunity to do so, I never considered music as a career. On the day we selected the instruments we would play, we were brought down to the cafeteria, which was also the auditorium, where the stage was. We were greeted by the school music teachers who asked us to come up on stage, take a seat, and then they began talking about the different instruments found in an orchestra or a concert band. The orchestra was mostly made up of string instruments, while the band had several categories, including brass, woodwind, and percussion. They showed us each of the instruments and told us a little bit about them. We were then asked to consider all that we had heard and write down on the piece of paper we were given the instrument we most wanted to play. As only a certain number of students would be able to play each one, we were also told to write down a second choice in case our first choice wasn't available.

I quickly decided that I wanted to play the flute. It seemed like it would be fun to play. My youngest brother, Chris, who was two years ahead of me in school, was in the orchestra and played the cello. Playing the flute meant that I would be different as I would be in the band. That was important to me. The biggest selling point, however, was that the case the flute came in was small, so it would be easy to carry back and forth to school. After watching my brother lug his cello to and from school, I wanted to make a smart decision. I wrote the flute down, and I didn't consider any other instrument.

I sat there, patiently waiting until it was my turn to tell the teacher the instrument I had selected. I was very excited, but only until this girl Linda sitting right next to me looked at my paper and saw what I had written. She then wrote down the flute as well. I didn't like that she had copied from me and, as she was always picking on me because she was much bigger than me. I didn't want to spend time with her. I didn't tell Linda this, of course. Thankfully, she was called on first, and when she said flute, the teacher said that she could go ahead and learn to play that. I was so mad. Why couldn't she have picked her own instrument?!

It was my turn next, and when the teacher turned to me, I hid my paper under my leg and told her that I wasn't sure which instrument I wanted to play. She was my brother's teacher, and as most kids wanted to be in the band, few kids were choosing string instruments. The teacher asked me a few questions, and it was then decided that I would play the violin. That was it. I would be a violinist.

Learning to read music and playing the violin came easily to me. It was helpful that I also had private weekly lessons with a music teacher for several years in addition to lessons during school. By the time I was in junior high school, I was first chair in the orchestra, which means I sat in the seat immediately to the left of the conductor and closest to the audience. This placement is an indication that I was deemed to be the strongest violin player.

For several years, I was invited to participate in the Suffolk County Music Educators' Association (SCMEA) annual county-wide orchestra festival and compete against other violin players in the county. I was proud to have been selected for the orchestra and for having been asked to compete, but it did add a good deal of additional stress on me as much more practice was needed to learn several new pieces of music on top of the pieces I was required to learn for the school orchestra. I can't say I particularly liked participating, but I found satisfaction with having been selected and seeing my superior scores.

While living on Long Island, the school district that I attended was very large. My ninth grade class had 1,500 kids, which was drastically different from what I experienced when I moved to Fort Myers, Florida, at the end of that year. My new high school had 1,500 students in total. Another significant difference I encountered at my new school was in connection with the orchestra. To begin, it was much smaller than the one I had played in while living in New York, as there weren't many kids in the school. Also, unlike New York, where kids began playing an instrument in second grade, in Florida, they began in the seventh grade. Those five additional years of playing set me far ahead of the others in terms of skill, so much so that I didn't think I wanted to stay in it. I realized how nice everyone was, however, and I also felt a good deal of comfort from being around something so familiar to me as I worked to adapt to being away from all my friends and living in a new state. I continued to play throughout high school, but my skill level never improved above where it was when I arrived in Florida despite the additional years of playing.

While I liked playing the violin, I wouldn't say that it was my passion.

Before moving to Florida, playing an instrument meant practicing at home for 30 minutes each day, and for most of the time I played, I viewed this as a chore. Just another task or homework assignment that had to be done. I had committed to playing, and, as I was expected to do, I took it seriously.

* * *

MY DAD'S EXPECTATION OF FOLLOWING THROUGH ON commitments was on full display a few months after he had signed the papers allowing me to join the military. Upon arriving home one day that spring, my dad told me that I had received a call from a local community college. "What did they want?" I asked.

He told me, "They said that they had heard about your superior violin skills and wanted to speak with you about a scholarship."

"Wow, really?" I asked with surprise. "That would be great. Where's the information so I can call them back?" I inquired.

"I didn't take it down," he said.

"Why not?" I questioned.

"You decided to join the Marine Corps, so I told them that you were all set and wouldn't be interested in the scholarship."

That was it. There was no further discussion. While I certainly had never intended to continue playing the violin beyond graduation, I could not help but think that this was a lost opportunity. I came to call my decision to join the military the single best decision of my life. I have, however, periodically wondered how different my life might have been if only I had the chance to speak with the college.

3
ARRIVING AT
BOOTCAMP

My **ENLISTMENT DATE** IN THE
United States Marine Corps was set for
September 27, 1983, four months after
graduating from high school. I requested
this date as I thought this extra time
would provide me an opportunity to get
in shape, and, let me be honest, Bootcamp at the hottest time of the year
didn't seem like a good idea. I also know
I requested a date so far removed from
my graduation date, because I was
afraid. I spent my childhood trying to
stay out of trouble. I was a nervous child
who worried about everything and
lacked self-confidence. Given these
traits, I did not think I would even make
it through.

I arrived for Bootcamp on Parris Island, South Carolina, at 4 a.m. on
September 28. I was exhausted and more than a little apprehensive about
what lay ahead. My journey had started some nineteen hours earlier when I
boarded a Greyhound bus in Fort Myers and headed for the military enlistment processing center in Miami.

There were eight of us heading to Bootcamp from this processing
center. After the oath of enlistment, where we swore to uphold the Consti-

tution of the United States, the Marine who had administered the oath said, "Welcome to the Corps." Despite our nervousness, we all smiled with pride. After we completed the rest of the intake process, we were driven to the airport, and the Marines that had accompanied us shook our hands and wished us well.

We then began what I would come to call 'hurry up and wait' as we continued our long day's journey to Bootcamp. We arrived at the airport just in time for our short flight to Orlando, then endured a long six-hour layover before our short 1 a.m. flight to Charleston. I was more than a little weary when I arrived, which was counter to the wide-awake and surprisingly friendly Marines who greeted us. A big comfortable tour-type bus took us to a building not too far from the airport. We were told we would be waiting on the arrival of additional recruits. During the ride, the lights were on, and the Marines walked up and down the aisle chatting with us. If it weren't for the anxiousness that was continuing to build inside of me, I would have considered it a relaxing ride.

A hot dinner awaited us. "Better eat up while you can," one of the Marines said. "I am not sure when you will get chow next." The atmosphere was casual and laid-back, and the Marines did not appear to be in a hurry as we waited another hour or so for the additional recruits to arrive.

It was about 3 a.m. when we saw buses arriving. These were not the luxury buses we had been on earlier. These were like school buses but, not surprising, they were green. They looked old and, upon sitting down, felt that way too. The seats were hard and extremely uncomfortable. If they had ever had springs, they had long since worn out.

We were asked to board and take the first open seat. As the line began to form, I recalled the advice my oldest brother, Ronnie Bill, had given me a few weeks before. He had served in the Navy and told me it was important that I remember to never be first, never be last, and never volunteer. Happy to take this experienced advice, I purposely placed myself in the middle of the line. The first bus finished filling up with the person directly in front of me, and I became the first person to board the second bus. I sat, as instructed, in the first empty seat, which, of course, was the front seat. A male recruit sat down next to me. The two Marines who would accompany us to Parris Island sat together in the front seat across the aisle, and the rest of the bus filled.

As we began the one-hour journey into the night, a hush came over the bus. Everyone became lost in their own thoughts and fears of what awaited us. The lights on the bus were dimmed, and the Marines escorting us sat quietly. Exhausted from what was already an exceptionally long day, I fell asleep like many of the other recruits. When the bus stopped at the entrance to Parris Island, the palpable vibration of the rising tension and the chatter of those around me caused me to wake up. I, for one, sat up a little straighter in my seat as we came onto the base.

A few minutes later, the bus stopped again. We had arrived at a large, imposing building with several Marines standing outside of it. This was the men's training command. The two Marines that had been sitting across the aisle got up quietly and walked off. They never said a word, and they never looked back. A nanosecond later, a large, strong-looking male Marine came onto the bus. It was our first encounter with a Drill Instructor, and it did not disappoint.

After allowing his presence to be felt, he shouted, "All you men, get off the bus. GET. OFF. THE. BUS!" It was loud and startling. After the men ran off, the two Marines got back on and sat down. They stared straight ahead, still not saying a word. The bus immediately began to move. It was completely silent as we headed toward the women's training command where, I assumed, our welcome would be just like the men's. At this moment, I began to panic as it dawned on me that I was now all alone in the front seat. I would be first off the bus. What was I supposed to do when I got off? What had the first male done? I couldn't remember. Ugh. I had tried to follow my brother's advice, but, not surprisingly, I had failed.

These and other thoughts continued to swirl in my head until the bus stopped, and my Bootcamp experience began. I heard the female Drill Instructor before I saw her, and I immediately did so when she commanded us to get off the bus in a very loud, authoritative, and not-so-pleasant way. I was, of course, first off. I do not remember hearing anything about what I should do once I got off, so I just kept walking straight ahead. That is until I was stopped dead in my tracks by a female Drill Instructor. She had come out of nowhere and planted herself in front of me. She was just a few inches from my face. I can still recall what her face looked like as her mouth yelled at me. It was taut and tan ... and looked incredibly angry.

"Why are you not on the yellow footprints?" she demanded.

What yellow footprints? I was thinking, just as she took hold of my shoulders and turned me around where, much to my surprise and embarrassment, I saw the big yellow footprints upon which all my fellow female recruits were now standing. Not an illustrious start to my Bootcamp experience.

After a grueling eight-and-a-half-weeks, I graduated on December 1, 1983. I finished fourth in my Company, narrowly missing a meritorious promotion to the next rank, which was given to the top three graduates. *If you had just tried a little bit harder*, I heard my Inner Critic say when the results were posted, *you'd have been on that list*. My Inner Critic had been with me since early childhood and was constantly talking at me. It was this voice that prompted me to berate myself for coming in fourth. What I did not do, which was very typical of me, was praise myself for what I had accomplished.

As I expected it would, the test I had taken in high school showed an aptitude toward business and administrative work, so I chose the Military Occupational Specialty (MOS) of an 0151. My job in the Corps would be that of an administrative clerk and, after a few weeks of leave, I reported to Camp Johnson, a small base attached to Camp Lejeune near the east coast of North Carolina, for admin school. I found the school quite easy, given my enhanced typing and administrative skills learned during many business classes in high school.

I was handpicked for my next assignment and transferred to Henderson Hall, just up the street from the Pentagon in Alexandria, Virginia. I was to work as an administrative clerk at Headquarters Marine Corps located, at that time, just across the street from the base in the Navy Annex for the department which assigned Marines with the rank of Colonel to their duty stations. I loved my new duty station and the work I was doing. The people I worked with were great. I met many high-ranking Marine officers, and my work was important.

4

DAVID, THE BEGINNING

I HAD BEEN IN THE MARINE CORPS JUST OVER A YEAR WHEN I met David. It was his laugh that drew my attention first. It was a bit louder than the voices around him, low in tone and more of a chuckle than a laugh. David was around 5'7" with a stocky build, brown eyes and brown hair. In line with military standards, his hair was cut short on the sides and not too long on top. David had lots of energy and was comfortable sharing his thoughts and opinions with others. David was part of the large crowd that I hung out with at places like the Enlisted Club, the on-base pool, and in Georgetown when we would all go off base to party. He seemed to be well-liked. David was a cook, and as his assignment was supervisor of the chow hall, I saw him two or three times a day for meals.

We began dating in late 1984, bonding over our stories of difficult childhoods. I was attracted to him and appreciated the little things that he did for me, like when he decorated my barracks room on New Year's Eve. He had duty watch until midnight, so we were not able to go off the base with everyone else to celebrate. He wanted to  do something nice for me while I waited for him. I felt safe with David, supported by the fact that I retreated into his arms the night the repressed memory of sexual abuse as a child surfaced. I will always appreciate how gentle and caring he was during and after this dark and difficult discovery.

The spring after we met, David received transfer orders and was to leave in mid-July for a base in Tustin, California. As his departure came closer, I realized that I had become attached to him. David leaving was difficult, and I was happy to wait by the phone and talk with him when he called every few days. We had never discussed a future together until one Sunday morning, about a month after his departure, when he called.

"Heidi," he said. "I miss you and I can't live without you. Will you marry me?"

"Yes," I said right then and there. We were both extremely excited, and he promised he would come back east as soon as possible, and we would marry.

I didn't realize it would happen so quickly, but there he was calling me 24-hours later to tell me that he had been authorized a 72-hour pass starting this Thursday. The plan was that he would fly to D.C. on Thursday, we would marry on Friday, August 23, 1985, and then he would fly back to his base on Saturday. That was it. We were getting married in four days!

I knew I needed to tell my dad and Ann, but it took me another day to get up the nerve to call them, so they only had 3-days' notice of my upcoming nuptials. When I called, I was expecting to be challenged on why I thought I wanted to do this and told that perhaps it would be best to wait. None of what I thought might happen did. They never questioned what I said I was going to do. They accepted it without discussion, closed their business for a few days, and made the drive to be there.

The wedding was held on a beautiful summer day in late August in the small base chapel, and, as we were married, I was happy knowing that I was now someone's wife, as this meant I was no longer the unlovable person that I thought I was. I was going to have the life that I thought I should have. A life in which I would be protected and supported. We were separated again for a few months as I waited for my transfer to be approved. How exciting it was to pick him up from the airport in November when he came east to collect me. We made a stop down in Florida to see our parents and then had an adventure driving out to California to begin our life together.

I was excited to be married and sincerely expected that we would settle comfortably and easily into the flow of married life. My Prince Charming had come to rescue me, telling me that he could not live without me, and he had already shown me that he would support me and be there when I needed him. I had a fairy tale vision in my head, like Cinderella, of what married life should be like, and this vision was not at all what I had experienced growing up.

* * *

As was a consistent theme for me, life did not calm down as I expected. Instead, it became difficult and confusing. It seemed my fairy tale was not meant to be. Not long after I arrived in California, David began making excuses to not be at home. His usual excuse was that he was working. He also went out with his friends, and I was not permitted to go with him. He did go out without me when we were in D.C., but I thought it would be different now. I was beginning to understand that David drank a lot and, when we were together, he was always drunk.

When we hung with the group in D.C., I had thought of him as fun-loving. He was always laughing. In this environment, however, I found David to be an excessive drinker, intolerant of others' views, distant from me and others, and who acted as if he were superior to everyone. The few friends I had made did not like getting together when he would be included as they found him abrasive, intrusive, and a know-it-all. Once, when we were at a girlfriend's house for dinner, David — without being asked to help — went into the kitchen while dinner was being prepared and began tasting and seasoning the food. Understandably, my girlfriend was upset, found his behavior odd and took it as an insult.

During the fourteen months that we were together in California, David's regular absence from our home and his coming home drunk were both constant topics of our frequent arguments. I hated that he wasn't home, and I didn't like that he was out without me. I also knew he was drinking and driving. We lived in on-base housing, so we had to engage with the military police at the gate to gain entry to the base. As I so desperately wanted to control David's behavior, I did threaten on a couple of occasions to call the base police to tell them to look for his vehicle. If he were caught drinking and driving, there would be severe consequences from the military. I knew this and, while I was mad enough to want to, I never did rat him out.

David was turning out differently from the person I thought I had married. This was not the same man who had been so attentive to me back in D.C. I was upset and feeling quite unsettled. I had tied my self-worth to my marriage, and, given all that was happening, I was feeling quite worthless. I was feeling abandoned and helpless.

It was impossible trying to deal with David, and it didn't help that I didn't feel safe with him anymore. He didn't hit me, but his behavior was erratic and counter to what I had seen before we married. I tried to talk to him, but he shut me out and wouldn't participate. I tried talking, crying, and screaming at him, but these didn't work either, no matter how hard I tried to get through to him. All my efforts with David were failures, and I couldn't control what he was doing, so I began to employ the coping skills I had learned as a child. I would get defensive and angry but didn't show that to him or anyone else. I withdrew from him yet tried to give the sense that all was okay. I told myself that it was my fault, and I didn't hesitate to believe it.

On top of my mind spinning about all that I had, could, or should have done, I was also trying to deal with my Inner Critic. As he had done all my life, he took full advantage of my depressed state and let me know that it was, in fact, all my fault. He drilled it into my head that my marriage was failing because I was not the loveable person I wanted David to think I was. Who did I think I was, believing I deserved a fairy tale life? My Inner Critic was relentless, as always. I found him and the situation with David exhausting and humiliating. Of course, my marriage wasn't going to work out, I thought. I had brought the knowledge with me from childhood that I was not good enough for someone to stay with. People always leave.

David chose to cope with the difficulties we were having by leaving me in California just after the first of the year in 1987, staying with his parents while serving on recruiter duty in his hometown of Melbourne, Florida, before being transferred overseas in July. He never did return to California or me.

*　*　*

WHEN I MOVED BACK TO FLORIDA AFTER MY DISCHARGE IN September 1987, I was 22. I knew we would be divorcing but did not know when as he was now out of the country. To my great surprise, David contacted me at Thanksgiving to tell me that he was back in Florida for a few weeks of leave. He showed no interest in getting back together, and as I had already moved past our marriage, I told him that we should proceed with a divorce. He agreed, so I went down to the courthouse the following week. Given that we had no children and had already amicably split our marital assets, it turned out to be a simple process. I submitted the required paperwork and, explaining to the clerk that David would soon be heading back to his overseas duty station, the clerk was able to get the judge to waive the usual waiting period. Our divorce request would be heard at the end of that week. I contacted David, who was fine with this unexpected news.

While I didn't need him to, I readily agreed when my dad offered to come with me to the courthouse. As I noticed once I became an adult, this gesture was typical of my dad, who wanted to be supportive when and where he could. Parking near the courts in downtown Fort Myers could be difficult. Spots were hard to find, and most had a coin meter with a 2-hour parking maximum. Having dad there would be helpful as I wouldn't need to worry if I took a metered spot.

Dad and I arrived early, ahead of David. David was staying with his parents, who lived four hours away and, as he planned to drive roundtrip the same day, he told me his mother was coming with him to share the driving. It had been almost eleven months since I last saw David, so seeing him was awkward. I had only met David's mother on a couple of occasions, and I had never felt particularly comfortable around her, so, given this and the circumstances of this meeting, seeing her was also awkward. After waiting for them in the lobby, we went together to find the courtroom where we were told to report. The doors had not yet opened, and we stood in the corridor with the others who were also waiting.

As I expected he would, my dad had greeted David and his mother warmly and was now making idle chit-chat. He talked about the weather and asked about the drive. He talked about anything but the divorce, and I was grateful to have him with me. The doors opened a short while later. It was a typical courtroom with rows on either side and a bench up front and center. David and his mother went into a row on the right, and my dad and I moved into the row immediately behind them. A sheriff's deputy announced that the judge would be out in a little while and asked everyone that was there to appear before them to stay in the courtroom until called. He then told us that we could talk quietly while we waited.

As I sat there, my mind was working overtime. I felt sad about my marriage failing. Frustrated and let down over what could have been and wasn't. Why had David not fought to keep me? Why had he treated me the way that he had? I was thinking about how difficult it was to be here with him and his mother, and grateful that they were sitting in front of me and not beside or behind me. I also wondered how long it would be before the judge began and then, once the process started, how long before our case was called. As always, I was worrying and wondering about everything.

Sensing my tension, dad reached over and squeezed my hand, bringing me a sense of comfort. He then leaned over, pointing to his watch, and said, "I should go down and feed the meter so I can get back before you're called." I knew it was well ahead of the 2-hour time limit, but this was so like my dad. He would never wait until the last minute to complete something that had to be done. Before he got up from his seat, he leaned forward, asking if David had also parked in a metered spot, and, if so, he said he would be happy to take care of their car as well. As they had, he collected the information on their car and where it was parked and left the courtroom. I sat there alone, feeling uneasy and staring at the back of the heads of David and his mother.

Dad had only been gone a short while when the judge appeared. After settling in, he said he was ready for the first case. David and I were called forward first. The judge began by thanking both of us for our service and confirmed for the record that he had waived the waiting period in light of David's upcoming return to his overseas duty station. He reviewed the paperwork to be sure it was in order and then asked both of us to confirm that what was listed in the papers was correct. Once we both confirmed that it was, he told us that he was granting the divorce and that we would receive a copy of the final paperwork in the mail. That was it. It took three minutes. David and I walked out of the courtroom, single people once again, with his mother trailing behind.

My dad was not back yet, so we waited for him in the hallway. As we stood there in uncomfortable silence, David's mother decided that this was the time that she should say something. As she began, it was obvious that David had told her a bunch of lies about me and the reasons we were getting divorced. She started by saying that this was certainly a sad day and one which I should feel particularly ashamed about because it was my fault that David and I had married in the first place.

She went on to say, "Here was my son, just minding his own business, when you called to say that you couldn't live without him and asking him to marry you. He is a kind person, so he said yes. He spent the last couple of years trying to make you happy, but, in return, all he got was a home that was so unbearable to live in that he had to flee to my home to get away from you."

I was stunned. I glanced up at David. He was looking at the ground. David knew that all she was saying was untrue, but I wasn't too surprised as he had lied to me throughout our relationship. I was, however, very hurt. I didn't have it in me to speak up for myself to correct her version of events, and, as I felt a deep sense of failure, I didn't say a word.

Thankfully, it wasn't too long before my dad appeared. He was, of course, surprised to see us outside the courtroom, so I explained that we had been called first and that it had only taken a few minutes. We all walked toward the exit and, once outside, bid a stiff goodbye as they went to the left towards their car, and dad and I turned to the right.

"How did it go?" Dad asked after we were out of earshot of them.

"Okay," I said. "But wait until I tell you what his mother said to me." I was feeling a bit off balance and still digesting it even as I repeated her words.

When I finished telling him, my dad, predictably unpredictable, simply said, "Well, if I had known she was going to be like that, I would have had her go down and feed the meters." I busted out laughing as he hugged me around the shoulders.

* * *

I KNEW THAT OUR RELATIONSHIP HAD JUST CHANGED. TODAY was a difficult day. I was dealing with grown-up things, and my dad had been there supporting me the entire way. I felt like we both had a new view of our relationship and felt, at that moment, that we were becoming friends and were on more equal footing than we had ever been. This positive change in our relationship, I was sure, had to do with my recognition that despite my desire to have had a successful marriage, it didn't turn out that way, and I know that this failure changed me. Perhaps, my dad had also experienced this feeling in his own life, and it had impacted him in ways I did not understand.

Maybe this is what naturally happens between a parent and a child as the child grows, but I certainly never expected it, given how things were when I was young. I was an obedient and quiet child growing up, always looking to do what was expected to avoid any adverse consequences or knowing that I was in trouble for something. I didn't talk much unless I was spoken to first, and I certainly didn't have open dialogues or conversations with my father.

The new track that we found ourselves on was enjoyable and, for my father, enlightening and amusing. When I received my discharge, I had unfinished dental work. If I wanted the government to pay for it, I would need to get it taken care of within a few months. I had three impacted wisdom teeth that needed to be removed and, knowing how expensive that would be to pay for on my own, I went ahead and scheduled the oral surgery for January, the month following my divorce. While I had seven teeth pulled during my childhood, they had all been removed using only a local numbing agent. This time, however, I would be put to sleep with what they referred to as laughing gas.

As usual, when I don't know what to expect, and it is my first time doing something, I was nervous. Dad was with me, and on the way to the office, he lightened my anxiety by just making regular conversation about regular things. I appreciated this. The procedure was easy enough, and I didn't feel any pain, not even when I woke up. Being under the anesthesia felt amazing, and I had been commenting on it since we left the dentist's office. I was in and out of lucidity on the ride home and talking up a storm. Dad thought it would be good to stop and get a few milkshakes to keep in the freezer as I wouldn't be able to eat anything solid for several days. This sounded like a good idea, and while sitting in the drive-through of the Burger King on College Parkway in Ft. Myers, Florida, my dad learned something about me.

Still under the influence and uninhibited, I chose that moment to say to my father, "Dad, if I had known that drugs were this good, I would've done 'em." I said this in complete seriousness, so I could not understand why my father began laughing. With just that one sentence, I had revealed to him that while he may have caught me drinking beer a few times, his fear that I was doing drugs in high school — because I had a 24-year-old boyfriend who my father was convinced did drugs — was false. This was another touching and connecting moment with my father, in contrast to much of my childhood.

5

A FAMILY DINNER

MY CHILDHOOD WAS FILLED WITH CHAOS AND CONSTANT **change**, which started even before my parent's divorce was finalized when I turned five years old. Given my age at the time of their divorce, I don't have many memories of my entire family being together. Actually, I have only one; a dinner with my five older brothers, my mother and my father. This memory is incredibly special to me.

I was young at the time, but I have long questioned how it could be that I had only one memory of one dinner. Why not more? Why only one? Why this one? Is it possible that I made it up? I had thought about this one memory often throughout the years and in 2015, during a call with one of my brothers, the thought of that dinner came to me once again. Maybe, I thought, it *had* actually happened and, as all of my brothers were there and are older, they would remember it too. Given what had

transpired, who could forget it? While I so wanted to ask him, I began to ask myself, do I want to do something that may shatter the only family memory I have? If he didn't recall what I was remembering, that would be fine but, what if he recalled the dinner and what I thought had happened hadn't happened at all? What if it was completely different from what I thought? Could I live with a different understanding?

I decided to ask, anyway. I found myself providing my brother with a few details, then asking him if he remembered such a dinner. What? Did he just say yes, he remembers this dinner? Wow! This is great, or is it? If I shared the rest of the details from my mind, would he confirm them? The memory was so special, given how much the dynamics within my family would change in the next handful of years. There was always tension in our house, and everyone was always on edge. In this memory, however, we were just a regular family.

At the time of the dinner, the house was filled with animals. There were many dogs, most of the large variety. There were a few cats and the usual animals that kids like to have, including hamsters, birds, and guinea pigs. Any strays that my brothers found were brought into the house. There were more pets than a family should have, but that is what happens when you have a father who is never home, and a mother who cannot handle six children with an age range spanning over nine years. My mother let us do whatever we wanted. It was my father, when he was home, who was strict, did the yelling, and doled out the punishments.

It was this chaos that allowed the monkey into the house. It came to us courtesy of my second oldest brother, Keith. It seems that he had gone to the store that day to purchase a skateboard with money he had saved, and as he headed towards sporting goods, he cut through the pet department where he spotted this spider monkey. Having enough money to purchase it, he did and, instead of walking out with a skateboard, he walked out with the monkey. Really? A 13-year-old boy walks out of a story with a monkey with no adult present and no phone call to the parents? Yes. That is what happened.

As my brother and I continued to speak about that dinner, I was elated to learn that I had nothing to worry about. The dinner had happened exactly as I remembered it! Perhaps it was the dynamics in our house or the events that transpired, but the memory of that one dinner was perfectly etched in my mind.

* * *

WE ALL SAT AROUND THE RECTANGULAR-SHAPED TABLE IN THE brown paneled dining room of our high-ranch house on Long Island, New York. I was sitting between two of my brothers, with my remaining brothers across from me. My dad sat at the end of the table to my left and my mother was at the opposite end. Dinner began as it always did. We waited for dad to sit down and, once he had filled his plate with food from the dishes placed in the center of the table, we got ours and began eating. Dad did not know about the monkey yet. My guess is no one was planning to tell him, but the monkey had other plans.

As we sat there eating, it appeared, climbing onto the light over the table. All of us kids began laughing. No one was surprised to see that my dad was not amused. Our laughing stopped immediately when he raised his voice and asked, "Whose monkey is that?" I am not certain if my dad startled it or if it was just perfect timing, but at that precise moment, the monkey pooped in the butter. We all froze. There was a long pause before my dad loudly placed his two hands on the table and stood up. This was not going to be good. I shrunk down between my brothers and looked over at my mother. In a move that I have always thought, and have since come to know, was out of character for her, my mother leaned over with her knife and cut the butter in half, separating the good part of the butter from the part that, well, no one was going to touch now.

In a calm and soothing voice, she then said, "Don't worry Ron, he only ruined half the butter." There was another long pause. Also out of character, in our home where things easily escalated and spiraled out of control most of the time, everyone started laughing ... even my dad.

6

CHAOS AND CHANGE
BEGINS

**MY FATHER, RON, AND MY MOTHER, SYD, MARRIED IN APRIL
1955.** This was one month before my father graduated from college, two
months before he joined the Navy, and only six months before my oldest
brother's birth. I am the youngest of six and the only girl. I was born in
June 1965. My oldest brother, Ronnie Bill, was nine and a half when I was
born. Keith, the second oldest, was eight and a half. The fraternal twins,
Robin and Robby, were seven, and my youngest brother, Chris, was just a
year and a half old.

About six months before I arrived, my parents bought the house where
I grew up. I do not know exactly when my father stopped living with our
family, but it was before February 1970; so, I was no more than four and a
half when he left. I was too young to understand why he had gone but old
enough to have felt the tension and witnessed the numerous fights, both
verbal and physical, between my mother and father before he did.

After my father left, it was mostly my oldest brother Ronnie Bill, who
looked out for me. He was strong and capable, and he protected me. I
thought he was the strongest person in the world simply because one day,
he was bringing two tall-backed dining room chairs down the hallway from
one of the bedrooms, holding one under each arm. "Hop on," he had said
as he lowered one back down to the floor.

"Really?" I exclaimed.

"Yeah," he said.

Up I went! Didn't I feel like a princess sitting there as he continued
down the hall, through the living room, and deposited me at the dinner

table? He was like a superhero to me. He made sure I was looked after, and he kept my other brothers away from me on those occasions when they decided I made a good target for teasing.

Being so much younger and smaller, I couldn't do anything when my brothers turned their attention toward me. I know they only thought of it as playing, but they would hold me down and tickle me until I cried or, even worse, wet my pants. They also locked me in the closet. This particular closet was in the upstairs hallway, home to the vacuum and other tall cleaning items. When playing hide-and-go-seek, it made a good hiding spot, and, on numerous occasions, one or more of my brothers put me in it and held the door closed. In addition to teasing, my brothers liked to joke around and rough house. While I am too young to remember, I think it was their handy work that is seen in the only photo that exists of me with my mother. In it, I have two black eyes. I was around three years old, and I didn't look at all happy. I was always out-strengthened and out-numbered growing up.

* * *

A TELLING SIGN OF THE CHAOS AND CHANGE THAT WAS happening within our family was the number of absences from school that my brothers and I had in any given year. Looking at the absence records that I have for several of my brothers for the five school years before I entered kindergarten in September 1970, things must have been difficult as they were each absent an average of twenty-seven times each of those years.

My parents divorced in June 1970 and, as they did not want to disrupt our lives, they planned for us to stay in the house with our mother, who was given full legal custody of us. My father, who did not have any scheduled visitation, paid the bills and was allowed to see us periodically if he chose. Sadly, according to a letter from my mother's attorney in January 1971, my father had not seen us since at least the previous May.

As I entered kindergarten, it was obvious that whatever chaos was going on previously had escalated. During my first year of school, 1970 – 1971, I was absent forty-seven times, and my brothers, on average, were absent sixty-one times. Given this dramatic increase, it is not surprising that my mother, in May 1971, told my father she could no longer care for us.

It was shortly after this notification that I was sitting in front of the house when my dad drove by with his new wife, Joan. He was not planning on stopping but did so as I was sitting alone on the curb. I was just about to turn six. No one was with me, and there was no one else in sight. I was dressed only in one of my brother's white t-shirts, which fit more like a long dress. I did not have any shoes, pants, or underwear on, and it looked like I had not had a bath in a while. My father was none-too-pleased to find me outside without supervision and in this condition, especially since he gave my mother all but $50 of his salary each month to care for us. Having been compelled to stop at the sight of me, he located my brothers and found that our mother was not home.

As some of us seemed to need new clothes and we all looked like we could use a good meal, we were loaded into their car and went to McCrory's. Dad bought us shoes, shirts, pants, and underwear, which we were told to put on in the dressing room. The t-shirt I had on was put in the trash right there in the store. It felt like Christmas to me, and while I could dress myself, Joan asked if she could help me. "Yes, please," I replied timidly to this beautiful and gentle woman. We then went over to the lunch counter to get something to eat.

My dad did not like the way I looked, so he returned and took me to the doctor later that week. After examining me, the doctor said that I was malnourished and, if my diet weren't corrected, it could impact my physical and mental development. While I do not know how my dad felt about seeing his children with inadequate clothing, dirty, hungry, and lacking supervision, I am sure it had a lot to do with things changing.

At the time they had come by the house, my parents had been divorced just under a year, and Joan and my father had been married about six months. While there was no plan for the custody arrangement my parents had previously agreed upon to change, it did. In June 1971, just before the end of my kindergarten year, my mother moved out of the house, and my dad moved back in, bringing Joan with him. Except for a brief visit that I felt forced to agree to at age eighteen, I never saw my mother, Syd, again.

At the time she moved in, Joan was 26 years old and taking on a stepmother role to six children ranging in age from six to fifteen who, for several years, had been left to fend for themselves, lacked discipline, and did not know the concept of routine. Like my dad, Joan was strict and set high expectations. I suspect her military background made her this way. Joan was a Marine Corps officer and, before her marriage, had been serving in the

reserves. She was a junior high school English teacher and was nothing like my mother. Joan became a presence in my life and did all the things that a parent is supposed to do, including instilling a sense of routine and discipline.

With her short blond hair, Joan was petite at about 5' tall. When I think of Joan, I think of her hands first. Joan's hands were small but still larger than mine. Her fingers were slender, and the heart of her hands fleshy and warm. Those hands were so soft, and I found them to be a safe place to retreat into. Every night as I tried to fall asleep, I held onto them tightly, not letting go for fear that Joan would leave me too, as my mother had.

I began calling Joan "mom" shortly after she moved into the house. I am not sure if it was suggested or if I chose that on my own. I recall that it made her happy to introduce me as her daughter and have people see me calling her mom. Calling her this also made me feel secure at a time when I did not often feel this way. Shortly after she moved in, Joan made a promise to me that she would never leave me as my mother had.

7
THE DOGHOUSE

THINGS CHANGED DRAMATICALLY AFTER DAD AND JOAN moved in as they worked to put rules and structure in place. Being older and having had a great deal of freedom, my oldest brothers didn't much care for all these changes, which included a rigid schedule, chores, grade attainment, school presence expectations, as well as clothing and haircut guidelines that were to be followed without question, complaint, or being reminded. As there was nothing strict about our household before they moved in, there was much resentment about the level of discipline and strictness put upon us with their arrival.

A show of the discipline and control instilled by Joan and my dad can be seen in the dramatic improvement in our school absence records over the next several years. Our attendance was almost perfect, with the total number of absences for those of us living in the house numbering only six.

Following all of the rules that Joan or dad imposed was expected. Failure to comply always led to punishment, so staying out of trouble became a particular focus for me. Just rolling one's eyes was grounds for discipline, as was not doing chores, talking back, skipping or doing poorly in school, and, certainly, any act of defiance. Grades were expected to be all A's and, if we achieved this, there was a monetary reward. There was a punishment if we didn't, and even if only one grade was less than a B. The list of potential punishments was long and included being hit, being grounded, doing extra chores, going to bed without dinner, or weeding the rock garden when we got older. Not that any of the punishments were good, but being grounded was not fun at all. It was always imposed a week-

37

at-a-time, not by days, and extra chores were assigned as well. Also, when grounded, other than doing schoolwork, chores, or practicing our instruments, we were not allowed to do anything but sit on the desk chair in our room.

It became known in our house that everything had a place, and everything had to be in its place, or there were consequences. If an infraction was considered small, the corresponding consequence was small but still impactful. For example, I had to get out of the pool for the day because I didn't hang my clothes up on the hooks in the bathroom when I changed into my bathing suit. Some violations, like being willful or lying, were considered more severe and the consequence was being hit by my father.

When I was growing up, nobody questioned a child getting hit as it was just what parents did. I didn't know any kid whose parents didn't punish them by hitting or spanking. What I perceived was happening to other kids, however, was that they were getting swatted or, on occasion, I recall hearing of someone being 'beaten' by their dad with his belt. Everyone knew that being beaten didn't mean a full-on beating as it sounded. It was getting whacked a few times, and while this may have left some red marks that welted up a bit, any swelling only lasted a few hours. What was happening in my house was different. Getting hit in my house hurt, and sometimes some bruises took a while to go away. My memories of my father hitting my brothers and me are not good. When we got hit, it was usually with anger, and those were the ones that hurt the most. Thankfully, I don't remember getting hit too often, but those few memories linger still.

It was probably the fear of the consequences, having been convinced through experience that one did not want to risk being in trouble, that I was a good girl and followed the lessons I had been taught. If I did get into serious trouble where the consequence was being hit, it was carried out with one of two things. The first was with a 1x2 piece of lumber, but this wasn't nearly as bad as the other, a ping pong paddle. That was worse. When we got hit, it was usually done on a bare backside using the rubberized surface of the paddle, with its hard-protruding nibs, which always caused a significant amount of stinging and welting. My small stature didn't help as the paddle covered my entire backside, and after five or six hard whacks, it was uncomfortable to sit for a couple of days. The 1x2 produced longer-lasting bruising but was preferred. Perhaps it was the way it had to be held or its length, but it only connected with flesh on the outside of one butt cheek, which gave you the ability, afterward, to sit down leaning on the other cheek, which usually remained unharmed.

Once I was a bit older, maybe around nine, the hitting stopped, and other consequences, like weeding the rock garden, were added. Weeding was a miserable punishment as it was only done on Saturdays after completing our big weekly household chores, which meant that it interrupted playtime with my friends.

Weeding was high on my list of the worst punishments because I could never pick all the weeds, even if I were there for days. I would come to understand that it was never about getting every weed. It was about how much time I would be required to spend weeding before being told I was done — and this was in direct proportion to how much trouble I was in. I never knew how long I was going to be out there, so time went by very slowly. I did not think of myself as a bad child at all, but I did spend a good many days weeding, so much so that my friends will still bring it up occasionally, even all these years later.

* * *

WHILE THE CONSEQUENCES OF HAVING GOTTEN IN TROUBLE were one thing, finding out you were in trouble was a whole other matter in my house. I suppose that many grow up hearing the phrase 'you are in the doghouse.' In our house, however, the doghouse was literal. No, we were not sent to sit in a doghouse as punishment, but it was the way we knew that someone was in trouble.

As kids, we were not allowed to enter the house by the front door or through the garage. We were required to come around the back of the house and use the door that led into what we called the mudroom. It was not really a room but more of a small area where the heating system and water tank for the house were located. From this small space, you could enter the downstairs bathroom and then into the rest of the house. The mudroom is where we were required to take off our shoes and coats. Coats were not allowed to be worn indoors as we were told we would overheat and that we could get sick. Shoes were also not allowed as dad and Joan did not want us tracking dirt and mud into the house. I understood this, but I was resentful as they wore shoes in the house. It was a clear example that 'do as I say and not what I do' was alive and well.

When standing in the mudroom, you could not see the small wall to the left of the door that led from the bathroom into the hallway. Every time we came into the house, before we even took off our shoes or coats, the first thing we all did was lean over, holding onto the edge of the wall separating the mudroom from the bathroom, and take a peek at that wall. I was jealous of my older brothers as they had the advantage of being taller, which meant this was easier for them to do. We leaned in, as we were not allowed to walk into the bathroom with our shoes on, and we couldn't wait to look at that wall.

What we were so interested to see on that wall was a doghouse. The entire piece was about 14" long, 5" tall, and was a flat wooden decoration. The doghouse itself, located on the right, was painted brown with a red roof. It had an oval doorway painted black and, toward the top of it, there was a hook. To the left of the doghouse were six small hooks, and from each one hung a wooden dog. Each dog was painted a different color. Across the front of each dog was a rectangular box with a white background and, within this box, our names were written. We each had our own dog. If our dog was hanging in the doghouse, we knew we were in trouble, but just didn't yet know for what. So much for innocent before being proven guilty.

Upon seeing my empty hook, I often wanted to turn around and walk back out the door ... but there was nowhere for me to go. I would just be brought right back, and then I would be in more trouble. It didn't matter who was in the doghouse as the mood in the house was always strained when any one of us was in trouble, and it wasn't unusual for more than one of us to be in the doghouse at any given time.

The changes and control instilled when dad and Joan moved in, paired with dad's physical punishments and short temper, proved too much for some. It wasn't long before there were more departures from our house.

My four oldest brothers left within a few years. It started about the time I turned seven, in 1972, with Keith, the second oldest who was fifteen. With his independent spirit, he had run away from the house on a few occasions after spending a good amount of time in the doghouse. His punishments were usually from acts of defiance like talking back, not cutting his hair, or skipping school. He didn't like the control imposed upon him and was very vocal about it, so he decided to leave the house and move in with our mother. While he spent a little bit of time living with her, he left her house within a year and made it on his own from there.

Ronnie Bill, the oldest and my protector, also ran away from the house and went to go live with our mother just a few months after Keith left. He was almost seventeen. Ron was the tallest of the boys and had a distinctive wave in the front of his dark brown hair, similar to the one my father had.

Robby, the oldest of the twins, was constantly in trouble, and, in May 1973, he requested to go live with our mother. He was just fifteen.

Within a few months, Robin, the younger twin, ran away from home when Ronnie Bill and Keith knocked on his bedroom window in the middle of the night, encouraging him to leave. They knew how hard dad was on him. As Robin would later tell me, after a fight with dad, he crawled out of the window that night. He regretted what he did soon after he left but did not know how to fix it.

While Keith, Ronnie Bill, and Robin would not return to the house to live, in February 1974, about nine months after he had left, Robby came back. This was short-lived, as only a few months later, my father kicked him out and told him to go back and live with his mother. I couldn't blame my dad for sending Robby away as he had been trying to get Chris, who was ten years old at the time, to smoke marijuana.

That was it. By the summer of 1974, within three years of dad moving back into the house with Joan and only about two years between the first one leaving and the last, the four oldest boys were gone and would not return. I grew up without having any sort of a relationship with them and, while I was getting older without any type of relationship with my mother, my brothers did have one with her. While they had years of a relationship with my father before they left the house, it ended, except for a few brief conversations or letters after they were gone.

The boys leaving was one of the other difficulties about the doghouse. As the boys left, their dogs were removed. So each time I walked in, I was reminded that there was one less person in the house.

8

FOUR YEARS OF
STABILITY

ONCE IT WAS JUST ME AND MY YOUNGEST BROTHER CHRIS left in the house, life began settling down into a rhythm of stability that I had not experienced since that very brief period just after dad moved back into the house with Joan four years earlier. My dad seemed a bit more at ease after the chaos of my oldest brothers leaving the house was over. There were no changes, however, regarding chores or expectations. The lessons in how we were required to conduct ourselves also continued.

One lesson we were taught was that one does not talk openly about their personal thoughts or views. An example of this occurred when I was around ten years old. I was with my dad. We parked in the school's back parking lot and headed into the cafeteria so he could cast his vote on a school referendum. I held his hand, as I was required to do out in public. Not only was this for my safety, but it also made it easier for him to let me know if I was doing something wrong. One squeeze of the hand was all it ever took.

As we made our way across the parking lot, I saw one of my classmates coming out of the building with her parents. As we passed each other, she asked, "Is your dad going to vote yes?" Whatever this particular referendum was, everyone seemed to be talking about it leading up to this vote. These, however, were not topics discussed in my house, so I didn't know if my dad was going to vote in favor of it or not. Without thinking, I looked up at my dad and asked, "Are you going to vote yes?"

Never looking down or breaking his stride, his response was short and direct, "It is nobody's business but mine who and what I vote for." That was it. He never said another word, and through these types of interactions, I was clearly taught the rules of the house.

There was also no discussion of personal feelings, emotions, views, or opinions. There was no questioning why decisions were made, and there was no debating a different aspect or side when an opportunity for opposing views presented itself. It was clear that the children were expected to accept what adults did and said without question. There were also a lot of secrets, and, if we knew them, we were not allowed to talk about them — either in or outside the house. Growing up, given all the expectations, the lessons that were being taught, and the changes and chaos I was experiencing, I tried to be seen as little as possible, spoke only when necessary, and always did as I was told. I was a people-pleasing and obedient child — learning not to have a voice.

* * *

THE YEAR AFTER MY OLDER BROTHERS LEFT, CHRIS AND I BEGAN attending a Lutheran church with a teacher with whom Joan worked. Dad and Joan did not attend, and I was resentful of this as it seemed like more of the despised 'do as I say, not what I do' requirements. We were told to call this man Uncle Rich, and his wife was to be referred to as Aunt Ginny. They were both very active in the church. We would attend this church for several years, even taking classes to make our confirmations and going to vacation bible school for two weeks during the day for a summer or two.

My brother Chris was due to receive his confirmation in the spring of 1978, and I would follow a year later. Before this, however, we needed to show proof that we had been baptized. As my dad said we had not been, my brother and I were baptized shortly before he was confirmed. How disappointing it was to learn, many years later, that I had been baptized soon after I was born ... and that my father either did not know or did not remember it.

* * *

WHILE WE LIVED IN WHAT I WOULD CALL A MIDDLE-CLASS neighborhood, it began to dawn on me that we didn't have much money, or at least that was my thought the day I discovered that we were drinking powdered milk. I was young, maybe seven or eight, and it was hard for me to comprehend that we were poor.

After Joan came to live with us, the routine was that our plates were made up for us, and we were required to eat whatever was on them. Dinnertime was usually difficult for me. I was a very picky and slow eater. On many occasions, I didn't finish all that was on my plate before my brother completed his chore of clearing the table, so my plate was put in the refrigerator to become my breakfast the following morning. My least favorite day of the week for dinner was smorgasbord night, the night when all the leftovers from the prior six days were heated up. After dinner, any remaining food was saved for this once-a-week leftover meal, even if only a spoonful or two. To this day, I am not a big fan of leftovers.

Meals were always eaten in the dining room. Our high-ranch home was two stories, with the front entrance halfway between the upstairs and downstairs. Upon stepping into the house, a short flight of six stairs headed up, and another flight led down. Up the stairs and straight ahead, at the back of the house, was the small galley kitchen. The dining room sat just over from there. With its tri-colored green shag carpet, the living room was immediately to the right. My brother and I were only allowed in this room if we were invited to say hello to company or on special occasions, like Christmas.

The hallway on the left led to three small bedrooms and a bathroom. The bathroom, diagonally across the hall from my dad and Joan's room, was considered their bathroom, and we had to traipse all the way downstairs to use what was always referred to as the downstairs bathroom. I was afraid of the dark growing up, and I hated going all the way down there in the middle of the night. I also resented not being able to use their bathroom when it was right across the hall from my room. *What would it hurt if I used it?* I would think … but I never did. It was against the rules.

Down the stairs, the family room opened to the right and was located at the back of the house. Tucked away at the front of the house, off the family room, was an all-purpose room. It used to be a bedroom when my older brothers were living with us but, after they left, it was converted to this space by reducing the wall shared with the family room to waist-height. The downstairs was painted an upbeat yellow to coordinate with the yellow and orange shag carpet. This, along with the double-wide garden window that my dad installed, helped to brighten up an otherwise dark area.

Each Saturday, at 8 a.m., if we weren't already out of bed, dad or Joan came into our room and threw back our covers to wake us. This was our big chore day, and before we were sent out to play, we had to get through our lists. Unlike most parents I knew, who simply asked if a chore had been completed, our chores had to be carefully inspected to ensure they met expectations.

Our list of chores included stripping the sheets off our bed, washing them, and then putting them back on the bed. We had to dust and vacuum our rooms, then clean either the downstairs bathroom or the family room. The bathroom was small with only a sink, toilet, and a stand-up shower, and it was definitely easier to clean than the family room, which was about three times larger. It was not only the size that made the family room less desirable to clean; it was how it was furnished and decorated. Closest to the stairs, there was a large couch with end tables, a reclining chair and table, and a large organ my father played fairly regularly. At the other end of the room, on the wall facing the backyard, the large greenhouse window was chock-full of various plants.

The wall at the far end of the room held homemade bookshelves surrounding a free-standing wood-burning stove set upon a platform of red bricks. The wooden shelves themselves were made by my dad out in the garage. They were not mounted to the wall, but instead were held up by decorative white concrete blocks. The blocks were 4" thick, about 14" square, and they had a design cut through them that looked like a flower. These blocks were typically used outside, and while they looked pretty, my knuckles were constantly raw from knocking into the rough concrete when dusting the shelves and trying to move around the many books, records, plants, and knick-knacks that filled them.

* * *

WHEN IT CAME TO CHORES, 'IT'S NOT GOOD ENOUGH, YOU WILL have to do it again' were words I heard frequently. Joan always conducted the inspections. I never thought of Joan as being mean, but she was strict and had exceedingly high expectations. I was around ten years old when, one morning, I was waiting for Joan to come down and inspect my work. My brother was next door cleaning the bathroom, and my dad, as usual, was outside in the garage. Chris was always better and faster at everything, including eating, chores, homework, climbing trees, and even coloring. There was no end to his talents and abilities — and my lack thereof. The bathroom was the last thing on my brother's Saturday morning chore list.

During inspections, Joan didn't talk much. She would wander around the room, pointing at obvious things that had not been done or dragging her finger across shelves, then looking at it to see if there was any dust. Perhaps her military background made her conduct it this way, but I didn't much like it. As she started inspecting my work, the first thing Joan did was to point to the dirty dust rag that I had left on the floor, which obviously

46

signaled that I had not fully vacuumed the room. She then took a quick look around at the dusting and announced that there was much more work to do.

What an idiot for having left the rag there. I was mad at myself, and my brother didn't help my mood when he poked his head out the bathroom door to laugh and stick his tongue out at me. After a few minutes of feeling sorry for myself, I picked up the rag and walked around to check the dusting. I put the dust rag in the laundry and went to grab the vacuum again. While I didn't think it needed to be vacuumed, I knew Joan would be listening for it.

As I was coming back down the stairs, struggling again with the vacuum, which was too tall and too heavy for me to easily handle, Chris was coming up. He took great pleasure in telling me he was done, and, unlike me, he would soon be out of the house. He also used it as an opportunity to shove me, causing me to stumble and let go of the vacuum, which hit the wall with a huge bang. I froze, knowing what was coming. Joan yelled out, "Heidi, be more careful. Don't go putting marks on my walls!" My brother made another face at me, satisfied that he had gotten me in trouble, and continued up while I continued my struggle down.

When Joan came down to inspect Chris' work, I told her I was ready as well. Not unusual for my brother; he was told that everything was in order. Joan came into the family room and began looking at the shelves along the back wall and then went around the rest of the room. She said, "Heidi, I am disappointed in you. This is the second time today that I have looked at what you have done, and I can see that you did not put any care into doing this right." I wanted to protest, but talking back was not allowed. Joan looked at me and said, "I will give you one more chance to do this correctly. If it is not, you are not going out today. You will be grounded for the entire week, and you will be assigned the family room again next Saturday."

Feeling defeated as I watched her head back upstairs, I sat down on the floor and began to cry. I knew, for sure, I was going to put in all my effort, and I would still end up in trouble.

It wasn't until he was kneeling in front of me that I realized my dad had come in from the garage. Ignoring my tears, he lifted me back to my feet and said, "I want to teach you something."

"Okay," I said, sniffling and wiping my tears. He told me, "I always had a hard time getting a room fully dusted when I was your age, but I learned a secret about how to do it, and I want to share that with you."

"Really?" I ask. "What is it?"

He began to explain, "The first thing is, you must start in one corner and work your way around the room in an orderly way, so you won't miss anything." That certainly sounded like a much better way than absent-mindedly jumping from dusting one thing to the next, I thought. "Also, just picture a speck of dust floating down and landing on a surface," he said. "Then all you have to do is to clean where the dust lands. So, go ahead. Pretend to be dust and show me all the places that you could land," he finished.

Just like that, my chore had been turned into a game. It was so much fun to go around the room, showing dad all the places I could be found. I was on the top of the plant leaves, the legs that stuck out from under the couch, the top of books, and the ears of the porcelain dog that sat on the shelf. When I slowed down a bit, my dad said, "I have something else to share."

"What, what is it?" I asked excitedly.

He then revealed, "This secret can also be used when cleaning other things too, like the bathroom." I smiled broadly, knowing that this was going to help me get a passing grade on chore inspection the first time, get outside to play earlier than ever, and maybe — just maybe — allow me to finish before my brother. My dad hadn't let me off the hook and still expected me to do my chores well, but he taught me a different way of thinking about accomplishing them. As he looked down at me, he asked, "Now, do you think you will be able to dust this room and have it pass inspection?"

"Yes!" I shouted with confidence.

"Good girl," he said as he headed back down the hall toward the garage.

"Dad?" I called after him.

"Yes, sweetheart?"

"Do we have to tell Chris this secret?"

"No," he answered with a smile, understanding exactly why I would not want my brother to know. "We can keep it between us."

9
A SUMMER ADVENTURE

THE RHYTHM OF OUR STRUCTURED AND RESTRICTIVE LIFE rarely ever changed. What a thrill it was when, in 1977, we experienced a summer-long adventure. I was 12-years-old, and each morning I awoke, laying on the ground outside in a sleeping bag. I stretched to get the last remaining sleep out of me, clasping my hands and stretching my arms straight up over my head. I looked like a boy with my short haircut. My clothes certainly didn't help. My pajamas consisted of a hand-me-down t-shirt from one of my brothers. I was a tomboy. I never was a girly girl.

I was surrounded by sand with some short tufts of weeds here and there. I always awoke early and could see the sun, just coming up, beginning to hit the water in the canal just a short distance from where I lay. *Looks like it is going to be another beautiful day*, I thought, looking up at the sky, which  had a few wispy clouds and was growing brighter. I looked in the other direction and saw the back of our unfinished summer home — just the shell of a small two-story house. When finished, it was to have three bedrooms and two baths. At the time, however, there were no walls, electrical, heat, insulation, or plumbing. A work-in-progress then, it was a labor of love project for my father and Joan's dad, the only grandfather I had ever known.

The prior year, along with her parents, Joan and my dad purchased the land I slept on, located on the eastern end of Long Island. They worked with a contractor to build just the shell and, as my father and Joan's father were skilled in all that would be needed to finish the interior, they planned to complete it over the summer and into the fall.

Everything was outside to allow my father and grandfather to work on the house without interruption or things getting in their way. The only time we went inside the house for any length of time, other than to do work, was if it rained. While my parents took possession of the only tent we had, my brother Chris and I were willingly relegated to sleeping outside under the stars. All our cooking and eating was also done outside. We lived out of coolers and did most of the cooking on a small coal barbeque. I was always hungry when I woke up that summer. It must have been all the fresh air and the very active days.

Despite the change of venue, the first order of business each morning was, of course, chores. While everything felt more casual, the regimented environment with order and process continued. First up was to prime the water pump, where we got our water for cooking and bathing. I so loved this task. It was fun and, unlike my other chores, it never felt like work, although it was not easy. My short, petite, and frail frame made it hard for me to raise the arm of the pump so, especially at the beginning of summer, it took quite a bit of time to coax the water up from the ground. I turned it into a game. How many times would I have to pump it today before the water started trickling? How many more before there was a steady flow? Maybe one less than yesterday, I always thought hopefully.

While we had chores to do at the house each day, Chris and I usually volunteered to spend time helping our father and grandfather as well. They had their own projects so we each had one-on-one time with them. I enjoyed working with my grandfather. He always made me feel like I could do everything he was doing. One day he was working on plumbing. "Here," he said, "would you like to try?" as he handed me the blowtorch.

"Really, can I?" I asked excitedly. That large tool spitting fire was much too big for my small hands, so he held it with me as we soldered a pipe together. It was both exhilarating and terrifying to hold it. In between requests to fetch him supplies or other tools, grandpa would tell me stories of when he was growing up. He was born in Czechoslovakia and immigrated to the United States when he was one year old. His father was a woodcarver and made the most beautiful furniture. Grandpa was good at anything that he could do with his hands, including plumbing, electrical, fixing radios, and anything mechanical. Like my father, grandpa knew so much about so many things.

While they would only come out for the day, my grandparents spent a good deal of time with us that summer, allowing me to watch my grandmother cook and tend to the small garden she had planted. She was a fabulous cook, having learned from her mother. Her parents were born in Austria and met here in the United States. Her father had been a farmer in the old country and her mother, a housekeeper. I can still smell the rhubarb pie she often made that summer.

Once our morning chores were done, my brother and I spent our days hanging out together and keeping busy. We explored the neighborhood, looked for frogs in the swampy reeds at the edge of the water, and spent time out on the water in a rowboat. We hiked deep into the woods down the street to hunt for blueberries, eating most of them before we made it back to the house. We also took long bicycle rides, sometimes to Jabreski's Junk Yard, spending hours wandering among all the old things that had found their way there. Jabreski's held many strange things to look at, and the owner didn't mind us being there. When it was hot, we would go for a swim in the canal. We also went clamming with our feet and hunted for lobsters at night. We did a good deal of fishing, so we set up a trap each night to catch bait. Sometimes we would catch an eel, which was always exciting, but it was often also sad as, by the time we opened the trap and realized we had caught one, the darn thing slithered away directly toward the water, disappearing over the bulkhead. Man, those things were fast! I always wondered how they knew which direction the water was.

Setting the table for dinner was also my chore, and I liked it this summer. I spent time with my dad as he worked to get the fire started so the cooking could be done. I always found an opportune time to ask if we could make smores that night. He always said yes. He would make the fire a little bigger and keep it going for longer, which helped keep me

warm on the nippy summer evenings before it was time to slide into my sleeping bag.

Clear and vivid memories of those long, lazy, and warm summer days spent doing whatever and those cool summer nights sleeping soundly under the stars remain with me. My grandmother standing there, holding vegetables from her garden. Joan making sandwiches for lunch. My dad, starting the fire and showing me how to roast a hot dog on a stick. My grandfather, whispering a bit of wisdom in my ear that was meant only for me. My brother, on his bicycle, riding in front of me down the road to our next adventure.

* * *

Life was extremely good that summer. While things had settled down with the chaos of my brothers leaving a couple of years behind us by then, the strictness of life and the weight of expectations were always there, as evidenced by what happened when I returned to school just after that beautiful and peaceful summer.

It was the fall of 1977. I was 12-years-old, in seventh grade, and a member of the school chorus. Our teacher informed us that in a few weeks, we were going on a field trip to New York City to see *Annie the Musical* on Broadway. The musical had opened the year before and was such a hit. I loved the music, and it would be so great to see it. Oh, what fun, I remember thinking!

There was, however, a cost for the trip, and I knew that I would be expected to pay it. As I made my way home that day, I worked out how I was going to do just that. If I put together what I had already saved, the allowance that I would earn each week over the next several weeks, along with the money I would get for every A I expected to receive on my next report card, I would have enough. My parents, however, would need to lay out the money ahead of time, and this is what I thought the sticking point would be on whether I would get to go or not. I was hopeful, though, that all I had figured out would get them to see how much this trip meant to me.

I was so excited when I presented the permission slip to Joan and explained, before she even asked, just how I was planning to pay for it. It felt like her response to my request was given before I had even fully presented my plan ... and the answer was no. No, you can't go. This response was so counter to my excitement to attend. It might have been easier to understand if it was because I had not yet earned the money, or even if it was because it would be a school night, and we were never allowed to do anything but homework and practice our instruments on school nights. The reason the answer was no was because neither my dad nor Joan would be willing to drive to the school to pick me up at midnight.

In trying to salvage the opportunity, I said, "I can have someone else's parents drop me off." Nope, that was not okay either. They were not comfortable with me being driven home at that hour by someone else, and their sleep would still be disrupted as they would have to be up to let me in the house. That was it. I wasn't going. I was incredibly upset but knew better than to cry and carry on as that could mean being punished.

I swallowed my disappointment, but it never left. While I have no way of really knowing how many times I have thought of the disappointment since then, I would guess it has been in the hundreds. While I could have taken an opportunity to see a version of *Annie* on Broadway later in life, I never did. It just wouldn't be the same. Andrea McArdle was the original Annie, and that is who I wanted to see. She was almost the same age as me, so I looked up to her. It seems a bit silly that I have carried this around with me. It is probably time to let this disappointment go.

10

LAST ONE STANDING

BY THE FOLLOWING SUMMER, 1978, LIFE AS I KNEW IT CHANGED yet again when my brother Chris was placed into a group home by child protective services. He was 14-years-old. His demeanor and behavior had changed, and he began skipping school and acting out. There were several incidents, and it was after the last one that he was taken into custody by the courts. Like my four oldest brothers, Chris would not return to live with us.

I turned thirteen the month Chris left, and since it was just me in the house and I had no contact with the boys, I began to think of myself as an only child. My father was still married to Joan, but all was not well. While I did not know why, things were tense. I spent a lot of time in my room, trying to be as quiet as possible and doing my best to blend in with the furnishings around me.

Outings were rare, and excursions with just my dad were few and far between, but on one particular day that school year, my father took me to a parade. It was so nice to be out with him doing something fun. The tension that was palpable in the house was left behind, and my father was in an incredibly happy mood. My naïve young mind thought this was because he was alone with me.

We had fun watching the parade and, when it was over, my father told me that we were going to say hello to one of his friends that had marched in it. He told me his friend played the drum in a fire department band. I remember thinking that was pretty cool as we walked through the crowd to find this person. We found his friend, drum on the ground, taking off the parade costume they had been wearing.

First, my dad introduced me, then turned to me and said, "Heidi, this is my friend Ann." I remember thinking it was weird that he had a female friend, but then he added that they worked together at school. We didn't stay long, and after a few minutes of watching them chat, we said our good-byes and I was happy, once again, to have dad all to myself. As we walked away, my dad asked, "Do you like Ann?" *I just met her*, I thought. I didn't know if I liked her or not, but what did it matter? I wasn't going to see her again.

Joan would live in my childhood home for eight school years. For the first seven, I was absent 11 days. As they had in the past, my absences continued to be a telling sign of the chaos, change, and difficulties I was experiencing. In my eighth-grade year, 1978-1979, I was absent nine times. Dad and Joan were both schoolteachers and, during that year, I spent a good deal of time alone with Joan because my dad rarely made it home from school until after I had gone to bed. I did not know or understand what was happening between them or why my father was not coming home, but I didn't ask questions as I was taught.

I knew Joan was terribly upset over what my dad was doing, and one night she came into my bedroom and woke me up. She said, "Your father is on his way home, and when he gets here, there may be yelling." She went on to tell me, "If you hear me screaming, I want you to leave the house and go over to Mrs. A's house and ask her to call the police." I was scared, and I could tell that Joan was also scared. While she didn't say it, I knew that she was concerned about my father putting his hands on her in anger. It had happened once before. They had fought, and dad shoved Joan, causing her to fall through a jalousie door and puncture her eardrum. Thankfully, I did not have to leave the house that night, but there was much yelling. The fighting between them was increasing. I felt alone and vulnerable, but there was no one to turn to.

I turned fourteen the following summer and, as I had done for the first time the prior summer, I was going to sleep-away camp. Unlike the year before when I went for one three-weeklong session, I was going for two back-to-back sessions, which meant I would be gone for six weeks. This was not something I had asked to do, but when the arrangements were being made a few months earlier, I recall being happy to go for that long. The tension had only gotten worse, and Joan and my dad, when he was home, spent most of their time engaged in nasty arguments or ignoring each other entirely.

As they had the prior summer, dad and Joan were to drive me the six hours to camp. Surprisingly, things were much better by the day I left for camp. I wasn't feeling any of the fierce tension, and even the yelling and fighting had stopped, despite school having been out for a few weeks and them being home together every day. During the drive, I sat in the back seat, feeling happy as I watched Joan reach over from the passenger side and put her hand on my dad's arm for a few moments.

When we arrived at camp, they helped me unload all my gear, and then we ate lunch in the mess hall with all the other campers and their parents. It was good to be together as a family. As Joan and my dad departed, there were hugs, I love you's, and wishes for me to have a wonderful time. As he always did, dad opened the passenger door for Joan and, as they drove away, I waved intensely at them until they were out of sight.

While things seemed better, I knew that they were still not right, and I found myself anxious at camp. My anxiousness persisted, and one week into the second session, I asked that my parents be called to come and pick me up. My camp counselor said they had been called, but it was four long days before they arrived. As they pulled up, my dad was driving the car, and as expected, there was another person with him. It was not, I quickly realized, the woman with the soft hands that I called mom. It was not the woman who had taken care of me and loved me for the past eight years. It was not the woman who had provided me a sense of security and the stability that had been lacking from my mother. It was not Joan. It was Ann. It was the woman from the parade. The woman with whom my father worked. "Ann is my girlfriend," he told me. He also told me that he and Joan were divorcing. "All of this was worked out while you were at camp and, there is a change at the house to tell you about as well," he went on. "Joan has moved out and has taken her things with her. Ann has moved in."

Just like that, it was done. There was no discussion. There was no advance warning. Not one question about how I felt was ever asked, nor was I asked if I was okay with what was happening. I am sure, like all the other changes that had happened in my life up to that moment, I was expected take this in stride and just accept what was. The six-hour ride home in the car was difficult for me. I kept wanting to ask about Joan, but I didn't dare. I knew better than to question anything. I wasn't feeling comfortable, but I couldn't speak up.

A few days after I arrived home, my father drove me over so I could spend a night with Joan, who was now living full-time in our summer home. This was not something that would come to be a regular thing. We had a long talk about what had happened. I felt safe with Joan and wanted to stay, so I asked her, "Can I come and live with you?" Her response was, "You need to be with your father." I cried, telling her that I didn't want to go back to that house and that I wanted to live with her. That is when she said the words that would break my heart. She told me, "You cannot come and live with me. You need to go home." As it turned out, Joan broke the promise that she made to that scared little 5-year-old girl, who was now a scared fourteen-year-old girl. She left me too.

* * *

In an instant, life had changed, yet again. Everything felt upside down, and the stability I had with Joan in my life was gone. But, as I had learned to do so well, I was the good girl I was required to be. My voice stayed silent, and I pretended that all was okay. What choice did I have? I was a child who was taught to do as I was told ... and if I didn't, there were severe consequences. My mother had left my life long ago. All my brothers were out of my life, and I had no way to contact them. Joan was no longer available to me. I didn't have a choice. I didn't have anywhere to go, which meant that I had to stay. This also meant that I had to stay silent because if I spoke up I might be told to leave too.

Ann had left a husband and her three children behind to be with my father. Two girls, ages eighteen and nineteen, and a boy of thirteen. I did come to develop a close relationship with one of Ann's daughters, Patti, and typically just call her my sister when referring to her. As they did visit with Ann at our house, I didn't feel too much like an only child anymore. This feeling was short-lived, however. About six months after Ann moved in, my dad informed me that the three of us would be moving from New York to Florida over the upcoming summer. Once again, life as I knew it was going to change. After the move, Ann's children remained with their father in New York and visited us in Florida somewhat infrequently. I was back, once again, to feeling like an only child.

After we moved, I was away from my friends, Joan, and all things familiar, but I had much more freedom than before as dad and Ann, having only been living together for about a year, were busy settling into the new life they wanted to create for themselves. My newfound freedom was also in part due to a new job and the acquisition of my driver's permit. I was fifteen and, from that day on, I worked virtually full-time until I left for Bootcamp.

I received my learner's permit at age fifteen and my full driver's license at sixteen. Dad and Ann had two cars so, once I got my learner's permit, I was allowed to use the second car if they weren't using it. They both worked at the same place and usually drove together, so I had the car almost all to myself. That worked well until I got into an accident. While I was fine, the car was not, and I got into a great deal of trouble for wrecking it. What I got in worse trouble for, however, was telling the doctor at the hospital not to call my dad as he would kill me. My father was furious that I would tell someone that.

As I was continuing to work and we no longer had the second car, I begged people to drive me to work or would take a different bus from school to get there. Thankfully, I didn't have to do this for long as I had saved a good deal of money. When the owner of the restaurant where I worked told me that his father was selling one of his cars, I bought it.

Dad and Ann worked at a marina and spent a good portion of the day at work. They often stayed after it closed to have a few drinks with their new friends. With their schedule, along with school, work, and the fact that I now had my own car, I took full advantage of not having to be at home very much.

11

CHRIS GRADUATES

WHILE THE ATMOSPHERE IN THE HOUSE WAS DIFFERENT when we moved to Florida, just like in New York and before Ann moved in, things could change on a dime. While I had more freedom, there were still lines I knew better than to cross. Talking with any of my brothers was off-limits. Speaking with Joan without them knowing was off-limits. Hiding something from them was off-limits.

As I had grown up in such a restrictive environment, I did things that I would consider sneaking around. Also, I did lie on occasions when I wanted to do something that I knew I wouldn't have been allowed to for reasons that I thought were too constrictive and arbitrary. One such occasion was when I skipped school, called out sick from my job as a cashier at Kmart, and drove 3.5 hours to the Naval Recruit Training Command in Orlando, Florida, to see my brother Chris graduate from Naval Bootcamp. This was in the fall of my senior year of high school. It was 1982. He had sent me a letter a few weeks before telling me about the graduation and asking if I could come. He also wanted my dad to come, but I knew better than to ask dad about that possibility, so I never mentioned it.

When we moved to Florida, Chris, still in the custody of the courts and living in a group home, had been granted permission to visit us on two occasions. Once in August 1980 and again in February 1981. Those visits had gone so well that it was decided that he would come live with us full-time after he graduated from high school in June. That never happened. Sometime after he visited with us, there was some kind of falling out between Chris, dad, and/or Ann, and, just like everyone else, he was cut out of our lives.

While I wasn't willing to open up a discussion with my dad about attending the graduation, I went anyway. It was an extremely long day, but I was so happy to have seen my brother. I missed him. I am not even sure what time I made it back to the house that day but, immediately upon my arrival, I knew something was wrong. As I walked in the front door, I could feel the tension and found my father and Ann in the living room. I knew that they knew where I had been. *How had they found out?* I thought. I was so naïve thinking that my mail was private, but I would come to learn that many letters were sent to me by family that were either never given to me or were opened, read, sealed back up, then given to me. This must have been one of those times.

Ann, with a larger physical presence than my father, was closer to the front door and somewhat in front of him. She asked, "Where have you been?"

"At work," I answered, clearly understanding from her question and tone that she knew that that was not the case, but not willing to tell them where I had gone.

"No, you weren't," she replied.

"Yes, I was," I responded, still committed to not telling the truth.

She took a step closer, now only about three feet from me, and asked again, this time in an angrier tone, "Where were you?" I knew I was caught but I also didn't really know if they knew where I had been so, again, I decided to lie and said I was hanging with my friends or something. "No, you weren't. We know you went up to see your brother graduate from Bootcamp."

I felt like a trapped rat and had no choice now but to admit it. In a voice that was a bit defiant, however, feeling like I had done something I should have been allowed to do in the first place, I said, "Yes, I did go to see Chris, and what's so wrong with that?" As my exchange of words with Ann escalated; my father remained silent. I began walking towards the short hall to the right that led to my bedroom, and as I rounded the corner I saw a large cardboard box, maybe two feet by two feet across and about three feet tall blocking entry into my bedroom. I noticed it was filled and, as I rushed to try to look inside of it, I yelled over my shoulder, "What is this?"

Ann was right behind me and began yelling, "If you don't want to follow the rules of this house and you prefer to be with *those* people, then you can just leave. Your things are packed. We will be putting you on a flight and you can go live with your mother."

I turned toward her, surprising myself with what I said. I shouted, "You can't tell me what to do! You're not my mother." At that moment, I felt a shattering within me as she slapped me across my face. It hurt both physically and emotionally, but not as bad as the hurt I felt when my father just stood there. He didn't say a word. I was so angry. I said something to him like, "Are you going to let her do that to me?"

All he said in response was, "You shouldn't have done what you did." I stood there bewildered. Dad, still standing behind Ann in the narrow, cramped hallway, touched her shoulder, gesturing for her to back away from me. They disappeared back into the living room together.

It took me a moment to turn back toward my room. To confirm what I already suspected, I glanced around my room before looking into the box, and it was a mess. There was hardly anything left on my shelves and my drawers, still open and in disarray, were empty but for a few things absently hanging out of them. I began to sob. How could he have let her hit me? What had I done that was so bad as to warrant my belongings being thrown into a box, being slapped by my dad's girlfriend, and being told I was going to have to live with a woman whom I had not seen or spoken to since the end of kindergarten over eleven years earlier? I didn't think they were bluffing, and I fully expected that I would be leaving the house shortly. I just couldn't understand why I couldn't have a relationship with my brother just because they didn't have or didn't want one.

It wasn't lost on me that what was happening was not just about skipping school and seeing my brother. There was something much bigger behind this, I knew. Unfortunately, as with other times, I knew there were secrets and information that I wasn't being told, I would never find out what it was really about, and I was certainly not able to ask anyone.

I climbed over the box and into my bedroom, and sat down on the bed. I was numb. I was tired. I was scared. And my face hurt. I just sat there waiting to be told what was going to happen next. At some point, much later, my father came into my room. He stood in front of me and told me that what I had done was not okay, but that after discussing it with Ann, they had decided that I could stay. He conveyed that I was 'skating on thin ice,' a term I had heard many times growing up, and that I was expected to 'tow-the-line' going forward. I was also told that I was not to have any communication with any other members of my family unless he knew about it. Message received. There was no way that I was going to jeopardize being thrown out of the house, no matter how scared I was to stay there, to be sent to live with a mother that I didn't know. Dad told me that I could unpack my things and go to bed.

From how the conversation with Ann went, it was evident to me that she was the one who had thrown all my things into the box. Record albums and perfume bottles broken, torn and wrinkled items, clothes, shoes, and other things mixed together. Everything was a jumbled mess, and some of my things were ruined. I was fuming as I was straightening all of it out. I was also afraid. While I had seen Ann get mad before, this was the first time she had behaved at this heightened level of anger or had been physically abusive. I was afraid for my well-being, especially since my father did not come to my aid.

* * *

ONCE AGAIN, A TELLING SIGN OF THE DIFFICULTIES I WAS experiencing at home showed in my absences from school. During my first year in Florida, obviously struggling to handle all that had happened, I had thirteen absences — along with my first F ever. My grades in my other major subjects were C's and D's. It wasn't a good year. Thankfully, in 11th grade, I had only two absences and received A's and B's overall. After the incident with Ann at the beginning of my senior year, I buried myself in a full-time work schedule, stayed out of the house as much as I could, and distanced myself from both Ann and my dad. While my grades were pretty good, as they needed to be for me to graduate, I cut school frequently and had thirty-one absences during my senior year. It was a clear indication of the continued chaos I was experiencing. I was also feeling the familiar emotion of loneliness.

There was no longer anyone for me to talk to and nowhere to turn, which may also be why I decided to join the military. Not unlike why countless others join, the military would provide me the opportunity to escape all that I disliked about my childhood. While I thought I was the only one that had lived through terrible things, I would soon meet David. As it turned out, David had a past that led to our failed marriage. There were demons he didn't want to face, including memories he had also hidden down deep inside — and a strong desire to keep them there.

12

A LETTER TO DAVID

When I walked away from my marriage to David, that all too familiar feeling of loneliness was present. Given my childhood experiences, I always had a longing to be accepted and not to be — or feel — thrown away. I hadn't felt accepted by David, and I certainly felt like he had thrown me away. I also felt like a failure and came away from our broken marriage more securely wrapped in the belief that I was unwanted, unlovable, and not worthy of a peaceful and beautiful fairy tale life. My experience with David added to the hurt my heart was still holding onto from my childhood. To protect it, I simply added to the height, width, and thickness of the walls I had been erecting and using as protection for many years. I was making myself impenetrable.

While I thought I had left David in the past, in 2004, I received a call from my father letting me know that David had reached out looking for me. "What did he want?" I asked, quite perplexed as our divorce had been finalized seventeen years earlier, and I hadn't spoken with him in many years.

"He says he owes you money and that he wants to speak with you," was the answer. "Does he owe you money?" my father asked.

"Probably ... but why is he calling me now?"

"He left a phone number. Would you like it?"

"Sure," I said, taking down the number as he recited it. Curious, I reached out to David. "Hi," I said awkwardly. "I heard you called looking for me because you owe me money?"

"Yes," he replied. "I wanted to see if maybe we could get together and talk?"

"Why?" I asked with defensiveness and distrust.

"Well, I've been thinking about us and there are some things I need to say. I can explain when we get together. Would you be open to meeting me?"

My curiosity had the better of me, and I agreed to see him. We planned to meet in Philadelphia, where I was going on a business trip, and I hung up feeling a bit apprehensive but still curious.

We met in the lobby of the hotel where I was staying. David was staying nearby with a friend who happened to live in the area. It was late, around 9 p.m. We went into the busy hotel restaurant and found a quiet booth in the back. I was uncomfortable. David seemed a bit nervous and quickly dove into the reason for wanting to meet.

"I am an alcoholic," he stated. "I have been in recovery since around the time we split up. I am not sure you realize how much you helped me see a better way to live. It is because of you that I went to AA and got sober." I sat there stunned. I didn't know what to say and, in his nervousness, he just kept talking. "I came to tell you this and to make amends," he said. I didn't understand the context of what he meant by amends, and he must have seen a confused look on my face. He stopped and said, "Maybe you don't know what I am talking about, so let me explain." He told me about the twelve steps of the AA program and explained that one of them was to fix the wrongs that one had done in the past. Meeting with me, he went on, was his attempt to do that. He then went on to say, among other things, how sorry he was for the way he had treated me.

As he had not yet brought up owing me money, I finally asked, "Why do you think you owe me money?"

"Well," he started. "After you got out of the service, but before we divorced, I was receiving additional funds from the military for your support as I was overseas. I should have sent that money to you, but I didn't. Also, when I left California, I left you with all of the bills."

"Oh, I see," I said. "How much is it?"

"Oh, I don't know. I would have to figure that out."

The conversation continued for a bit and, as we were wrapping up, he asked if I had any pictures of our time at Henderson Hall where we had met.

"I'm sure I do," I replied. He asked if I could send him copies as his had been lost in one of his moves. I told him I would.

So many memories came flooding back to me after that conversation. These memories and the information he shared with me — which provided insight on things that had happened during our marriage that I had not previously understood — were not sitting well with me. While he had said he wanted to meet with me because he owed me money, he never mentioned it again ... and I never received anything from him. This was also not sitting well with me. It took eight months for me to make copies of the pictures and, as I prepared the package to send to him, I decided that I needed to write a letter to David to share my feelings with him.

July 16, 2005

Dear David,

Let me begin by apologizing for how long it has taken me to send the pictures you requested. I sincerely hope you enjoy them, and they bring back nothing but happy memories.

They certainly brought back a lot of memories for me. When you and I met up, it had been so long since I had thought about that time in any detail. The pictures, on top of our conversation, brought a lot back. How sad a period that was for me. I was so anxious to start my life and to find happiness and peace. I thought I had. You were so funny, handsome, and caring when I met you. I thought you would always be there to protect me, and I would never have to worry again.

I'm not sure where this letter is headed, but I just felt strongly that I had to respond to your visit. I have promised myself (let's see if I can actually keep it) that I will not go back and change what I write. I think it is important that you hear, and I get out, a number of thoughts that I've had in my head. I'm sure that some of these things will be hard to hear. I can't help that, but I am sorry for any hurt you may feel from any of what I write.

I was so angry at you for so long. I didn't know or understand what had happened. How could someone who called me up from California to say they couldn't live without me and wanted/had to marry me right away, be so mean and so uncaring? You left me at home so many times. I had people (Bob Stoner for one) tell me they saw you out at a bar with a girl. It took him a long while to tell me, but he did so only after I told him we were through. By then, thankfully, there were too many other things that it didn't matter. You lied to me all the time. About where you were going, your parents, friends, and you made up stories. I couldn't understand all of that. You once told me your parents had a home on the water with a boathouse. You said they were cool, and if we went to visit, they would let us spend the night in the boathouse together. You and I know these things aren't true.

It must have been so difficult for you to pick up the phone and call my father to see if you could find me. It must have been more difficult to meet up with me and to say what you said. I must admire you for that. I have several people I wish I could explain things or apologize to, and I don't know if I'll ever have the courage to do that. Perhaps one day.

Anyway, at first, I couldn't figure out why you called. What did you want from me? Why would you tell my father that you thought you owed me money? Was that your way to get me to call? I'm still as insecure and naïve as I was back then, but I am much stronger. "I will always be okay." That has been how I have survived. I say that less often now, but for years I said it all the time. It was the only way I could get through. I understand your need to share your story with me and your desire to have me understand. I know you didn't offer it as an excuse but an explanation. I appreciate it. I don't, however, know if I buy into all this AA stuff.

Two things bothered me about the reason you wanted to talk to me. The first is ... How could you come into my life after so much time to help yours when you may be hurting mine in the process? What if I had things going on that had me in a place where I couldn't handle hearing what you had to say?

I know I told you this, but you need to understand that you looked at that time in your life as a start upwards. I looked at it as a confirmation of my failures. My past was never going to be behind me. It was always going to be there. I wasn't going to be able to rise above the things my family made me live through. I wasn't ever going to be able to trust anyone completely enough to take down the brick wall I built to protect me. There was then, and is now, a big part of me that knows I have a lot of good things to offer. There was and is a big part of me, however, that thinks I am nothing but "a big pile of shit" that doesn't deserve to be at peace. Being at peace, frankly, is more important than being happy.

While I did enjoy our conversation when we met up last year, when I had time to dwell on it, it brought back some ugly stuff I didn't want to have to think about again. Things like the fact that I sold your wedding ring for $14. If I went back to Tustin California today, I could bring you directly to the store where I went. You left me for *recruitment duty in Florida and didn't take your ring. I felt guilt for a long time for doing that. I had no right, but while I'd like to apologize, I can't. I would do the same today. I was so hurt at the time.*

The other thing I don't get is this requirement to try to make amends when possible. You called me because you thought you owed me money. Then, you never offered to pay me back any of the money you owed me. I could care less about the money, but how can you get beyond this without making a wrong right? How can you expect to forgive yourself or have others forgive you if you don't do that?

Fundamentally, I think I have a problem with this program. I am glad, however, that you found it and that it has been good for you. I know your coins mean a great deal to you. It shows a sustained accomplishment that I cannot begin to understand. I know you wanted me to have your sixteen-year coin, but I am returning it to you now. I don't need it. It only serves to remind me of things that should have been. Your failures made me fail. I'm angry at you for that.

Why did you call? Why did you call now? I don't understand all of what you were trying to accomplish, but I do hope that you felt you succeeded.

David, please know that the purpose of this letter was not to bring you any hurt. I needed to get these thoughts out so I can move on. I'm not angry with you anymore. Things happen. I have a better understanding of the reasons now. I'm glad you found the help you needed. I'm sorry I couldn't help you at the time. Please know that had you told me, I would have tried.

I hope you have found peace and happiness in your life. Our past leaves clues on how to navigate the future. Perhaps we can both use the past to make our futures better.

Take care, be well.

THE CONVERSATION WITH DAVID, AND MY TIME REFLECTING ON it, helped me put some things behind me — or to at least put them in a context that made sense out of what I could not previously understand. While I still have many concerns about AA, I am grateful that David had the courage to reach out and that I used my voice to tell him my thoughts. All of this has helped me to reflect more easily on that time.

13
JOHN AND CHILDREN

I MET JOHN BEFORE I WAS EVEN DIVORCED FROM DAVID. JOHN was an officer in the Marine Corps stationed on the same base where I was. I met him at a monthly gathering called "Bosses' Night," when enlisted personnel can bring those they report to to the enlisted club for a few drinks after work. David had left about eight months prior and was currently stationed overseas. I had told him already that I wanted a divorce, but nothing had been done to facilitate this request yet. When I met John, I was on what is called terminal leave. I was still on active duty, but I was ending my service obligation using my remaining vacation time. John was tall, almost six-foot, with big, soft, round brown eyes, and a medium-toned build. He was friendly and very handsome. We talked for a little while, and then I left the gathering.

A friend who worked for him called me the next day telling me that John had asked about me and wanted my phone number. While officers and enlisted personnel are not allowed to date, my enlistment was ending, so I told him to give it to him. It was a bit amusing when John called. I didn't even know his real first name as, in the military, someone's first name is their rank, so, for me, he was Captain. Still holding tight onto the need to feel loved and wanted, I was happy that someone was looking to spend time with me.

John came to pick me up and took me to dinner a few days later. We talked about many things that night, even learning that we grew up not more than four miles from each other on Long Island in the same style house. It took just that one dinner. I was smitten, as was he. He told me later that he had called one of his sisters and told her that he had just returned from a date with the girl he was going to marry. We saw each other a good deal over the next few weeks before I left to head back to Florida in October 1987 after my discharge. I was 22-years-old.

I left California not knowing if I would see John again as, at this time, I was still married to David. With the surprise of the quick finalizing of the divorce, however, John came to Florida to visit me. During this visit, he asked if I would come back to California to live with him. I immediately agreed and moved back out to be with him at the end of January 1988.

Our relationship was easy and fun — a direct counter to what I had experienced with David — so I chalked up the marriage to David as a mistake. An impetuous decision that was made when I was too young to know better. When John proposed just a few months later, I said yes, and the wedding was set for January 14 of the following year. We remained in California until he was discharged in October, then headed back home to New York to get ready for the wedding. I was fully expecting that we would settle into a beautiful life, and I was anxious to do just that hoping that, just maybe, I could have a fairy tale life after all.

John came from a close Italian family. Everyone lived near to one another, and they usually gathered on Sundays for a big family dinner. He had one brother in college and three sisters who were married, and all had or would soon have children. We had both found jobs by the time we married, and John even joined the local Marine Corps Reserve Unit to continue to serve and earn extra money to help us purchase a home. By the following November, we had purchased a home just a couple of miles from his parents' house, and I was beginning to hint about starting a family. John felt strongly that he wanted to wait, so we decided to shelve that discussion for another year or so. The next year went by quickly as we settled into our jobs, married life, and began a few renovations on our home.

We had begun the tradition of alternating the Thanksgiving and Christmas holidays between John's family in New York and mine in Florida. Thanksgiving 1990 had us in Florida. We had just arrived home after our long two-day drive back when there was a knock at our door. It was John's parents delivering a message to him. They told us that his military unit had been trying to reach him and had left several messages on our answering machine, but when they didn't hear from him, they called his parents, who were listed as emergency contacts. John needed to call his command right away.

As John went into the other room to make the call, his parents and I sat down in the living room nervously waiting to hear what this was all about. John came back a short while later. "I'm being activated," he said flatly. "I need to report this coming Wednesday in support of *Operation Desert Shield*." The Reserves hadn't been activated for many years, and it wasn't something I ever thought would or could happen. No one knew what to say at that moment, and I began processing the fact that my husband was going to Iraq, an area of unrest. We had not even been married two years yet. I shouldn't have been surprised, however, as life had continually shown me that just when I thought things would calm down, they don't.

On December 5, 1990, John was activated and left for the Persian Gulf the week after Christmas. He was on the ground close to the action when it turned from *Operation Desert Shield* to the fighting of *Desert Storm*, which began the following month on January 17 and ended, thankfully, just 43 days later, on February 28. I was terrified that John would not return but, thankfully, he did after about six months of active duty. He was deactivated and returned to his civilian job, and we worked on getting settled back into our lives.

* * *

JOHN'S UNEXPECTED ACTIVATION MADE US BOTH REALIZE THAT life is short, and by the end of that year, John agreed that it was time to start our family. By the end of 1992, the following year, I was still not pregnant and consulted my gynecologist, who assured me it was not unusual for it to take more than twelve months. I was not at all convinced, and as each month passed, my stress level built. By the middle of 1993, I was still not pregnant, and my growing concern was making me irritable. My doctor decided to send me for a few tests. I had to lay on an ice-cold stainless-steel table for one of them while a large quantity of colored liquid was forced up into my lady parts using an air compressor-type machine. All the while, an external scanner tracked the liquid to see its flow. This test was extremely painful. It was so painful, in fact, that as we left the doctor's office, I told my husband, in a not so nice tone, "We are never having sex again." I was not joking.

It took a bit of time for the air that had been forced into me to work its way out of my body and for the thoughts of the pain to subside. Then, focused on the desire to have a child, it was back to trying. While painful, the test was helpful as it revealed that I have a tilted uterus which, my doctor told me, might be why it is taking longer to get pregnant. My feelings of guilt, knowing that it was my fault I was not pregnant yet, started to grow.

John and I had enjoyed an intimate relationship that was comfortable and spontaneous. As we began to get further into the process of trying to have children, however, the joy of our intimate moments faded. John worked in the city and, as such, had a long commute to and from work each day, and we now had the added pressure of having to defer our intimacy to the times that the ovulation kit said was most opportune. We were both trying to make the best of it, knowing that the end result would be a child. As time went by, however, keeping our spirits up became harder. By the end of 1993, still not pregnant, my doctor suggested that we consider my taking a prescription hormone shot each month which could enhance the possibility of my eggs being fertilized. The shot was given once a month, and we decided to try it. After five months, I was still not pregnant, and I was devastated.

I am a very private person when it comes to my personal life. We weren't getting pregnant, and I felt it was my fault, so I didn't want to talk about it. I had not been keeping his or my family updated on all that was going on. John, feeling under pressure to produce an heir that would carry on the family name and watching all his sisters easily having children, seemed happy to avoid the subject with them as well. By this time, John's parents had at least six grandchildren, and I began to feel depressed. It didn't help that we were being asked when we were going to have children on a consistent and regular basis. It was all incredibly stressful which, my doctor kept reminding me, was not helping the process.

After the shots didn't work, we met again with the doctor. During this discussion, it was discovered that there was one test that had not yet been done, and it could provide some insight. This was a test of John's sperm to ensure that he was producing them at the right level and that they were viable. When the doctor said this, I became angry and let this be known in my tone when I said, "We have been at this for two years, and NOW you think of doing this?" I was dumbfounded and remained upset throughout the rest of the appointment. John, as always, held my hand and did his best to reassure me that all would be fine. He was always so patient with me. He went to take the test a few days later, and then we waited to meet with the doctor. We both knew something was wrong by the look on the doctor's face.

He gently stated, "The test shows that John has only a small fraction of the sperm most men have." He went on to say, "Men, on average, have somewhere between 15 and 200 million sperm. John has only about 70,000. With this amount," he informed us, "it will be nearly impossible for you to get pregnant naturally." We were both numb.

I was ashamed of myself when I felt a huge sense of relief upon hearing the news, as I now knew that it wasn't my fault that I had not become pregnant. I am also ashamed by how I chose to break the news to John's mother. The next time she brought up the subject of getting pregnant, I took great joy in letting her know that it was because of her son — not me. What I said wasn't nice or called for. I wish I could have stopped myself from saying it, but I just couldn't. I had been feeling so anxious, and responsible, and so desperate for everyone to know that it wasn't me.

The desire to get pregnant was still within both of us and, at great monetary cost and emotional toll, we tried several different approaches hoping for success. One avenue we tried was artificial insemination, which is when the sperm is placed into the uterus by a doctor. The goal is that the sperm not having to swim to the egg themselves would result in a pregnancy. Five months of trying and still no pregnancy. We stopped to catch our breath and regroup as the next step would be to try the same procedure again using donor sperm. We took a few months to come to terms with this, allowing our fragile and raw emotions to get back to a level where we felt ready to try again. Then, we had to work through the process of selecting a donor.

We underwent another five months of artificial insemination with donor sperm and still no luck. It was now around mid-1995, and we decided to take a break until January. Our emotions were shot, and we also needed to save money as the next step, our last resort, was to try in-vitro fertilization with donor sperm. This is where one or more eggs are extracted from me and, in a petri dish outside the womb, they are inseminated with the sperm and placed back inside of me with the hope that at least one of the eggs becomes fertilized and produces a baby. While a small portion of the prior procedures was paid by insurance, we would have to pay the entire cost of this procedure — around $15,000 per cycle.

We went through a few months of trying invitro. A few months of daily shots for five days to boost my hormones and do all that could be done to prepare my body to become pregnant. Nothing. No pregnancy. Not one of them took. Failure, again. That was it. I was done. I was emotionally, physically, and mentally spent. I am sure John was feeling the same way. To cope, I withdrew from him and into myself and kept myself busier than ever. Once we began using donor sperm and it didn't work, I was back to believing that it was my fault. From as far back as I could remember, I had said, even writing this in a high school memory book to a friend, that I did not want to have children. So, when all that we had tried did not work, I just knew that God had taken me seriously. It *was* all my fault. In the spring of 1996, John and I stopped trying to have children and tried to make a life without them. I was thirty years old.

14

BUSY, BUSY, BUSY

WORK, WORK, WORK. BUSY, busy, busy. That has been me since I don't remember when. Well, I guess, high school. I worked all through high school, usually holding two jobs and maintaining a full-time schedule. I continued the trend of working two jobs even when I went into the military, working a second job for at least two of the four years I served.

When John and I moved back to New York in late 1988, that is when I *truly* became busy. Along with the process of trying to get pregnant, during the next decade, I worked on settling into married life and renovating and decorating our new home. I also held several second jobs to earn some extra money for the household. I always felt like I wasn't doing enough, and as I learned in childhood, being busy every moment of the day was what I was supposed to do.

In high school, I had expected to have a career as a secretary or administrative assistant and, when we returned to New York, I took a job at Allstate Insurance typing insurance applications into their system. My time in the Marine Corps, however, had taught me that I was capable of much more, so I decided to work towards earning a degree and seeing what the world had in store for me. I had taken a few college classes while in the service, but I was still far from having the required number of credits to graduate. As it seemed daunting to work towards a bachelor's degree, which would have taken five or six years to complete going part-time, I decided to first obtain my associate degree at the local community college — and where, when I was young, I had spent many hours riding my bike around the campus.

Allstate Insurance was a large company with over 50,000 employees, so there were always opportunities to move up into a different position. The organization had a formal program called the Job Opportunity Program to facilitate this, and open positions were posted on a job board. Most days, as I came down the hall after having lunch, I would look at the new postings. One day, about eight months after I began working there, one of the jobs caught my eye. The title was Human Resources Representative, and the listed duties were similar to a good number of those that I had performed in the military. Excited about this possibility, I completed the necessary form and submitted it, as required, to my manager. My manager came back with the signed form but pointed out that it wasn't likely I would get the job as I didn't have the required four-year degree.

As I did have four years in the military, I submitted the form anyway. I was interviewed by the Divisional Human Resources Manager, Fred Wolfe, who had been with Allstate for over 30 years. This is who I would be working for. He was friendly, approachable, and I enjoyed our conversation. As it turned out, Fred had served in the Army and, as he told me during that interview, "Your time in the military is more valuable than any degree," and he offered me the position.

After less than a year at Allstate, I officially had a career in Human Resources and not just a job. I would go on to spend almost five years at Allstate, leaving, at my request and with a lay-off package, during a time of significant downsizing due to advances in technology. I would be out of work for two years, strategically using the time and the money I had received from the lay-off package to complete my associate degree.

In 1995, I went back to work, grateful that my four years of human resource experience and my newly acquired degree had helped me to obtain a next-level up position at Nikon as an Employee Relations Specialist. In that role, I was responsible for coaching and counseling both managers and employees to improve morale as well as behavior and performance. Less than a year later, and just a few short months after John and I stopped trying to have a child, I was promoted to head the Human Resources function. I had practically begged for the job after my manager, the former head, left. I did not yet have my bachelor's degree, nor did I have nearly enough years of human resources experience for the position.

When I received the promotion, there were two stipulations. The first, given I lacked significant experience, was that if I couldn't successfully do the job after six months, I would be fired. The second was that I was required to complete my degree as quickly as possible. Along with this perceived pressure from the company, I also put pressure on myself as I knew that if I could successfully do this job, I would be set for life in a solid career.

Thankfully, I was already enrolled in an accelerated weekend trimester college degree program at the time of the promotion. This schedule was helpful as it allowed me to have my weeknights free and take a full load of three classes. I am a rule and expectation follower, and I had a plan on how I was going to earn the necessary credits and graduate in the spring of 1998. To finish my degree on schedule, along with taking three classes during that semester and the next, I was also working on earning an additional nine credits through PELA. PELA stood for Prior Experiential Learning Assessment and was a program in which a student could write an extensive scholarly paper showing how their prior work experience provided them with enhanced skills and abilities related to the degree program in which they were enrolled. As an example, I was writing a paper on how I developed and facilitated training on effective recruitment. While it was on-the-job learning, it also related to my degree. While writing for these credits sounded like it would be easy, it wasn't. The papers were required to be lengthy and detailed, and I would need to provide substantial back-up and obtain letters, in this case from a prior boss, supporting my direct involvement and what I had learned.

* * *

IN EARLY NOVEMBER 1997, SOMETIME BEFORE 9 A.M., THE HEAD of Production knocked on my open office door and said good morning. I was sitting in my chair staring in the opposite direction, and I am sure he thought that I was looking at my computer, which was situated on the credenza behind my desk. I wasn't. I was lost in what I was feeling. There were a million things that I needed to do, and I couldn't seem to get enough gumption to do even one of them. He began talking before I even acknowledged his greeting. I slowly turned my chair around to face him.

He stopped talking, reached behind him to close my office door, and then said, "What's the matter?" While I had tried to muster up some energy to get what I imagined was a pained look off my face, it obviously had not worked. I was immediately embarrassed and tried desperately to collect myself, but I couldn't. Tears welled up in my eyes, threatening to roll down my face. I felt so ashamed. There was no crying at work. Work was a place where you must hold things together and not display any emotions.

'*Dammit, Heidi,*' I cursed myself as I began pinching and then twisting the skin of my thigh through the material on the skirt of my tailored business suit. As it had on several other occasions, I was hoping that the extreme discomfort I was causing myself would override my emotions. It didn't work.

He sat, not saying a word, as I took a few deep breaths and dried my tears. When I had collected myself sufficiently, he asked, "What's going on, is everything ok?"

"I don't know," I replied. "I came into work and while nothing significant has happened, I am feeling so overwhelmed. I have so many things going on, and I don't know what I should do next. Quite frankly, I am not sure how to get through the day."

I surprised myself with what I had just admitted and was further surprised when this man, a bit older and someone who had his act together based on all I had seen of him since I began working with him, said, "I have been where you are."

"Really?" I blurted out, more of a statement than a question.

"There was a similar point in my life, and I sought the help of a therapist." He said that the therapist had helped him work through some things and had provided him with tools to navigate life's difficulties. "Would you like his name?" he asked.

"Yes, please," I replied immediately. He left, returning a few minutes later, and handed me a piece of paper. As he turned to leave, he simply said good luck. That was the first and last time, in the five years that we worked together, that we spoke about anything that was not work-related.

After he left, I got up and closed the door to my small office. I walked back, sat down, and, after a moment, resigned to the fact that whatever was happening within me was not something I could figure out how to fix on my own, I picked up the phone and dialed. I had never been to a therapist before, but here I was, leaving a message letting them know who I was referred by and stating I needed to speak with him. I hung up and just sat there, still lost about how to get through the day.

When the therapist, a licensed social worker, called me back a short time later, I was still sitting motionless in my office chair. When I answered the phone, trying to act all business-like, I thanked him for the return call and asked if I could see him that day. I wasn't surprised when he asked me to give him an understanding of what was happening and why I felt the urgent need to meet with him. As I opened my mouth to answer him, I began to sob, and it was through this sobbing that I described how I was feeling. He agreed to see me at 6 p.m., and I hung up the phone, grateful that I would be seeing him later. I went through the rest of the day in a fog trying to get tasks accomplished. What I did not do that day was tell my husband how I was feeling. This was my fault as I had put too many things on my plate, and it was my job to deal with them.

* * *

I ARRIVED AT THE ADDRESS THE THERAPIST GAVE ME AROUND 5:50 p.m. As I had been raised, being on time meant being early. It was a house and the two-car garage had been converted into an office. I found the entrance around the side of the garage and stepped up the two wooden steps. With my hand on the doorknob, I took a couple of deep breaths, not knowing what I would find beyond the door. I entered a small room where soft music filled the air and darkness filled the corners. It wasn't overly inviting but comfortable enough. I could hear hushed voices coming from behind a door that was directly in front of me, so, suspecting that I had successfully found the waiting area, I took a seat on the small couch.

A few minutes later, the voices disappeared, and, within a few moments, the door to the inner space opened. A man smiled warmly at me as he said, "Heidi?"

"Yes," I said, with a smile on my face as I rose from the couch.

"I'm Tom," he said. "Come on in." I followed him into his office, which felt more like a small living room with a couple of overstuffed chairs and a loveseat. The therapist, average in height, weight, and build, was maybe mid-forties and carried himself in a way that conveyed confidence. There was no desk. The room had no windows, and it felt tight, dark, and cold. He motioned for me to sit on the leather loveseat to the right, and he sat on an upholstered upright chair opposite me.

I was nervous and made idle chit-chat as we sat down. He then looked directly at me and asked, "What can I do for you?" I gulped a bit, and as my insides shook with apprehension, I began speaking in a soft but direct manner.

"Well, I'm not sure, but I'm having a hard time getting through the day. I guess I just have too much going on. I am sorry to bother you."

"Well, why don't we start with your telling me all that is going on in your life."

"Sure," I said, continuing to wear the smile that had been on my face since he had first greeted me.

In a matter-of-fact way and with the belief that the number of things that I was doing was normal, I began. "First, I am the head of Human Resources for Nikon. It is a high-level job for a big company. There are about four hundred employees scattered across five locations, and this is the time of the year when we hold open enrollment meetings for employees to decide on which insurance coverage they want for next year. There are a great many changes, so we're holding informational meetings in each office. I traveled last week, and I travel again next week. I am then home the following week as well as the week after, which is Thanksgiving week. I leave the Monday after Thanksgiving, not returning home until Friday, and then I travel the week after as well. And, of course, on top of my travel schedule, my regular work needs to be done."

As I spoke, I looked in the direction of the therapist and, while I looked him in the eye occasionally, I found myself diverting my eyes, looking at some far-off point to the left of his face. I was trying to decide what he was thinking about what I had said so far. Was he bored with what I was saying? Was he going to stop me and say something like, "So what? Most people have too many things going on?" He was hard to read, so I continued with a bit of discomfort. "Besides work," I started to say.

But I didn't finish this sentence as he interrupted, asking, "Before you go on, may I ask you a question?"

"Sure," I replied flatly.

In a tone that was not accusatory or negative but inquisitive, he said, "I am reflecting on our conversation earlier today and how you sounded. I am trying to balance that with what I am seeing and hearing from you now. Given how you were earlier, how can you be smiling? How can you be talking to me in a manner that seems like any other discussion you might have during the day?"

"Because that's what I'm supposed to do," I replied quite easily.

"What do you mean?"

"This is how I was raised and how I live my life. No one else needs to know that I am not doing okay and, certainly, no one should be burdened with my problems."

"Is that the way you feel right now," he asked. "Like you're being a burden to me?"

"Of course," I quickly replied. "I'm embarrassed. I'm an adult. I'm expected to manage issues that arise and, especially those that are my fault. I put too much on my plate. This was my own doing."

"Okay," he said, clearly trying to process what I had said, but allowing me to continue.

"I am also enrolled in college to complete my bachelor's degree by next spring. I am taking a full load in an accelerated program. I attend classes every other weekend, on Friday nights, all-day Saturday, and Sunday mornings. I have an extensive paper to write for each of these classes, and, in addition to this, I am trying to write papers to earn an additional nine credits for what is called Prior Learning Experience. I must say, while this all sounded doable back in August when I registered and when classes began in September, I am now at a loss over how to successfully get all this schoolwork done. I still have two weekends of classes left, along with final exams and papers to write."

Still with a smile on my face and the same matter-of-factness in my voice, I continued. "I, of course, also have my personal life. My marriage, my home, and the upcoming holidays. I love the holidays, and every year, the day after Thanksgiving, I put up my Christmas tree along with all the other Christmas decorations. It has also become a tradition that my husband and I host a holiday party at our home on the first Saturday of December. We invite friends, family, and work colleagues. This will be the sixth or seventh year that we had held this party, and people look forward to it."

I paused here as, while other things were going on in my life, I had just covered the major ones. He looked at me and said, "That certainly is a lot."

"Yes," I replied. "But it's not that unusual for me. I always have a lot on my plate." He then asked me a question that, while simple and one which I answered immediately, I would come to reflect on quite often.

He asked me, "What do you do when your plate gets full?" Without any hesitation, and in a voice that sounded surprised by the question for the answer was obvious, I stated, "I get a bigger plate."

"And when that one gets full you ...?" his voice trailed off, waiting for me to catch on. As the question sunk in, I slowly and hesitantly responded with something that sounded more like a question than a statement.

"I fit it on the plate that I already have?" He just looked at me for a moment. "I guess I do have a lot going on and, perhaps," I admitted, "there is a bit too much."

"So, what can you do about that?" he asked. "What can you take off of your plate?"

"Nothing," I replied. "It's all important and I have committed to doing it all." My response was stated a bit more adamantly and more defensively than I had planned.

"Okay," he said, "What can you get others to help you with? What about your papers? You mentioned earlier that you would be handwriting them during your upcoming travel, but then you would have to type them when you returned home."

"Yes, that's right."

"Well, could you get someone else to type them for you? Perhaps you could hire someone," he suggested. "Or even ask your husband." Hmmm, I sat there thinking for a moment. My husband was good with the computer, and he did a good deal of typing himself. This could work, I thought, and if he agreed, it would save me many hours of work.

"Yes," I said. "That could work."

"Now, what else can we take off of your plate?"

"Nothing else," I said, still resisting this possibility.

"What about not hosting the Christmas party."

"Oh, I can't cancel that," I immediately replied, adding, "People expect us to have it."

"How much work goes into planning and hosting?"

"A lot," I admitted. He asked me to estimate how many hours I spent on the party planning and hosting. "Easily twenty hours or more," I responded.

"Wouldn't that time, just for this year, be better spent on school or other tasks?" He asked, reminding me that most of the items, like school and extensive travel for work, were temporary but would still be around for another five or six weeks. "Given how you sounded and what you said to me earlier on the phone, why not consider canceling it just for this year? Just to relieve some of the pressure." He was, of course, right. I was still experiencing that overwhelming feeling just explaining to him all that I had to do.

I sat there for a moment and then answered, "I'll consider it."

As I drove home that evening, I reviewed all that we discussed. The idea of having my husband help with the typing was a great suggestion, and I was sure that John would be glad to help. As for the party, he was right about that. The hours that would be spent on that could be put to much better use this year. The party needed to be canceled.

I arrived home around 8 p.m. My husband was not surprised by such a late arrival as he knew I was busy at work these days. He didn't ask me where I had been, and I didn't mention to him that I had been anywhere other than at work. As we sat down to eat dinner, I decided to let him know my thoughts on the party. I explained that while it was disappointing, I just had too much on my plate and that I should be focused on work and school now. He said he completely understood, and that was that. I went to bed that night feeling lighter than I had felt in weeks.

15

AN UGLY RESPONSE

THE NEXT COUPLE OF WEEKS FLEW BY IN A HAZE. THE FOUR-day weekend at Thanksgiving helped me to get things organized for work and school and gave me time to put a to-do list together of all that I needed to accomplish in the next few short weeks before the school semester ended. The list was still long and, while I was still not sure how I would get it all done, I felt good about the decision to cancel the party. With a lot of help from my husband, we even put up the Christmas decorations and our tree, as usual, the day after Thanksgiving. The light feeling continued.

As Sunday and the weekend were winding to a close, my husband came into the bedroom to find me packing for the business trip I would be on for the next five days. He cheerfully said, "I want to tell you something."

"What is it," I asked as I continued to fold items into my suitcase.

He started with, "Well, I know how much you look forward to the Christmas party each year, and while I know you said you wanted to cancel it, I wanted to do something special for you. So, I have made all the arrangements, and we are still going to have the party next Saturday night." I stopped in my tracks. Please tell me I had not just heard him say that. I know I should have been appreciative that he would do something so thoughtful, and it was sweet, but I became immediately enraged.

"What do you mean the party isn't canceled?" I stated this in a loud voice with a tone that made it clear I was extremely unhappy.

"Well," he said tentatively, "I sent out the invitations two weeks ago."

"Who's coming?" I demanded to know.

"The usual crowd."

"Show me the list," my voice straining with the desire to yell. He looked at me for a moment and then went downstairs to get the list. I looked it over and immediately saw that names were missing. "What about food? Did you order it already?"

"Yes," he replied, quite happy with what he had done as I stood there incredulous.

"Can you show me the order slip?"

"Sure," he said, handing it over.

Immediately critical, I cried out, "This isn't enough food. What else were you planning on serving?"

"Just chips and dip."

My need to control the outcome and ensure that everything went the way I thought it was supposed to go got the best of me. This was, literally, the last thing that I needed at this moment. I had been feeling good not too long before this, but now ... now I felt like I was going over the edge. Why was life always this way for me? Just when I thought that things would calm down, they didn't.

At some point in the conversation, I asked about my parents.

"They are also coming," he announced quite proudly.

"What?" I exclaimed in disbelief.

"Yes, they are driving up from Florida. Isn't that great?"

I couldn't hold anything back any longer. "No, it is not great," I yelled. "None of this is great! I canceled the party because, as I told you, there was too much going on, and I just didn't have the time to do it."

"Yes, I know. That is why I am doing it for you."

"So, what?" I said, spitting my words at him. "I'm just supposed to not ask any questions, let you handle everything, and try to enjoy the party even though there won't be enough food, invitations weren't sent to everyone that should have been invited and, on top of this, my parents are coming at a time when I have too much to do already?"

"Yes," he answered slowly, clearly not understanding why I was upset.

"When are they arriving?" I demanded.

"They said they will be here by Friday evening and will leave on Monday morning."

"So," I continued to spit my words, "I am leaving at 5 a.m. tomorrow. I will get back around 6 p.m. on Friday, and they will be arriving at about the same time?"

"Yes," he replied slowly.

"And then," I continued, "they are leaving Monday morning, so they will still be here when I leave for my next trip on Sunday afternoon. I am then gone for five days, returning on Friday late afternoon, and I will be at school that entire weekend, beginning Friday night. Plus, it is the weekend when all my papers are due and during which I take final exams. Do I have this correct?" I demanded he acknowledge all that I was experiencing and feeling at that moment.

"That's correct," he replied quietly, finally seeing how extremely unhappy I was.

* * *

LIKE EVERY OTHER TIME THAT I HAD FELT OVERWHELMED, I felt helpless and felt like I was going to break. Also, just like every other time, I did what was expected. It took a bit of time, but I dried my tears and stuffed all that I was feeling down deep inside. I apologized to my husband for my behavior and for overreacting, thanked him for his thoughtfulness, and then went about getting the tasks that needed to be done, done.

I knew that my reaction and current state of mind was not just because of all the to-do's that I had to get done. It was only the previous year that John and I had given up on trying to have children. We had talked about adoption, but we never pursued it, and the topic of children was buried within each of us. I know that I was silently suffering, and I expect that John was also.

I knew I should have told him that I was having difficulty getting through the day and that it was severe enough for me to see a therapist, but I couldn't. I just felt like such a failure for not being able to conceive — and now not to be able to get through an ordinary day of life. It was all just too much for me, and I could not find a way to open up to him or to bring myself to talk with him about anything I was feeling. We continued forward as a couple but separately, each in our own world. Our marriage didn't survive. We divorced after eleven years.

As I had after my first failed marriage, during my marriage to John, I continued to add to the protective wall that I had been building. With each challenge we faced, I allowed my exterior to harden, adding depth and strength to the internal wall around my heart. It wasn't fair to John or us, but I needed to in order to continue to survive this life.

At some point, long after my marriage to John ended, I became resigned to the fact that I would never have children. It was emotionally difficult to grasp that this was the case, but one day, at around age forty, I knew that I was finally past this particular hurt and disappointment. It is a blessing that I did come to terms with it as, if I hadn't, it would have been devastating when I learned in 2012 that there had been a water contamination incident on Camp Lejeune. During certain years, including the one that I was there, anyone stationed there, or at Camp Johnson where I had been, had been exposed to harmful toxins. Many were now experiencing a lengthy list of serious medical conditions. While there were a great many conditions that people were suffering from, including kidney and bladder cancer and Parkinson's disease, the one that may have impacted me was infertility.

16

MEETING BOB

I WAS THIRTY-FOUR WHEN MY MARRIAGE TO JOHN ENDED. IT was the fall of 1999 and I moved to a small town on Long Island about forty minutes from the home John and I had shared. I spent most of the first few months in my small, bottom-floor apartment of a two-story house. I was so sad and cried a great deal over my second failed marriage. I couldn't believe that it had happened again. I felt like I tried so hard to make it work, and it just didn't.

In late December, as the difficult year was drawing to a close, I finally had enough of myself. It was time to get out and explore the beautiful quaint downtown area, which was only about a half-mile down the hill from where I was living. While I intended to have dinner at one of the restaurants, as I drove through town I was suddenly feeling very vulnerable and not confident enough to sit and eat by myself. Instead of heading home, however, I told myself that I could still go into one of the restaurants but get take-out instead.

I picked a place in the middle of a small strip of storefronts. It had a large front window and, when I looked inside, I could see that the place was not very big. There were two tables in the front window, three tables down the left side, and room for maybe three or four more in the back. In addition to the tables, there was a bar. In fact, most of the place was taken up by the large wooden bar, which sat along a good portion in the middle of the right-hand wall. It was a Wednesday, about 4:30 in the afternoon, and I had the day off.

As I opened the inner door to the restaurant, I stopped for a minute to figure out where I should go. There was just one other person at the bar sitting about a third of the way down the long side of it. A few of the tables had people sitting at them, and, seeing that the short end of the bar was open, I decided to head to the corner next to the wall.

I was now directly in front of the tables which sat in the front window. I was not planning to stay long so, instead of sitting down, I stood. This allowed me to put my back to the wall and, from this vantage point, I could see out the front window while also seeing anyone coming in the front door and take in all the tables throughout the small interior. I had not previously spent much time in bars but, for a year or so before we divorced, John and I would eat lunch at the bar of a local Italian restaurant a few times a month, so I was comfortable enough.

The bartender greeted me right away, and I asked for a draft beer and a menu. As I stood there waiting for her to come back, I took the opportunity to look around. This certainly felt like a hometown local hangout. There were photos and other memorabilia, like a police officer's badge, hanging on the large far wall and, on the wall in the back, there were caricature drawings, I assumed, of locals and regulars. I observed the bartender greeting a few people who walked in by their names, and the waitress was standing talking with the folks at a nearby table in a way that indicated that they knew each other well.

I ordered my food quickly and, while I sipped my beer and waited for my order, I overheard the bartender talking with the man at the bar about a football pool. As had been the case since high school, I was a huge football fan. I immediately spoke up and said, "Can anyone get into the pool?"

"Sure," she replied. "Do you live in town?"

"Yes," I answered. "I just moved here a few months ago."

She introduced herself along with the gentleman at the bar. I told them my name and then set about picking a few football boxes as I chatted with the gentleman about the town and local happenings. He was extremely friendly, indicated that he was a regular patron of the restaurant, and told me I would need to meet his wife and that I should come to the house party they were throwing in a couple of weeks. I thought this was so lovely, and I told him I would be sure to stop in again to meet his wife.

Bob walked in as I handed the bartender back the large square cardboard paper, which now had my name in several of the boxes. I was immediately drawn to him and found him to be handsome, sexy, and friendly. The bartender greeted him by name, and then, as he looked over at me with his round red face and his beautiful blue eyes, she introduced the two of us. I would find out later that the only reason he even looked at me was that I was standing in his spot. The corner spot is where he usually took up space when he came in, which, I would also find out later, was virtually every day.

As these three locals began chatting, I excused myself to go to the bathroom. I was feeling a bit out of place and was hoping that my food would be there when I returned. Thankfully, it was, so I paid my bill and left.

The truth is that I fell in love with Bob the moment I met him. Another truth is that he was married when I met him, but I didn't know this at first. The third truth is that, while I met him in a bar/restaurant, I didn't know he was an alcoholic. Just these three truths would have made for a difficult relationship, but when you add our own insecurities and brokenness into this mix, it was the perfect recipe for something that would not end well.

I would return to the café a few times over the next few weeks. Bob was there every time. He introduced me to his friends and other people that he knew. He didn't have a wedding ring on, and he never discussed a wife or a family. Nor did anyone else. It would be many weeks before I found out he was married. Sadly, I decided to be with him anyway. I was still so desperate to be loved, cared for, and wanted. Bob and I would talk a great deal about our pasts and what we wanted for the future. About six months after we met, having spent as much time together as we could, Bob and I decided that we would go away together for a few days to see if we thought the relationship would be something that might work or if we should stop seeing each other.

Unfortunately, by the time that trip came, it was known to his wife and others that we were together. I had decided to be with Bob based on information that he shared with me about the state of his marriage and his relationship with his wife. While he lied to me about many things, especially at the beginning, I was somewhat comforted to know that the information about the state of his marriage was correct, as it was corroborated by his wife during a conversation that the two of us had shortly after she found out. Bob told me that he had been unhappy in his marriage for many years, and he had even told his wife that if he ever won the lottery, he would leave her. He did win the lottery, splitting a 4.5-million-dollar prize with a friend about two or three years before I met him. Bob and his wife decided to divorce, and, in the divorce settlement, he gave her all the remaining lottery payments.

After the decision to divorce was made, his parents were told, and I committed myself to make the relationship work. I tried doing just that for many years. I had a lot of guilt for being with Bob and much regret. It was already known that we were together when I found out many things about

Bob that I had not known previously. While I knew that he had a relationship with someone before he met me, also while he was married, I later learned that it was still going on. I believed the lies that he told me the day I found out, along with the lies he told for the next several years. All in all, Bob would cheat on me for the first two-and-a-half years of our relationship. I was still, however, stubbornly staying and trying to make it work. I loved him and thought that was enough. As I have come to define my actions on this and many other things, I was trying to put a square peg into a round hole.

From the beginning, I allowed circumstances and behaviors to happen that I had previously indicated to myself and others were not okay. Things like having an affair with a married person. This was not okay, but I allowed myself to do it. Being in a car when the driver had been drinking. This was not okay, but I allowed Bob to do it. Being in a car when the driver was drinking while driving the car. This was not okay, but I allowed Bob to do it. Allowing someone to cheat on me. This was not okay, but I allowed Bob to do it. Allowing someone to lie to me. This was not okay, but I allowed Bob, his friends, and others in his family to do it. Allowing someone to take advantage of my generosity. This was not okay, but I allowed Bob and others in his family to do it. Allowing someone to manipulate me using both their words and actions. This was not okay, but I allowed it from many.

I let my love for Bob and my longing to be in a successful relationship override everything that was not okay. I also let the unhealthy part of me override my thoughts when things came up that were not okay, and, in the process, I became severely broken. In truth, I had come into the relationship with Bob already broken. I just didn't describe it as that. What I told Bob was that I felt like I was a piece of shit. While he would deny it years later, he told me he felt the same way about himself. Kindred spirits, I thought, trying to make things right in our world without regard for what we were doing to ourselves as individuals, to each other, and certainly without any regard for others.

* * *

MANY QUALITIES ATTRACTED ME TO BOB. HE WAS A gentleman. He would open the door for me and help me into his truck. He would hold my coat, help me into it, and then flip my hair up and out so it was not stuck inside my collar. Bob said sweet things at times. One time he said to me, "I can't wait to meet your dad." I was surprised by this and asked him why. "Because he's important to you," was his answer. That melted my heart. Bob had a way of saying things that were exactly what I needed to hear. At times, the hair on my arms stood up as I got goosebumps feeling the depth of what he was saying. I would come to understand that those times, which were infrequent, were when he was being emotionally vulnerable with me. Most of the rest of the time, he was emotionally unavailable.

Bob always held my hand and, as we entered a room, he would put his hand on the small of my back. He was also a great slow dancer. How I loved being in his arms and recall, early on, asking if he could promise me that we would dance one slow dance every day for the rest of our lives. Of course, he said, making that promise. He would come to break it.

Along with all his wonderful qualities, Bob was a drinker. He would drink every day and was very much a creature of habit. We hardly left the small town we lived in other than to go to work. I did try, for many years, to keep up with him. As I explained to my brother one day, I tried to be a professional when it came to drinking. I just couldn't do it. I didn't have it in me, and I couldn't keep up. I began to despise going downtown. Everything in his life, which was also my life, was centered around alcohol.

As they had been before we met, things continued to be busy in my life. About five years after we met, Bob and I moved into a house we purchased together. We immediately began four different major renovation phases, taking place over three-and-a-half years, on the 3,500 sq. ft. house and property. We had both been working in New York City for a few years by this time. We lived way outside of the city on Long Island, and my roundtrip commute to work was three and a half hours. The commute was on top of the executive-level jobs that I held, which also took up a substantial bit of my time, as did my frequent out-of-town work trips.

In addition to my busyness outside of the house, I spent an overabundance of time making sure that everything was in order in the house as well. Bob was very particular about just about everything. His clothes. My clothes. The cleanliness of the house. The organization of the closets, drawers, and garage. I thought that the more time I spent ensuring all was in order, the more it would help the feelings of not belonging, not feeling settled, and not feeling adequate that I was experiencing. It didn't. It only added to it. I was spending all this time making sure that everything was perfect and the way I thought it should be. The unfortunate part of this was that the more I did, the less Bob seemed to care about what I was doing in support of the house and how he wanted it. In turn, I began to put less and less value on myself, tried even harder, and kept myself busier, continuously looking for acceptance from Bob to confirm that all I was doing mattered.

Despite all that had transpired, Bob and I decided to get married after seven years of being together. I had told him over and over again from the beginning of our relationship that I didn't want a mediocre marriage so, when he proposed, I thought he was ready to settle down because that is what he told me. I was hopeful that we could calm into a quiet happy marriage. For the first five or so years we were together, we had been living in a small house that I owned, but in which Bob said he never felt at ease. It was about a year before he proposed that we had purchased our house, and now that we had a place we both owned, he said that he was in a happy place and looked forward to coming home from work, fiddling around in the garage, having dinner together and, on occasion, going downtown for a cocktail and dinner. This description was vastly different than how we had been living, which was him going to the bar after work and my getting off the train a couple of hours later and meeting him there for a bite to eat before heading home to bed to do it all over again the next day. I believed what he said to me, however, and we married.

Nothing changed, and in the end, it was Bob's drinking and the impact of his drinking that ruined what I thought could have been a beautiful and secure relationship. In the beginning, we would dance together every night. There was intimacy. There was talk of past regrets and hopes for the future. It was all changing, but it was happening very slowly. I am not sure how I could be so alert and on the ball at work and in all my extracurricular involvement yet miss that my marriage was not a marriage at all and that Bob's drinking had become so destructive to our relationship. I would come to learn that alcoholism is a progressive disease, and it does change a person over time. It also changes the people the alcoholic is with over time. I didn't see this happening to me either.

While I didn't see all that was happening to Bob, to me, or us, I felt it, though, and these feelings grew stronger over time. It was a feeling of sadness. It was a feeling of being alone. It was a feeling of isolation. It was a feeling of everything spinning too fast to keep up with. It was a feeling of inadequacy. It was a feeling that I was crazy. It was a feeling of guilt. It was the feeling that everything I did was wrong. It was all of these feelings and more.

17
A MILESTONE
BIRTHDAY

I TURNED FORTY-FIVE IN JUNE 2010. AS IT IS AN INCREMENT of five, I considered it a milestone birthday. As I do each year, I took a moment to reflect on my life. Bob and I had been married for four years, together for over eleven, and I continued to keep myself busy. On this birthday, I focused on where I was now, where I was headed, how I felt about my past and the present, and what the future might hold. The answer that I was formulating was heavy. Life was not good. I was not good. I did not feel like I was in a good place at all. In reflecting on my prior adult years, it wasn't like everything was great with them. Well, I do remember when I turned twenty-eight in 1993, I felt great for some reason. Most years, however, were just fine, or they were not fine, and I had clear reasons or, perhaps, excuses for why this was.

On previous birthdays, I would reflect and say to myself, things will be better next year or after _____ things will improve, filling in this blank with whatever time or circumstance I desired. I was viewing a good life only as a future possibility — as if it were going to happen, just at a later time.

This check-in, at forty-five, was quite different. Something wasn't right. I had accomplished a lot in my life but, different than in previous years, I was tapping into how I was *feeling* about my life rather than focusing on what I had accomplished. I was looking introspectively, which was not something I had ever done. The only thing I was focused on, and what would not leave my mind, was that something was off. This really could not be what life was about, could it? Was this really it?

This question was not new for me. I had experienced similar thoughts in the past, the most notable being when I was around eight or nine years old. I do not know why I can recall this particular moment so vividly. Perhaps it was a reflection of whatever chaos was happening in my life at that time but, on that day, I was walking home alone from the stores just down the hill from my house. I had just come down the steps alongside the movie theatre, making my way along the large brick façade of the side of the building. At that moment, I stopped and was overtaken by the thought that life made no sense. I found myself standing there saying, aloud, why would God make us go through all this stuff and then we just die? I remember looking up at the sky as if I were going to find an answer there. I did not get an answer that time, nor did I get one any other time, as I never asked anyone to help me understand. With all that had happened to and around me then, in my young life, I did what I always did — I tucked the question and all that came with it away deep inside. Then, suddenly at forty-five, I realized that this question had never left me. It had always been floating behind the busyness of everyday life.

My life was all about work and getting tasks done. It was about making sure everyone was happy with me and that I wasn't in trouble with anyone. As the 1990s had been, the 2000s were just as busy. I had a good career and was the head of Human Resources for a large national law firm. Early in the decade, I attended classes to earn my Senior Professional in Human Resources certification. Shortly thereafter, I began teaching a course that prepared people to take that same certification test. I would teach that course every other Saturday during the fall and spring semesters for about nine years, beginning in September of 2002.

Having decided to continue my education, on alternating Saturdays for the next three years, I took classes towards earning my master's degree. Later in the decade, having completed my degree, I began to teach in that same program and would do so for nine years. I was also active in my village government, having been appointed by the mayor to serve as Chair of the Zoning Board and also as the Superintendent of Highways. I was an active participant in the local Marine Corps League, a veteran's benevolent organization, and I spent a good deal of time serving and supporting my surrounding community by attending funerals, ceremonies, parades, awarding scholarships, and talking with school groups.

I was making a nice income. My husband was making a nice income. We had a beautiful home on the water, which was the envy of many of our friends and family, and I could spend whatever money I wanted to. There was, however, no real enjoyment despite all that I had, and there was no sense of satisfaction with all that I had accomplished.

The concept of life being all about work and tasks was not new to me. I was raised by a father that was always on the go. Always in constant motion. When I was growing up, dad was always focused on something I refer to as 'get a task, get it done, and get another.' This trait, if one can call it that, I learned from him. My father never sat down to relax. He was always in the garage and always focused on getting his long and never-ending list of routine tasks associated with keeping a home and running a business completed. Here I was at forty-five, feeling like I imagined he must have felt at some point. There was always something to take care of. There was always something that had to be done. I was a hamster on a wheel, as my brother Keith would say. I did not feel like I was gaining anything and, with an understanding that the goal in life is for one to be happy, I was searching for that feeling, yet it was elusive.

This was not the first time I was questioning my life and its value. It happened on one other occasion about nine years before this birthday and, at that time, I remember thinking that if someone told me that tomorrow would be my last day on earth, I would be okay with that. I wasn't suicidal, and I did not want to bring harm to myself or anyone else. My support for being okay with my life not continuing was quite simple. If life tomorrow was going to be the same as today, why did I need to stick around? I thought of life as vanilla. Anything good that happened was fleeting and could never be counted on to last. All the bad that was happening was the norm, as it had been since I was a child, so I adapted to it by smoothing it out so it didn't look or feel so bad. Life became something that wasn't great, and it wasn't awful. It just was, and it wasn't going to change. Life was doing, reaching the next goal, building a career, establishing a home life, being a good community citizen, not making anyone mad, and not getting in trouble. It was also about, among other neutral and unpleasant things, avoiding or living with the chaos of life created by me, by circumstances, and by those that occupied my personal life. Life at that time was the same as it had always been. It was just full of stuff, problems, and chaos. There were no feelings of joy, nor a focus on life being filled with happiness or enjoyment.

On this milestone birthday, I was working in mid-town Manhattan, and each morning I would take the 6:53 a.m. express train into New York City. I would switch to the subway to arrive at my building by around 8:15 a.m. While it was a good hour and 45 minutes each way, I was thankful that most of it was on the Long Island Railroad, because I would have what I call "captured time," making good use of it by grading student papers, writing papers, and completing homework for the courses I was taking, or just catching up on work. There was always something that I had to get done, and I used every moment of my day to check items off the never-ending and exhausting list of tasks that had to be completed.

The NYC subway system, at 8 a.m. during the week, is crowded. I am jostled at every stop it makes before mine as commuters squeeze around me or even try to go through me to get on or off the subway car. I had begun to recognize that every morning I was grumbling under my breath. It was never loud enough for anyone to hear, and my words were not based on kindness. The tone that I heard in my head and the words that came out of my mouth were filled with negativity and judgment. If someone bumped into me or pushed past me as if they were more important than me and their need to get somewhere must take priority, I muttered the same thing every time, "*Ah, so I see it is all about you today.*"

I had a feeling of heaviness and was also feeling bitter from the burden of all the responsibilities I had taken on, all that was expected of me, the tasks yet to be done, and the requirement that I am expected to do all of this well and not complain. It was quite evident, focusing on all I was seeing, thinking, and feeling about my life at this time, that something had to change. Finally, at forty-five, I knew I could not continue to live like this — especially in light of 'The Incident.'

18

THE INCIDENT

THE INCIDENT HAD HAPPENED AT WORK JUST A FEW MONTHS prior, and it had been weighing on me ever since. I tried to excuse my behavior by telling myself that it was justified. I could not, however, get my mind to accept this and to reconcile what I had done. It all started when I asked someone if they would do something for me. It was a very simple, straightforward task. It was a work-related request, and the individual I asked was a manager who worked for my organization. I knew her well. I was the head of Human Resources, and, having worked at the organization for about 6 years, I had long ago recognized this individual's deficiencies and had tried to work with her manager to address them.

The events that led to The Incident were rather ordinary. I did not usually conduct interviews, but one of the owners of the organization had a position that had been filled twice, then quickly vacated when the new hires quit. The owner, who was known to be a bit difficult, felt it was poor hiring that was causing the turnover. To help ease an escalating issue, I told him that I would personally conduct the interviews. During the process, I found a candidate that I knew would be a great fit for the position and who would be able to handle the challenges of working with this particular individual as her boss. My concern was getting the owner to go along with the recommendation as, understandably, he was a little apprehensive given the recent turnover.

As the manager had experience hiring for this type of position, I asked if she would meet with the candidate as well. It was a tactical move on my part as she was known to the owner and would be viewed as a credible source of information. As the candidate had all of the necessary credentials along with an adaptable, pleasant, and outgoing personality, I expected to easily get the manager's support, and then, if needed, I could use it to convince the owner to hire this candidate. When I made the request of the manager, it was a short conversation. I asked her to meet with the candidate for ten or fifteen minutes and then let me know her thoughts.

I was in my office when she came by and told me that she had met with the candidate. "And?" I asked. "How did it go?"

"I liked her. It was a great conversation," she answered.

Eager to get to the end result, I asked, "So, based on that, I assume you would be okay with us hiring her?"

"Well," she said. "I was after I met her, but then I decided to call a manager I know at her prior employer to see what she thought of her and, based on what she said, I don't think we should." My blood pressure shot right up. What? Why would she do that? I was saying this to myself, all the while outwardly remaining calm.

To her, I said, "Did the candidate work directly for this manager you know?"

"No," she said. "This person was only recently promoted to that position."

Why? I asked myself. *Why would she call someone that this person did not report to and who was not even a manager when the candidate worked there.* My blood was beginning to boil, and my anger was stirring.

Maintaining my composure externally, I said, "Well, what did this person say?"

"She gave me an ear full," the manager replied. "She said the candidate was difficult and that she had been fired." This didn't sound right to me as I had had a lengthy conversation with the candidate as to why she had left, and I had been satisfied with the explanation.

Given this, I asked the manager, "Did you ask the candidate why she left?"

"No, I didn't."

"So, you have nothing from the candidate to compare against what you heard from the manager? Is that correct?"

"That's correct," she said.

"Did the manager tell you anything else?" I asked.

"No, that was it."

"Well," I said. "If you had asked the candidate, you would have had a chance to understand that she was laid-off not because of any issues, but because there was a merger of two entities and, as is not uncommon, layoffs were necessary, and her position was impacted." My questions, more rhetorical than actual questions at this point, continued for a few more minutes.

"Well," she said, "in the future, I will keep that in mind but, as for the position, let me know if you want me to meet with any more candidates." I told her that that would not be necessary as I still supported the hiring and was planning to go to speak with the owner. That was when it happened. That is when The Incident began.

It started when she said, "I've already spoken with the owner." *Huh?* My brain thought quizzically.

"What do you mean that you spoke with the owner?" I asked a bit slowly.

"I spoke with the owner, the one that you had me interview the candidate for."

The anger I had been feeling was rising inside of me and was becoming outwardly visible. My voice lowered and slowed even further. "What do you mean you spoke with the owner?" I asked.

"I thought it would be helpful," she said, appearing clueless as to why I had asked the question.

My anger was getting to a point where I might not be able to fully contain it much longer, as evidenced by the tone of my voice changing when I said, "Why would you do that?"

"I thought that he would want to know my thoughts," she said.

My anger was now caught in my throat as I said in a slow and deliberate cadence in what should have been clear to her was an angry tone, "Did I ask you to speak with the owner?"

"I thought I was being helpful," she repeated.

Had she not answered my question?! Oh, she was going to answer my question, I asked and answered myself internally before I said to her, "That isn't what I asked. I asked you if I had asked you to speak with the owner." All my frustration with her from over the years was boiling up and coming out through my voice and demeanor.

She responded by saying, "I won't do it again. Next time I will just come to you."

I wanted to scream, and, in my own way, I did. In a very low and extremely indignant voice, I said, "Again, that isn't what I asked you. Why did you go speak to the owner?" I felt like I was spitting nails. She just looked at me with a blank expression. I repeated my question, "Why did you go speak to the owner?" My voice felt like it was coming from someone else. It sounded like a growl. If she had attempted a response, I do not recall it. Nothing she could say would have satisfied me. My tone of voice was now full-on nastiness. She had it coming, and I just let loose. With ever-increasing rage, I just kept repeating the question. I even leaned across my desk to get closer to her so she could feel my words as I looked her straight in the eyes and spoke at her.

I knew I had crossed a line. Not in what I was saying but in how I was saying it. It had turned personal. I was being nasty, and, quite frankly, I did not care about how I sounded or even what she may have been feeling. I was being inappropriate, and it was uncalled for, but I do not think that 'I should stop talking now' ever entered my mind. What did enter my mind at some point was that she was going to go complain to someone. I kept talking. I didn't care. I was the head of Human Resources. She had frustrated me for far too long. She deserved what she got from me and, even though I had never acted this way ever before, I would get away with it. My boss trusted me. I was livid when she left my office. I just could not believe that she had failed to follow through on such a simple request, and her actions would cause me to have to go back to square one in the hiring process.

Trying to put The Incident behind me, I went about my day, even stopping into my boss's office to let him know about something unrelated. As I turned to leave, he mentioned that the manager had stopped by to complain about how I treated her. I told him I wasn't surprised and that I had expected her to go to him. Without providing any context of what had transpired, I just told him that I was pretty direct with her and that I was unhappy because, as usual, she messed something up.

His response was something like, "That's what I figured." I walked away, realizing, as I had expected to, I had gotten away with some seriously horrible behavior. I truly didn't feel like myself and had the thought that, perhaps I had just seen my true self for the first time. That was a scary feeling.

The Incident and the conversation with my boss sat with me. I could not let it go. It would not leave my mind. I was right back in the moment, and I could feel the meanness coming up from deep inside of me. It dawned on me that I had treated her in a way that was similar to how I was treated growing up when I was being punished. While I did not physically hit her, I was delivering a punishment, and I was doing it with pure anger. I felt awful about how I had behaved. The Incident, as well as everything else I was feeling and dealing with, swirled around in my head throughout my forty-fifth birthday.

On this birthday, I was acknowledging that my mind was always in motion. I was constantly scrambling to catch up and be ready for what was coming next. What did I have to do? Who needed what done? How could I control how much my husband was drinking? I was not living in the present moment on any regular, consistent, or focused basis. Life was always about what was coming next, what may come next, or what had just happened. I was feeling anxious, which is not unlike how I had felt for most of my adult life. I worried about everything. It seemed that just when I stopped worrying, something would happen that would cause me to realize that I had to keep my guard up. My thoughts were negative, and the one consistent feeling that I had was anger, which was how I reacted to anything that happened that I did not expect or that didn't go the way I expected it to. Life was busy, and it was rushed, and it was unenjoyable.

PART TWO
SOMETHING HAD
TO GIVE

*"People have a hard time letting go of their suffering.
Out of a fear of the unknown,
they prefer suffering that is familiar."*

—— *Thich Nhat Hanh*

19

BITTER, NASTY, AND
UNHAPPY

I **WALKED HESITANTLY INTO THE ROOM**. THE MAN INSIDE gestured for me to sit on the couch which sat against the opposite wall, across from the door. I walked over tentatively and sat down, wishing I were anywhere but there. He attempted to engage me in idle chit-chat, trying to relax me. The voice in my head, always analyzing and ever critical, was at it as usual, and I did not hear anything the man said. As had been the case since the moment I sat down, I was looking down at my lap. My hands were clasped so tightly together that they were turning white. With my arms stiffly tucked into my sides, I was holding my knees together to stop my legs from shaking.

I am not sure how long it took me to notice that he had stopped talking and was just sitting quietly, but he continued to sit there in silence even after I realized it. The only sound I heard was the tick-tick-tick of the small wind-up clock sitting on the bookshelf across from me. I knew he was looking at me, but it was a long while before my need to always be polite and to do what was expected got the better of me. I finally looked up at him. He smiled and looked at me for a moment. Then, he leaned forward in his chair and, in a low and kind voice, gently asked, "Why are you here?"

I was in the office of a licensed social worker. It was September of 2010, and the moment that brought me here had occurred a few weeks earlier. I had been at work, and I just felt like I could not hold it together. I felt angry, not unlike many other days, but ... also different. I was reaching the apex of my tolerance for how I was feeling. I was the head of Human Resources for a large national law firm and, while I knew better than to lose my cool at the office, 'The Incident' with the manager a couple of months earlier remained fresh in my mind.

As had been the case for years, I was feeling resistant, defensive, and inflexible. I had always been a private person, hiding my secrets and not letting people get too close. I felt like the way that I had been surviving life was finally catching up to me, and as if I was a very tightly wound ball of string that might unravel at any moment. My usual trick to calm myself was to stand in a bathroom stall when things were a bit too much for me at work. That wasn't going to work for me today. There wasn't anything extraordinary about the moment that pushed me to the realization that I needed to leave the office and take a walk around the block. This was a huge tell that I was not okay. I never leave the office. Not ever. Not in all my years of working have I ever felt the need to just get out. This time was different.

I took the elevator down to the lobby of my mid-town office building and headed out the front door. I turned right, planning to loop around the block, but I didn't turn right again at the next corner. I just kept walking. I was on autopilot. I had no destination in mind and, had I not run into a person I worked with, I am sure I would have just kept walking for who knows how long. I was heading in the direction of downtown Manhattan, and he was heading uptown, toward our office. He got my attention by stepping in front of me, and then, after the usual exchange of pleasantries and greetings, he asked me what I was doing so far from the office. A bit perplexed, I glanced up at the street sign to see that I was, indeed, farther away than I expected to be. Losing track of where I was, I had walked over a half-mile. I responded in a lighthearted way that I was just getting a little fresh air, using a smile to hide the pain I was feeling. It was never okay for me to let someone know that something was not right in my world. He winked and said, "That's a lot of fresh air," then moved around me to continue his walk uptown.

I stood there for a long moment. Where *was* I going? This question was barely in word form in my head when I suddenly realized where I was headed. I began walking again, this time with purpose, still in the direction of downtown.

* * *

SOME NINE YEARS EARLIER, IN 2002, I HAD ATTENDED TWO OR three appointments with the licensed social worker whose office I now occupied, but I had stopped going. Mainly, I stopped because I was ashamed that I had felt the need to go in the first place. I was raised to be tough. I was raised to handle all that life threw at me. I was raised not to count on others as, I had learned so well, they could not be counted on. I also stopped because, as was usual for me, just spending a little time talking about the immediate issues had brought my feelings back down to a manageable level where I felt I could move forward. So, overriding my gut, which told me I should keep going, I canceled my upcoming appointments in a voicemail message and continued on with life. While much less intense, my reasons for seeking help were essentially the same back then. I felt over-whelmed and unable to handle all that I was expected to handle. This was the case when I went to see a therapist in 1997, again in 2002, and all these years later, needing help again. Or was it that I needed help *still*? Even though my mind did not register where I was headed, my subconscious led me toward his office. I knew I needed to see him again. Something wasn't right, and that something was me.

I could not remember his name, but I did recall exactly where his office was located. When I arrived at the building, I looked through the directory for a name that looked familiar. Recognizing it right away, third from the bottom on a list of about twenty names, I hit the buzzer to gain entry into the building. There was no answer. Still standing in front of the building, I took out my phone, looked his contact information up online, and called. The answering machine came on with the typical message telling me to leave my name, number, reason for my call, and someone would get back to me. Figures, I thought, as I felt my anger again. I left a message and, burying whatever was bothering me way down in that place where I hid lots of thoughts and feelings, I headed back to my office.

Between that moment and the minute I walked into the office for my appointment, I was continually reminded that the lid that had been covering that hiding place must be so worn out from use that it was no longer holding back its contents. Everything was bubbling up, and I was having a really difficult time hiding the anger I felt inside.

It would be four days before I received a call back. He apologized for the delay and told me that most therapists close their offices the last two weeks of August for vacation. The therapist said he had listened to my message, so he knew I wanted to schedule an appointment. He said that he did not have access to his full files at this time, so he could not recall the details or extent of our prior visits together. He did say, however, that he recalled that I was in a relationship with someone who was a heavy drinker.

"Yes," I said. "That is correct." I was amazed that he remembered that fact, given the many years in between.

When I responded that I had married him, he only said something like,

"Oh, I see." But the way he said it made it clear that he was not surprised that I had reached out to him again. We made an appointment for almost two weeks later and, even though I knew I had no intention of doing so, I promised him that if I needed to speak with him at any point prior, I would give him a call, and we could chat over the phone. I made it through, and I now sat in front of him as he waited for me to respond to his question.

He knew I heard and understood the question, but even after several weeks of waiting, I was slow in responding. My mind was still jumbled with what to say and what not to say. My Inner Critic was hard at work telling me that I had all this time to prepare, yet here I was unprepared and wasting this man's time.

Unsure exactly where it came from and how it was able to make its way past my Inner Critic and my need to maintain control, but I will be forever grateful for the tiny voice that came from somewhere inside and said to me, *'Now is your chance. Go for it. You are at the end and can no longer survive here. There is no alternative than to speak up and see if he can relieve your pain.'* As I opened my mouth to talk, from the same place the tiny voice had come from or, perhaps, somewhere else entirely, I heard myself speak these words, "I've become a bitter, nasty, and unhappy person. I don't know how I got here, and I am beginning to think that this is who I am." Then, I started to sob, knowing that what I had just spoken was the precise essence of what I felt about myself and had been feeling for quite some time. I was obviously in a very delicate state, and, after this initial meeting, I began seeing this therapist, whom I referred to as My Guy, weekly.

* * *

FROM THE VERY BEGINNING, I WANTED TO UNDERSTAND HOW long the process to feeling better would take. On several occasions, I tapped on the face of my watch and asked him, "So, how long before I feel better?"

"It'll take some time," was usually his answer. As I am a 'get a task, get it done' kinda gal, I decided to change my tactic with him after a few weeks of not receiving what I felt was an adequate response.

I went into a session and said, "So that I know what I need to do to get me from where I am now to wherever it is that I am headed, could you go through the steps that I will need to take to feel better?" That time, the response I received from My Guy was much more direct than he had been previously — and also very different from what I was expecting.

His reply was, "You should feel better about where you are in about a year."

That answer caused an immediate response from me — one filled with fury, dismay, and defensiveness. In an incredulous tone, my voice boomed, "A YEAR!? What do you mean a year? I can't continue to feel this way for another year!"

He went on, "Heidi, there isn't a checklist, and you need to have patience as it will take time."

At that moment, I began to realize and digest the reality that I was on a road that was, apparently, very very long. I'm not sure how long I expected it would take to fix whatever it was that was wrong with me, but I was very sure that had I known how long it would take to get to a place where I was feeling better, I never would have gone to see My Guy in the first place. That might seem counterintuitive, but I know myself. I had simply assumed that unless I was really that screwed up and abnormal, which is what he had now confirmed, there would be an easy and, most certainly, quick solution. Work through whatever the process to fix it is, and it is fixed. Apparently, this was not the case for me.

* * *

DURING THAT FIRST VISIT, MY GUY RECOMMENDED THAT I read the book *Co-Dependent No More* by Melody Beattie. I went right out and purchased it, and on Sunday of the three-day Labor Day weekend in 2010, my husband Bob found me sitting on our back deck reading it. He sat down on the lounge chair across from where I was sitting and asked, "What are you reading?" I showed him the cover of the book and, as I had not previously told him, I briefly filled him in on my decision to speak with a therapist and that he had recommended I read this book. I went on to tell him that one thing I recognized from what I had already read is that I try to control things.

"No, you don't," he said, disagreeing with me.

While it felt great to hear him say this, I fessed up and said, "No, I actually do." Understanding now what the concept of controlling was, I explained an example of it. I told him, "Think about this ... I try to control your drinking. Every day, as the afternoon goes by, I begin to focus on and fret about what train I will be able to get on. If I take the 5:45 p.m., I get home at 7:00 p.m. If I take the next express train, I get home at 7:50 p.m. I rush through my meetings, push conversations off to the next day, and run through Grand Central terminal to get to the subway to catch the earlier train. So, you see," I continued, "I have been trying to control one hour of your drinking by being on that earlier train."

As I was having a hard time coming to terms with the fact that I so desperately needed to be seeing My Guy, I purposely did not provide Bob with much information. I didn't need his judgment on top of my own. Still, with only the little bit of information that I shared with him, he asked, "Well, what about me? Does this mean we're getting divorced?" I had not begun going to a therapist to get a divorce. That was not something that was on my mind. I went because I was feeling lost and broken, and I needed to fix myself. I knew Bob very well and this reaction, focused on him without regard or concern of anyone else, was the norm. While it saddened me that he didn't consider my feelings, it reconfirmed for me that he would not be available to help me through whatever I was facing.

As I continued reading the book, I uncovered more descriptions of what it means to be co-dependent, which resonated strongly with me. In one section of the book, there were a handful of pages outlining behaviors that could indicate that someone is co-dependent. The behaviors were broken down into sections such as weak boundaries, control, dependency, and denial. As is my process when reading this type of book, I underlined the behaviors that rang true for me. There were many, and my list included the tendencies: do not feel content, happy, or peaceful with themselves; desperately seek love and approval; gradually increase their tolerance until they can tolerate and do things they said they never would; feel different from the rest of the world; takes things personally; feel terribly anxious about problems and people; settle for being needed; and one that I did all the time, apologize for bothering people. Once I had gone through the full list, underling those that described me, it provided a visual of how many of the behaviors I had. It was a lot.

While I did not recall previously reading this book, it is interesting to note that I had. Sometime the following summer, while cleaning out a few closets, I found a book that had an old-fashioned homemade cover on it. I didn't know what it was until I opened it. It was another copy of the co-dependency book, and I immediately recalled that My Guy had also recommended the book to me back in 2002. I turned to the pages which listed all the behaviors, and, not surprisingly, I had also underlined those that resonated with me back then. I rushed to get the copy I had read more recently so that I could compare the two. Sadly, when I did, there were many more underlined in the more recent copy.

This discovery solidified for me that I had never taken the time necessary to fully deal with my issues. I would get a quick fix to make myself feel a little better, stuff all the rest deep down inside, and continue on with life. This visual showed me that my issues had never gone away and had, in fact, gotten worse. Much worse. This was a severe reality check. I had been avoiding the situation I was now going through all of my life, dealing with issues directly and fully and not backing down from facing them head-on. No wonder I felt exhausted all the time. This was hard. My situation felt a bit hopeless, and those first couple of months were agonizing. My brain felt like it was stuck in a roundabout with no exits. Thoughts came into my mind and festered repeatedly, and I found it difficult to figure out how to get unstuck.

20

ALANON

As was the norm for my life, just when I thought things were calming down or settling into a rhythm, something always happened to shake things back up. The something that happened this particular time was that Bob required emergency open-heart surgery only about eight weeks after I had started seeing My Guy. Here I was going through my own crisis and having difficulty coping with life, but I willingly put my needs aside and made his my priority as I always did.

After a five-day stay, Bob came home from the hospital and began a slow recovery. Given his job in construction and his need to use his arm and chest muscles, while he was ready to resume regular activities about ten weeks later, he would be out of work for almost five months. Three weeks to the day after getting out of the hospital, his brother and his family arrived in town for the Thanksgiving holiday. The very day his brother arrived, Bob went downtown with him for cocktails. Bob's doctor had told him that his lifestyle — drinking — was a contributing factor to his heart issues, so I had been hopeful that he would decide to stop drinking or certainly curtail the amount. This was the biggest issue in my relationship with Bob. I kept hoping that he would change, and he kept showing me and telling me that he was not going to.

When he left the house with his brother that day, just like every other time he did something I didn't think he should, I kept thinking I must be the crazy one. I was feeling disappointed and frustrated — and much less optimism for a future without the influences of alcohol.

At the time of his surgery, Bob had been having blackouts for quite some time. While I ignored it for a while, I began to point it out and would, instead — with a bit of attitude in my voice — say something like, "Yes, I know. You told me the same story last night," cutting him off mid-sentence. Bob did not believe me and began to call me a liar. Just a few months after his surgery, after yet another discussion in which I was called a liar, Bob revealed that he had begun to keep a log a few months before his surgery. He told me that he began it as a way of proving to himself that his blackouts were not happening and that he was ultimately going to present it to me as proof that I was, in fact, a liar. Then, he let me know that because I had taken such good care of him after the surgery, he was reminded of how loving I was and decided that he would forgive me for making up the stories.

He had vowed to himself after his surgery that, as soon as he could get out to the garage on his own, he would take the log from where he had hidden it and destroy it, which is what he had done. He was telling me this now, he said, because he was mad he had destroyed it. According to Bob, if he hadn't, then he would have had a whole lot of proof that I was, indeed, a liar.

I asked Bob to explain to me what he kept in the log. He told me that after an evening out which, of course, meant that he was drinking, he would take out the logbook and write down the things that he had said. He went on to say that this way, when I brought something up later saying it was something we had previously discussed, he could get the log out and, if it wasn't in there, he would have proof that I was lying. I asked him, "When did you document the items we discussed? Was it when we got home?"

He answered, "No, it was the next morning."

I shook my head and muttered, "A lot of help that does. When you blackout, you can't remember anything — and even if you thought you could retain information from that night, you certainly could not recall it by the next morning." He disagreed, and we continued a conversation that went on and on with no resolution.

I was resentful of Bob for all the drinking he did. I was resentful of him for his lack of caring about his health, and how that could impact me, and for all the money he spent on his drinking. I was also resentful that there was no intimacy in our relationship because the drinking cut him off emotionally, and physical intimacy was not possible because of the effects of the alcohol. After we got married, I can count on one hand, and that's being a bit generous, the times that we had sex. It was not that I wasn't interested. I was. It was that Bob would turn me down, put me off, or be unable to.

* * *

IN ADDITION TO OUR THERAPY SESSIONS AND OTHER TOOLS, My Guy encouraged me to go to Alanon. He told me that it could help me get support and would be a different way to cope with Bob's drinking. I did not want to go. No way would sitting in a room listening to other people complain about their issues help in any way, I thought.

For several months, at the beginning of each of our sessions, My Guy would ask, "Did you go to a meeting this week?"

And each week, I would say, "No, and I am not planning on going to one." At the end of each session, he would — again — suggest that I consider going ... and I would walk out of our meeting without providing any response. This same ritual happened week after week until one day, four months after our sessions began, I finally went to a meeting.

It was a new year, and I decided to give it a try. During the Alanon meeting, someone said, "If you don't want to come back, your misery will cheerfully be refunded." That line stuck with me, and I began attending meetings, but it wasn't consistent. When I did attend, I would never raise my hand to speak, nor would I engage with anyone before or after the meeting. It would take me seven months to finally get the courage to stand up and speak. There had been an incident with Bob the previous evening, and at noon the next day, I went to a meeting across town from my office. I was so upset with the events of the night before, and even though I felt that it could be helpful to speak about it, I didn't find the courage to do it. I held back tears during the entire meeting, then headed back to the office and buried myself in work.

Later that day, my husband called and, despite what had transpired the evening before, he acted like nothing was wrong. I, of course, had a tone in my voice, and he finally asked me, "What's the matter?"

"What do you mean, what's the matter? Do you not remember what happened last night?"

"Oh, yeah, I need to call my son and apologize to him," he said.

"What about me?" I inquired. "Don't you think you need to apologize to me?"

"What for?" he asked.

I was instantly over-the-top angry. How could he be so insensitive? How could he not understand or see that I deserved an apology as well? I told him that I didn't know where I was going, but I would not be home after work. I also said that whenever I did make it back to the house, he should probably avoid me.

* * *

WHAT HAD TRANSPIRED THE NIGHT BEFORE BEGAN WHEN I stopped into the local Mexican restaurant to pick up dinner and ran into his youngest son and his girlfriend. It was such a beautiful evening, and Bob and I had talked earlier in the afternoon about eating dinner outside on the deck.

"Would you like to join us?" I asked them.

"Sure," they replied and said they would see us shortly.

As I arrived home and walked in the front door, Bob was walking in the sliding-glass door from the back deck, and I could see instantly that he was drunk. I went from happy to be home and looking forward to a relaxing evening on the deck, to instantly mad. Bob being drunk was certainly not an unusual occurrence, but now I was trying to figure out how I was going to take back a dinner invitation so that his son wouldn't see Bob in this condition.

Before I said anything, he saw my face and asked, "What did I do?"

I said, "Well, you drank too much, and I just ran into your son at the takeout place, and he and his girlfriend are coming over here to have dinner with us. But you're trashed."

He then raised his voice and said, "How could you invite them over to this house without asking me first?"

"What, am I supposed to ask your permission anytime I want to invite somebody here?" I inquired, clearly not agreeing with what he had just said.

"Well, what if I didn't want anybody here?" he asked.

This fighting distracted me from calling and, the next thing I knew, they were knocking on the door. Needless to say, it was a very awkward dinner. They could see that Bob was drunk, and I was not doing a good job of covering up how embarrassed and unhappy I was. I knew they had seen him drunk on many occasions, but this was a bit more than usual. This was a slur your words and stumble as you stand up kind of drunk. My tolerance for this continued nonsense was extremely low by this point.

* * *

AFTER I GOT OFF THE PHONE WITH BOB THE NEXT DAY, I realized that I needed to go to another Alanon meeting, so I went onto the internet and found one close to home that I could make if I left the office on time. It turned out to be a parent meeting, which is a meeting for parents who have children who are alcoholics. Not exactly the group I was hoping for, but I knew I needed to go, regardless. When I walked in, I was comforted to realize that I was exactly where I needed to be. This was a group of nurturing individuals and, while I never spoke a word, it must have been written on my face that I needed to be there. These beautiful people, sensing that I was not open to talking, did not try to force me into it, and a few stopped for a moment to say hello, just put a hand on my shoulder, or nodded at me with an understanding smile. I left the meeting feeling a bit calmer ... but still livid.

By this point in our relationship, Bob and I were living in separate rooms, and when I got home that night, he was already in the guestroom, and the light was off. When I woke the next morning, my mood had not shifted. I was still furious, so I decided that I should attend yet another Alanon meeting. At lunchtime, I walked to the same meeting I had attended the day before. With the knowledge that I was only making it through because of the people in these meetings, I finally raised my hand to talk. You don't always get called on, and I was grateful when I was.

Through the tears streaming down my face, I said, "The last 36 hours have been rough, and I know that the only reason that I am okay at this moment is that I have attended three meetings in the last 24 hours, and it is because of the kindness and support of strangers that I have made it till now." I went on, "I have been attending meetings for about seven months, and this is the first time I have ever spoken. I heard someone say months ago that they have been coming to Alanon for seventeen years, and I want you to know that I silently said to myself that there was no way that I would need to come to Alanon for that long. I apologize for those thoughts because I am only now beginning to understand why this could be. I thank those of you here in this room for being here, however long you've been attending, because today I really needed you, and you were here."

It was this experience that convinced me that attending meetings was helpful, and I saw value in them. While inconsistently at times, I attended meetings on a somewhat regular basis for the next couple of years.

21

BUILDING A
FOUNDATION

ANOTHER SUGGESTION FROM MY GUY WAS FOR ME TO KEEP A
journal. While I did not write in it very often, and my first entry was dated
almost three months after our first session, the early entries show that my
logical mind was trying to make some sense of my issues and come up with
possible solutions, including refocusing my mindset to help me move
forward. My first entry centered on trying to figure out just a few things
that I could concentrate on and commit to doing every day to help myself. I
also needed to figure out how to love and feel good about myself, feel more
trusting of others, and feel more loved, accepted, and supported by others. I
wrote:

---

*I don't know if these things are even possible given the life I have at this
time. Everyone in my life is cut off emotionally. No one ever asks me
how I am really doing, and any kidding and most conversations are
negatively focused. Most everyone in my life is a drinker or they are
married to a drinker. How do I move forward? It will take focus and a
strong desire to fight through the negativity coming from my Inner
Critic. Even if I am slowly moving away from where I have been, I
have absolutely no clue where I am headed.*

ON THE SAME DAY AS THIS ENTRY, I WROTE A LIST OUTLINING
the items that were bothering me or areas I needed to change. There were
many, including:

- *Do not do or continue to do things you are uncomfortable with.*
- *Do not let people cross your boundaries.*
- *Discuss what your feelings are and focus on your feelings.*
- *Each day focus on what you did well and what you feel proud of.*
- *What didn't you do well and what can you learn for next time?*
- *Go to Alanon meetings to help you not feel as crazy or alone.*
- *Decide what you want to do and decide what you don't want to do.*
- *Have fun (well, first figure out how to do this).*
- *What makes you happy?*
- *What makes you unhappy?*
- *Which people do you want in your life?*
- *Which people do you not want in your life?*

THIS JOURNAL ENTRY WAS THE BEGINNING OF THE FOUNDATION
I was building for a bridge that would get me from where I was to a place I
had never experienced nor thought possible before. I was looking for a place
of joy, peace, and a sense of self. Over time, I came to accept that my
moving forward was going to be a gradual process of awareness, acceptance,
and change. I would first need to understand my own thoughts, feelings,
and actions — and the reasons for them. I was beginning to understand
that I alone was responsible for these things and that others could only
impact my peace if I allowed them to. I was also beginning to understand
that I could choose how I would react to any given set of circumstances,
that feelings are triggered by thoughts, and that I could influence them. To
help me, I began to repeat the phrase, on a very frequent basis, "I cannot
control the first thing out of my mouth, but I can control the second." This
was helpful as it allowed me to stop the flow of a negative interaction and
change it into a positive one or, at least, a neutral one.

As I prepared for the weekly sessions with My Guy, I would jot down
my thoughts and things I wanted to speak with him about. I jotted them
down in my journal or emails to myself. These writings helped me formu-
late the words that would allow me, with My Guy's help, to define the

issues that I needed to work on. I found this extremely helpful, especially during those early months. They also enabled me to better judge my progress along the way. I wrote down when I was extremely unhappy. I wrote that I had a short fuse and found it hard to control myself at times. I wrote that I did not have the feeling of belonging within my relationships with family, my husband, and others. I wrote about needing answers and guidance and that I was willing to do the work. My entries clearly showed that I had a sense of urgency and needed 'this' to be fixed very quickly. Early journal entries show that my thoughts were scattered and very unfocused. I jumped from one to another, forgetting what the last thought even was. While I had lots of good insights written down in my journal, I was in too much pain and too unfocused to notice them or realize their value at the time.

Several discussions with My Guy centered on expectations, and I discovered that I absolutely projected my expectations on myself, others, and situations. I was always thinking ahead about what may be, what should be, and how something will or should look, feel, or sound. What I began to understand was, because of this, I was usually disappointed in people, events, and things as they couldn't possibly measure up to the expectations that I had pre-set in my mind. I knew I needed to focus on being in the present moment, and I recognized that this was not happening as I was always busy thinking two steps ahead.

When I began my journey away from brokenness, I was feeling overwhelmed. There was so much to focus on. So much to fix. My life felt empty. There was a void in my heart. I felt somewhat content during certain periods in my life, but the feeling never lasted, and I desperately wanted to have — and keep — that feeling. How would I be able to get to a place where I would feel differently without a checklist or some type of process? I felt like I was wandering aimlessly. I needed direction and inspiration. I turned to many places to get these two critical things, including Alanon meetings, a daily affirmation book, journaling, books, and sayings. I also watched movies. One, *Eat Pray Love*, was particularly helpful. Something that I had not focused on yet was forgiveness, and the movie discusses the idea that one needs to forgive themself before one can move forward. I was ashamed of so many things I had done. I was also embarrassed by many of them and had feelings of guilt about some of my life choices and actions.

* * *

IT TOOK A FEW MONTHS, BUT I WAS BEGINNING TO FEEL A BIT calmer and was usually able to keep myself that way. Considering where I had started, being an angry, fearful, and hostile person, I was happy with the small change. I was aware, however, that there was still much more to do and so many things to work on. At some point, I would need to begin dealing with how things I was encountering were making me feel. I was still just talking about them factually. I was not exactly sure how to make that shift because, by this time, I only really felt anger. Also, I must admit, it was easier to focus on everyone else's faults and issues, or what they had done to me, rather than turning the lens inward. Feelings are the hard part — but the things I would most need to focus on at some point. Now was not the time, as I was still fighting to get through each day.

As I continued working with My Guy, trying to implement all the tools and suggestions that he provided, I was still trying to come up with a check-list of to-dos to make the healing process easier to understand and carry-out. I used my journal and wrote about the things that were important to me and the things that were bothering me. One such list, written early on, was something I looked at fairly frequently over the next several months. Having to make such a list was uncomfortable for me, and focusing on these items did not come naturally. However, I knew that if I didn't take ownership of myself and my issues, I would continue to remain in pain with overwhelming feelings of despair, and this was no longer acceptable to me. My focus was to:

- *Stay calm.*
- *Don't control.*
- *Ask: What do I want to do right now?*
- *Ask: What do I not want to do?*
- *What is important to me?*
- *What isn't important to me?*
- *Whom do I care about?*
- *Whom do I want in my life?*
- *What makes me feel happy/fulfilled?*

AS HAD BEEN THE CASE FOR AN EXTENDED PERIOD, I FELT isolated and alone most of the time. I asked myself why I felt this way and what I was doing to contribute to these feelings. I recognized that I found most people in my life unsupportive. I didn't need many people in my life, just those who would support me and love me for me. It would take a bit more time to move this forward, but I was beginning to see that, at some point, I would need to pick which people would stay in my life and which would need to leave.

My feeling of isolation wasn't helped by the fact that I was literally walking through life with my head down. I wouldn't say hello to people that I passed, and I very rarely looked anyone in the eye, unless it was in the course of conducting business for my job. Also contributing to this was my consistent physical stance of crossing my arms. This body language kept me distanced from others and in a defensive mindset. I needed to change these things and find a way to open up and get my thoughts and opinions out.

I grew up in a house where there was no debate, your opinions were not solicited nor were they welcome, and open interactions and dialogue discouraged. Because of this, I found myself in my mid-forties, unable to truly tell people what I was thinking about things that were happening in my own life. How was I going to get my thoughts and opinions out? What could I do to begin to change this? What things could I do to make me feel safe enough to state my opinion? I thought a book club would help, but I never did seek an opportunity to try, which, among others I had thought of but never pursued, was a promising idea left on the table.

Life is certainly a journey of desire, focus, effort, and determination. It is also about continuous development and self-exploration. I did feel like I was making a small amount of progress for a good many months, but it wasn't consistent. I had glimpses of lighter days, but they were fleeting. My journey, however, took a momentous leap forward the day I visited the house where I grew up.

22

THE HOUSE WHERE I
GREW UP

It was March 28, 2011. I was
about seven months into the process of
fixing myself and, having decided that I
needed to do something more than I had
been doing to find a measure of peace, I
took the day off from work and took a
drive. Being in the car and driving is
something that I always find to be

soothing and helpful. I drove about forty-five minutes and found myself
sitting across the street from the house where I grew up.

It was painted yellow. Sitting up a bit on a little hill that was perfect for
sledding down after a snowfall, a sour apple tree was in the front yard. The
driveway, situated on the left of the house and leading to a one-car garage,
was just long enough to fit two cars in it. There was a pathway leading to
the shed and a gate to the backyard. There was a large cement patio in the
backyard where we would play what we called 'Round the World,' trying to
get the basketball into the net from different quadrants of the patio. We
also had many dinners on summer evenings, sitting at the round wooden
picnic table. There was a four-foot above ground pool with a beautiful,
unique deck that my father had designed and built. We spent many hours
in that pool. One birthday, when I was turning seven, I got to cut a ribbon
on the steps leading to the pool — officially opening it for the summer. I
loved that my birthday was the controlling factor. When Joan moved in, she
put in a large garden that ran from behind the shed to the back fence. She

planted tomatoes, cucumbers, zucchini, beans, and many other vegetables. One of our chores in the summer was to go out each day and collect up whatever was ripe.

As I sat looking at my childhood home, I grew gloomy, and tears welled up in my eyes. I was saddened with the realization of the number of years that had come and gone, and that I was still an unhappy person. Was I ever a happy person, I questioned? Had I ever experienced peace in my life? Was it even possible to have the things that I wanted so badly? When I got into the car earlier in the day, I had no plan for where I was going to drive, but I was on a mission to try to jumpstart my progress. Somehow, I thought that being here would help me remember things. Help me remember who I was when I was a little girl and help me remember events and memories that might provide clues as to how I got to where I am now. Perhaps in these, I would begin to find some wisdom and understanding that would help me.

Over the last few months, I had been thinking a good deal about my childhood. I couldn't recall many instances when I didn't feel pressure or unease. I do recall happy periods, but they were short-lived. As I looked at the house, I felt many emotions — but mostly, I felt empty as a flood of memories about that time in my life came back.

Growing up, I always felt like I was being watched. It was not unusual for Joan or my dad to go through our rooms when we weren't there. They were like surprise inspections. If anything was found that we weren't allowed to have, like candy or gum, it was laid out on the counter in the kitchen or at our place setting at the dining room table. This was a sign, of course, that they had been through our rooms and that we were in trouble. There were so many rules and requirements like, for example, when in trouble, you had to keep your bedroom door open at all times. There was never a feeling of freedom or any privacy.

This lack of privacy was most clearly illustrated when, for some reason, they became concerned that I was not washing my body well enough. The solution they came up with was for Joan to watch me take a shower. I was around seven or eight years old. I still remember her standing there watching me. I was embarrassed and uncomfortable, and I, of course, didn't go near my private parts, which, of course, became an issue. She was not happy and, as I stood there naked with the water still running, she yelled out to my father that I wasn't getting myself clean. I was so humiliated, and I felt violated.

* * *

I CONTINUED TO SIT IN THE CAR REFLECTING, AND WHILE THERE were a few fun memories that came to mind, most that I thought about were negative. Nothing was ever quite good enough. For example, if I received a B+ on a paper, the question was always why I had not gotten an A. Also, after getting our big weekly chores on Saturday done, we were sent outside to play, and we were not allowed to come back into the house before 5 p.m., except for lunch or to use the bathroom. That rule was not negotiable, not that any of them were.

The house was usually filled with tension, and there was a good deal of fighting and raised voices. When the adults in the house fought, while it was usually within earshot of us kids, it often happened out of sight. Sometimes the fights did not involve yelling. Instead, there was just a known tension rippling across an issue and the uncomfortable knowledge that there was a problem. That was exactly the case one night at dinner. Only my youngest brother Chris and I were living at home at the time. Meals were held in the dining room. My dad sat at the head of the table. Joan was to his left and closest to the kitchen. I sat to my dad's right, and Chris sat to my right. I was about 10-years-old. Joan had called us for dinner, and we sat at the table with the plates of food Joan had just put down in front of us.

What was expected to be a regular dinner, changed in a moment, which was not at all uncommon. You could have heard a pin drop when my father said in a questioning tone, as he pointed to his food, indicating that there was a problem, "What is this?"

Joan responded, "lamb curry." Without a word, my father got up from the table and went into the kitchen. When he returned to the dining room, he held the garbage can. He reached over and took my plate and threw it in the garbage can. He then snapped his fingers at my brother, signaling him to pass his plate as well. Dad tossed that plate into the can. Then, dad took his own plate and, as he dumped it into the can, it crashed into the others, and you could tell that one or more of them had broken.

He looked at Joan and, in a flat tone, said, "I told you never to make lamb." He then looked at us and said, "C'mon, we're going out."

It was startling to see my father speak to Joan this way but, as we were trained to do what we were told, my brother and I immediately got up from the table, not saying a word. My dad told us to put on our shoes and coats and meet him at the car. We rushed downstairs to get dressed, then made our way out the back door and around to the front. We were quiet when we got into the back of the car, and, for a long while, dad didn't say a word.

We didn't know where we were going until he finally spoke, and in a tone that belied what had just happened, said, "How does the Sizzler sound?"

Really?! That's where we're going for dinner?! Despite that it was a cafeteria-style restaurant, it felt fancy because we rarely went out to dinner and, when we did, it was usually to McDonald's. The Sizzler was a buffet-style restaurant where you walked in, picked up a tray, and, as you made your way down the line, you took what you wanted from the available assortment. My brother and I kept looking at each other like we had won the lottery. We were both so excited about where we were going that we didn't even think about what Joan must be going through back at the house.

Knowing how things have a habit of changing in a minute, my brother and I tensed as we got to the cashier with our trays. Our father was ahead of us, and we heard him say that he had left his money clip at home. Surprisingly, my dad remained calm and, as we already had our food, he simply asked the manager if he could leave us there to have our dinner while he got his money and came back. Given the year, no one thought twice about saying yes to his request. I don't know what transpired between Joan and my dad when he went back to the house. My guess is that he walked in, never said a word, picked up his money clip from his dresser and walked back out.

* * *

WHILE DAD KEPT HIMSELF BUSY IN THE GARAGE MOST OF THE time, Joan kept herself busy with the multitude of plants she kept in the house, the large garden she had planted out back, as well as with cooking and maintaining the house. Of all my memories with Joan, one stands out from the rest. It is one that, perhaps, influenced my decision to join the Marine Corps and my desire to help families in need during the holidays. It was nighttime, and I was sitting in the back seat of the car, trying to sit up a little taller so I could see all the pretty Christmas lights as we drove. I was excited because it was very unusual that I was out on a school night, and it was just the two of us. I was about 10-years-old, and Joan had on her Marine Corps uniform.

As we drove, Joan explained that we were on a special mission. She said that we were going to deliver toys to a family with children who needed some help. I was shy and did not like meeting new people, so I asked, "Can I sit in the car when we get there?"

"No," she said. "You will want to experience this." She went on to explain a bit more. "The Marine Corps Reserves has a program called Toys for Tots, and it collects unwrapped new toys for needy families within our community. The toys are then distributed to the families just before Christmas." She continued, "A needy family is one that is having a hard time financially, and without this help, they might not have a very nice Christmas."

"There are bags in the trunk as well as the three that are on the seat next to you" she continued. "When we get to the house, we will go in and meet the family. I will need to decide whether this family should get just the bags in the trunk or if I should also give them the ones on the back seat." She told me that my job was to bring the bags in and that unless she told me to also bring the bags from the backseat, I was only to bring the two from the trunk.

I was nervous that I would make a mistake, so I asked, "What will you say?"

She replied, "If I ask you to bring all the bags in and not to forget the bags in the back seat, then you'll know to bring them all." That made me feel better. She went on to say that one of the bags on the back seat was different from the other two. She told me that when I brought that bag in that I should give it directly to the woman we would be meeting and tell her that this bag was especially for her.

"Okay," I replied.

I went back to trying to look out the window at Christmas lights until we stopped in front of a house. Hmm, I thought. What were we doing here? If someone needed free toys, how could they be living in a house? There was even a car in the driveway, I noticed. This made no sense. Why would people in a house who owned a car need someone else to give them things for free. I didn't want to get in trouble for saying the wrong thing, so I kept these thoughts to myself.

Joan got out of the car and put on her uniform hat. She opened the back door and helped me out of the car. She took my hand, and we walked up to the front door. I could hear what sounded like a lot of people behind the door, and a female voice telling children to go wait in their room.

The door was opened by a man. He looked like I felt, nervous. As I came into the small ranch-style house, I was in the living room and saw something I had never seen before. A hospital bed was in the center of the small living room, and a woman was lying in it. Joan went over and said hello to her. I followed closely behind and, as I peaked at the women from around Joan's back, I thought that she did not look very good at all. It also smelled a bit in the house. I kept that to myself.

When the woman was done greeting Joan, she moved her head and attempted to get my attention. Joan moved out of the way, and my eyes connected with the lady's. She smiled and asked me to come closer so she could get a look at me. I did as I was told, even though I didn't want to. I slowly approached the bed, and she reached out and held me by my arm. I do not recall what she said to me, but I remember being so surprised by her comforting words. I liked her instantly, even though I now knew that she was why the house smelled. She asked if I wanted to meet her children and maybe I could play with them while she spoke with Joan. I smiled and immediately said yes as I didn't want to be near the smell any longer.

The woman called her four children out to meet me. One seemed to be around my age, and the rest were younger. They seemed happy and politely said, "Yes, mama," when they were told to take me to their room and play with me. When we walked into their room, I quickly realized that not only were they sharing one bedroom, but they also shared two beds. Unlike my room, which had lots of books, toys, and clothes, their room did not have much of anything in it, but, like mine, it was all very neatly kept. All of this surprised me, but, again, I did not say anything.

It seemed like I was in there only a few minutes when Joan called for me. When I arrived at her side, she looked down and asked, "Could you please go outside and bring in all of the bags that are in the car." She then added, holding my chin and looking me in the eyes, "And don't forget the ones in the back seat." I ran outside to do as I was asked, struggling to get the two large black bags from the trunk first. When I made it back inside, the nice lady asked if I would set them beside the small Christmas tree that was there. I did as I was told and then headed back outside. I brought in the next two bags and put them with the others.

Thinking that was all I was going to be bringing in, the lady asked me to come near her so she could talk with me. While I didn't want to smell her again, I did as I was asked. As I approached, she had tears in her eyes. She called me sweetheart, which I liked but at the same time, I didn't, as only my dad called me that. She then added that she knew God would bless me for the gift that I had given to her and her family, as without what we had brought, her children would not have had any gifts. I was a bit uncomfortable with the talk of God and by her thanking me. My mind also went back to the bad thoughts I had as we drove up, so I said the first thing that came to mind to get out of the conversation. I told her that I had to go back outside as there was one more bag especially for her.

As we drove home that night, I thought about how lucky I was that I didn't have a parent who was in a hospital bed in our living room. I also considered how happy the family seemed. I was too young to understand that the woman was most likely dying and that the Toys for Tots program may have helped provide a beautiful Christmas for her and her family — and that may very well have been the last one that they had together.

Joan would later tell me that in the bag that I handed to the woman were some gift certificates for food and personal items for her and her husband that Joan and my dad had purchased. I thought it was so nice that they had done something for someone else.

Beginning that year, as a lesson in helping others, we had to select one of our unopened Christmas gifts to donate to Toys for Tots. We weren't allowed to open it, so we never knew what we were giving away. It was always a beautiful and special part of Christmas, and each year I thought of the lady in the hospital bed in her living room and her family.

23
COLD AND HAPPY

As I CONTINUED TO SIT OUTSIDE MY CHILDHOOD HOME, MY thoughts turned to my dad. Nearly every single memory I have is of him working. He didn't have any guy friends. He didn't watch TV. He didn't follow sports. When he wasn't at his job as a teacher, he was always doing *something*. He did upkeep on the car. He worked in the yard. He spent many hours in the garage tinkering and putzing, as he called it.

While dad was strict, I loved spending time with him. He knew so many things, and I liked the things that he taught me. Although he did call me princess, he never treated me any differently than the boys. One time, he taught me how to siphon gas out of the car to use in the lawnmower. I can still taste the gas that made its way into my mouth when I didn't pull the hose out of it quickly enough as the liquid came up from the car's gas tank. Another time, I was around twelve, one of my chores was to bang one end of a metal 55-gallon drum out with a sharp chisel and small sledgehammer — a special thanks to my friend Janine, who gladly stepped in and did most of the work on that one.

As dad was always busy, other than errands, it was unusual for us to spend time together away from the house. So, it was extraordinary when dad asked me if I wanted to take a ride on the motorcycle with him in January, the year I was eleven. Dad and Joan had purchased two the previous summer and would take them out for long rides on Saturdays, leaving me and Chris locked out of the house playing with the other kids in the neighborhood. I immediately said yes, so happy that I would be going out somewhere with him. It was a breezy, crisp, and cold winter day.

My dad told me I should put warm clothes on, and then add my snow-suit, snow boots, and some warm gloves. For some reason, Joan and my youngest brother were out somewhere, so it was just the two of us. Excitedly, I ran up to my room to change my clothes, then rushed back down to the mudroom at the back of the house to put on all my snow gear. I found my dad in the garage, and he smiled at me as he took down Joan's helmet from the place where it hung on a peg and helped me put it on. I was smiling too.

I had only ridden on the motorcycle a couple of times, so my dad gave me some instructions before getting on. Hold on tight to the seat strap or him. Don't bang my helmeted head into him. Don't shift in the seat unless I told him I needed to first. When he leaned into a curve or turned, I was to lean with him. As we headed down the road a few minutes later, all the instructions I was given swirled in my head. I wanted to be sure not to forget one and ruin the day.

We hadn't driven too far before my dad pulled over into a parking lot. He turned the bike off and told me how to dismount. He then got off, bent down in front of me, and asked, "How do you like it."

"I love it!" I exclaimed.

"Are you scared?"

"No," I quickly answered.

He then said he wanted to take me to a special place. It would take about an hour and a half to get there, and we would have to go on the expressway.

"Are you okay with this?" he asked.

"Yes," I replied eagerly. Dad was going to take me somewhere special. My heart was so happy.

We got back on the motorcycle and headed east on the Long Island Expressway. I was a bit cold when riding in the neighborhood, but nothing like the cold I was feeling now. My small body was mostly hidden behind my dad, but the one thing I could not fully hide was my unprotected face. The cold wind felt like tiny icicle spears, and my face felt frozen by the time my father exited the expressway about a half-hour later and continued to head east on a beautiful two-lane road. The road held many treasures. There were beautiful old mansion-type homes. Some were in desperate need of repair, but the beauty of their original state shone through. There were large open fields and some big old farmhouses with moo cows, sheep, and chickens in the yard.

As we continued to drive, the land on either side of the road narrowed, and then, suddenly, the trees and houses disappeared, and a big wave of frigid air hit me. Off to my right, I could see the beach with the expansive Atlantic Ocean just beyond. The water, dark blue with the sun gleaming off the crest of the waves, was breathtaking. Even the smell in the air had changed. It was cleaner and lighter. It had also turned much colder. The wind was now coming from the side, and I was now feeling fully frozen. How much longer, I thought, as I closed my eyes, turning my face away from the wind and resting my head against my dad's back.

I knew we were turning as I could hear the turn signal my dad had switched on. As I had not seen or heard another vehicle in a while, I thought it odd that he would use it, but it was so like my dad. I lifted my head and opened my eyes as we made the turn into a parking lot, and that is when I saw it. Sitting up on a hill, a short distance away, was a very tall lighthouse. It was white with a thick brown horizontal stripe set against the backdrop of the overcast sky.

My father parked and, as I went to get off, my body felt frozen in place. It took a few moments to get moving, but we soon walked towards this massive, beautiful lighthouse.

"Where are we, dad?" I asked.

"This is the Montauk lighthouse," he replied. "We are at the very end of Long Island."

As the lighthouse was closed in the winter, we were not able to go in, but we walked up as far as we could and just looked up at it. Glancing over at my dad, he seemed to be mesmerized. I didn't ask why but, perhaps it had something to do with his time in the Navy. Lighthouses were something my dad loved his whole life.

After taking it in, dad took my hand and led me a short distance away to a steep rocky and sandy path that opened onto a beautiful beach full of smooth rocks. We walked together, not saying a word. Occasionally, I would let go of his hand, bend down, pick up a rock, and then run to catch up with him. It was extremely windy and, of course, still cold, but I was much warmer than I had been on the motorcycle. I felt light and free. This made me happy. I sensed the same in my dad, which made me even happier.

While it was going to be a very long and cold ride home, my insides were warmed by the events of the day and the time we had spent together. I was frozen again when we arrived home, and dad told me to go inside and, once he put everything away, he would come in and make hot chocolate. I didn't hesitate. I stopped in the mudroom to take my boots off but, being so cold, I kept my snowsuit on. I ran up the stairs and sat on the top step, waiting just outside the kitchen. As I sat there shivering, I felt like I was never going to be warm again. What I also felt was that I would never forget this day. What a beautiful adventure we had just experienced, and I was so grateful that my dad had shared such a special place with me.

24

THE LIST

MARCH 28, 2011, THE DAY I SAT OUTSIDE THE HOUSE WHERE I grew up, would be the last day that I wrote in my journal. I had spent a good deal of time that day thinking about my childhood, along with the memories and experiences that shaped me and my future, and what had become my current life. As I hoped, this visit did light some type of fire in me to more fully embrace and act on what My Guy was telling me to do and continue to fight to find my way through whatever was making me feel like I was not normal. I really was sick of my own whining. As had been the case for many months, I had so many thoughts swirling through my brain — but they still seemed random, scattered, and unfocused. As evidenced by my journal entry on that day, I was trying to focus on working through some things. How had my past influenced who I was now? How could I get joy in my life? What made me happy, and what made me unhappy? It was dawning on me that I had been living my life in a way that was very similar to how I was raised, and I was treating myself the way I had been treated. Sitting there, at my childhood house, I knew I couldn't live life this way anymore. I needed to find my way out.

During that visit, I wrote a list of what I wanted my life to look like. The idea for this list came from something that I had begun asking myself whenever I felt unhappy or stressed. What I had been asking myself, sometimes more than once a day, for several months, was 'What would make Heidi happy right now?' I had found that just asking this allowed me to focus on just the immediate moment in front of me. It also helped to calm me and put whatever was bothering me into perspective. Making a list of what I wanted was a positive action and had not been something that I had fully thought through previously. I had always focused more on what wasn't going well and what needed to change versus where I was headed and what I wanted. This list was so enlightening. I learned exactly what I was feeling about what I wanted my life to look and feel like. I wanted:

- *A smile on my face*
- *Satisfaction in my heart with the things that I do*
- *Be physically in shape*
- *Stop doing things that I don't want to do*
- *Be curious*
- *Try things*
- *Have faith in people*
- *Contribute in a meaningful way*
- *Take steps I am scared to take*
- *Know myself*

I WOULD REFLECT ON THIS LIST FAIRLY OFTEN OVER THE NEXT few months, even creating a more refined list in June of 2011. I printed it in color, the words on the left in blue and the words on the right in red. I printed it on a piece of paper small enough to fit nicely into my wallet when folded. This list was invaluable, and for quite a long time, at least two or three years, I carried it in my wallet and looked at it both in the morning and in the evening on the train during my commute into and back out of New York City. The first version I carried and read so often was:

Just for Today, I will ...

Stay present	*Not focus on tomorrow*
Make decisions for MY happiness	*Not focus on others needs*
Be true to the lines I draw	*Not go against my values/desires*
Be accepting	*Not be judgmental*
Focus on the journey	*Not just focus on the destination*
Experience the joy around me	*Not dwell on the past or insecurities*
Stay calm	*Not react*
Open up	*Not stay within myself*
Listen	*Talk less*

AT SOME POINT, I CAME TO UNDERSTAND THAT I SHOULD FOCUS on positive statements and that using the word 'not' would keep me from getting to where I wanted to be. I am grateful that I learned this, and within a few months, I updated it yet again. Not only did I want to focus on those things that were important to me daily, but I wanted to begin to concentrate on the future and refine what I wanted my life to look like. Quite extraordinary that something so simple could be so extremely helpful.

This list is still relevant today and where my focus remains. Except for the desire to be in a loving and supportive relationship with a partner where open communication and mutual respect are givens, there is nothing I would add or take away from this updated list:

Just for Today, I will ...	*What I want my life to look like ...*
Stay present	A smile on my face
Make decisions for MY happiness	Satisfaction with the things I do
Be true to the lines I draw	Be physically in shape
Be accepting	Be curious
Focus on the journey	Try things
Experience the joy around me	Have faith in people
Stay calm	Contribute in a meaningful way
Open up	Take steps I am scared to take
Listen	Truly know myself

The last few sentences of my final journal entry were very telling in terms of how the next several months would go. I wrote that I needed to find the courage to make myself happy. What would it take? How would I find that strength? I wrote that I was sick of whining about my life and that I should just 'ruck it up,' a term I learned in the military, which is how I had lived my life. This was why I always stuffed my feelings and my whining back down inside and avoided and ignored whatever I was feeling — because I believed no one cared and none of it mattered. What mattered then was not complaining, not being a burden to others, completing a task, getting another, and just getting on with what needed to be done.

The last words I journaled that day, and I wrote them in parentheses, were 'as if it were this easy.' This last statement hit me deeply. I realized that I was not at all convinced that I would get to the other side of the struggles I was facing. I was not convinced that I would ever be able to climb out of the hole where I felt stuck. I was not convinced that all that I was doing would really be successful or that I could ever get to a place of peace.

There have been many times in my life when something, a moment, a memory, a song, or even a conversation, has resonated so deeply that it moves me into actions that I've not previously undertaken, or has instilled some amount of strength or resolve that had not previously been within me. It is as if I get so sick of myself at times that I become willing to put more effort in because, Lord knows, I never felt like I was giving all that I could anyway.

This was what happened on the day that I sat outside the house where I grew up. I resolved to take back my life. I was completely committed and embraced what I knew would continue to be a very painful and arduous process that would take an incredible amount of strength and courage for me to get through. It was starting now, and it had to start with being completely honest with myself. I also knew I needed to start being completely honest with the one other person in my life who was creating lots of chaos for me, my husband, Bob.

25

THE LETTER

DETERMINED TO TAKE BACK MY LIFE, I SUDDENLY PULLED into a shopping center parking lot as I was driving home from the house where I grew up. My Guy had been encouraging me to write a letter to the universe about all that I was thinking and feeling. While it had been many months since he had suggested this, I still had not found the courage to write it. I was now calm, centered, and ready to write that letter. Parking out by the street, away from other cars so I would not be distracted or disturbed, I took out my journal and began to write.

What came out freely, easily, and with a directness I had not been able to muster for a good long while was not a letter to the universe. Instead, I was writing a letter to my husband. By that time, Bob and I had been together for twelve years, married for five, and, sadly, but feeling like there was no other choice, I had asked him to move out of our bedroom, and he was now living down the hall in the guestroom.

The letter flowed out of me in a river of feelings, disappointments, and hurt. As I wrote, tears streamed down my face, and I could see that I was finally recognizing and fessing up, at least to a small extent, to some of my own inadequacies and acknowledging that I had also contributed to our situation. I was revealing my pain, my unhappiness with where our marriage was, and my clear desire to have him hear me and to understand all that I was saying. The letter read:

Bob,

I love you. I've loved you since the moment I laid eyes on you. I want nothing more than to have a life with you that is peaceful and happy. A life where we are both able to be ourselves as well as being a couple. A marriage that is not mediocre – as I once explained to you.

I recognize that I may be difficult at times – I have strong opinions about things, and I will "fight" for things I feel strongly about. I also know that I am a caring and selfless person who puts everyone and everything else ahead of me most of the time. Over the past seven months, I have spent a lot of time getting to know myself better, recognizing the things I want to change, and working on changing them. Trying desperately to find peace and joy. My life became full of "stuff," lots of which are/were meaningless, unfulfilling, or something that was someone else's responsibility. I can no longer do these things. I must do for myself now. Find my happiness and meaning in my life. I need to recognize and change those things which are destructive, negative, and/or undermining my ability to be happy.

I sit writing this letter, still not wanting to say the things I need to say. I am afraid. I am already so alone, and lonely, and not hopeful.

The way our relationship is – I can no longer continue in it the way that it is. I can no longer be with you while you continue to drink. While I am sure you will find a way to, once again, twist what I have to say to make it all my fault, I am ready to deal with that. I am not perfect, and I am sure I contributed to where we are, but I can no longer wallow in my self-pity. I stand here willing to try to change what I need to change. It is obvious, however, that you are not in the same place.

You are an alcoholic – certainly, a high functioning one to the outside world, but not in "our" world.

The behaviors I can no longer tolerate include your choice to drink and not be with me. Your drinking impacts so many things about you and your life that I do not believe you even see. Your life revolves around drinking. When you will drink. When you won't drink. Scheduling your drinking. Making excuses to go downtown and drink. You are emotionally not there for me. You are a critical and negative person. You do not remember conversations – this is an almost daily occurrence now. You go downtown and then fall asleep on the couch. You tell me not to bring up the past. While I may be able to forgive, live with, or try to move past things you have done, I can't forget them.

They are hurtful and mean and are such a telling pattern when I look back.

I am desperately unhappy. I have accepted what I can only now describe as abuse – continually negative comments, non-supportive behavior, blaming everything and anything on me, being "mean" to me. It goes back to the beginning of our relationship. My world of possibilities for myself and my life was so big when I met you. All that has been closed. Our world is work, home, or a bar. I am so sad about what I thought we had and what could have been.

You once told me there was no one in this town for you to talk to. I understand that. I have always been here – you chose not to let me in.

I laid everything out for you at the beginning – my heart, me – everything. I trusted you completely. I had faith in you. Your actions over time, I realize now, have put me in a place where I can no longer trust you and I no longer do.

I truly want nothing but the best for you. I want you to be happy. It needs to start with you wanting to make a change. You need to get yourself help and get into recovery. I am not telling you what to do, although it may sound that way. I can no longer live in our life with you drinking. I am finding the strength to say this and, more importantly, to follow through because I need to for myself.

Bob, please consider what I have written. I will support you in your decisions, as I have always done. I do love you and know that there have been good times and loving behavior from you. When looking at the entire picture, however, I have mostly sad memories.

With love and kindness,
H

AFTER I FINISHED, I SAT THERE ABSORBING ALL THAT I WAS feeling about what I wrote. I was satisfied for having written it, but felt a deep sadness for all that was happening within my marriage. I was also feeling surprisingly matter-of-fact about it. It was what it was, and I had just put my reality on paper. What was now on paper were words that I had spoken to Bob before and some that I hadn't. The ones that I had said before were never taken seriously enough by Bob to have led him to make any changes, and, as I usually did, I accepted that. This letter, I felt, had a feeling of 'I am going to stand up for myself.' I wasn't feeling, however, that it would make any difference. I was unconvinced that what had just poured out of me would change anything. What I did know was that I was going to try.

* * *

IT TOOK ME TWO WEEKS TO GIVE THE LETTER TO BOB. I WANTED to give it to him sooner, but one of the things I had learned about living with Bob was that I needed to be strategic about the timing of conversations. Have it at the wrong time, and he couldn't participate because he had, was currently, or was headed to fix or get a cocktail. We both worked during the week, with Bob getting home before me every day, so I did not know how much he had drunk before I arrived home. Most Saturdays, I was at the college teaching and, even if Bob worked that day, he would get home before me or would have been home all day — so had either been at the bar earlier or was there when I got back to town. This left just Sunday morning as I would be able to see how much he had to drink the night before, and we were both usually home together until at least early afternoon.

While I was ready and determined to give him the letter, I was also scared. I wasn't scared of Bob; I was frightened by the future now that I was focused on confronting our issues as a couple and his drinking. "Can we talk?" I asked quietly, trying to ignore the 'oh what now' look that he shot me. We sat down in our large, bright, open great room that looked out onto the beautiful Long Island Sound. He sat down on the couch. I handed him the letter and then took a seat on the loveseat across from him.

I watched him as he read, my mind swirling with thoughts as I tried to figure out what he must be thinking. I had never confronted him like this, and as he didn't like to be directly spoken to about matters such as this, I remained concerned about how he would react. Not surprisingly, as soon as he finished reading, he immediately began defending his drinking and his behavior.

"I am not addicted to alcohol, and I can stop if I want to."

"No, you can't," I replied softly.

"Yes, I can," he insisted. "I went without drinking for several months after my open-heart surgery, so I can stop if I want to."

"That is not correct," I told him. "You stopped drinking for exactly four weeks and six days, then the day your brother came into town for Thanksgiving, you started drinking again. You haven't stopped since."

Also not surprising, he went on to explore how much wiggle room there was by asking me directly, "Does this mean I can't drink anymore?"

Knowing that if I said yes, it would set him off and probably end the conversation, I replied, "It isn't the drinking itself that is the problem. It's the behavior that comes along with it."

I was feeling proud of the way I was handling myself. I was not allowing him to provoke me, and I remained calm, focusing on stating my feelings and my perspective. This was progress, and I was thankful for the work I had been doing with My Guy. I told Bob about the behaviors that were not acceptable to me.

"Looking back," I said. "I am embarrassed to admit it, but I have accepted no intimacy, non-supportive and mean behavior, along with manipulation — and I have accepted all of this for far too long." I went on to tell him, "I am tired of feeling like there are secrets between us and that we cannot communicate openly and effectively." I even told him that I wished I had been able to recognize my own issues sooner as I would not have married him.

"I knew something wasn't right," I told him. "But I loved you and married you anyway, making that decision so as not to create waves and to just go along with what was expected of me given how long we had been together and how we got together in the first place. I wanted to trust what you were telling me about how life would be when we had a house together, but something was telling me that it wasn't the truth. I chose to believe it anyway." I told him, "From the beginning, I told you that I didn't want a mediocre marriage ...."

I didn't even get to finish this sentence when Bob interrupted me, saying, "We don't have a marriage, mediocre or otherwise." I sat there stunned by his words, silently digesting them. He wasn't wrong, but I had not yet admitted to myself that that was the case.

The conversation hit a lull, and, after a few minutes, Bob interrupted the silence and said with a defiant tone which claimed, 'you can't make me,' "I am not going to stop drinking. I could, but I choose not to. I like going downtown and having a cocktail or two each day."

"Bob," I said, clearly annoyed. "We would not be having this conversation if it was one or two cocktails a day. The truth, and you know it, is that you have at least eight or ten drinks a day. Please," I pleaded. "Please, stop drinking. Please get some help. If you can't do it for me, do it for your kids."

"I don't need help, and I do not need to recover," Bob stated adamantly.

Knowing the conversation was coming to an end as he only had a short tolerance for conversations like these, I took this last moment to say, "Bob, look, I think it would be good if you read the letter again. I need you to understand what I am saying. Please know," I added, "that for this marriage to work, I need to trust you. I took my walls down when I met you, but you have hurt me time and time again, so I rebuilt them. I know that hasn't helped us, but I can't take them back down before trust is reestablished." I ended the conversation by saying what I knew was my line in the sand but, as usual, saying it with a little gray in it versus the black and white feeling I had inside of me, "If you aren't willing to stop drinking, there is no hope that our marriage will survive."

26

UNTANGLING
FROM BOB

By November 2011, just six months later, I was 100% certain that my marriage was over. Nothing had improved since our conversation, and things continued to deteriorate. I knew it was time to end the marriage, and I approached Bob a few weeks before Thanksgiving. The conversation was not difficult for me to have, but it was extremely sad. Bob was quick to remind me that we were expected to host Thanksgiving dinner. I had spent many years doing only what he wanted and ignoring my own needs, and I was trying to be sure that I didn't ignore them anymore. While I thought, at the time, that I was being strategic, I gave in to what was a manipulative plea to delay this conversation. I thought that if I let him have this, he would allow us to pick the conversation back up afterward and move toward divorce. As usual, when I make decisions based on others' needs and ignore my own desires, I am left with resentment. I agreed to host Thanksgiving — but I did so begrudgingly and held a negative attitude toward it.

In the same conversation, in my way of always thinking two steps ahead, I expected that Bob would use the same argument about Christmas so, without him even asking, I told him I would put the conversation on hold until January. I knew I was being used. I knew I was being manipulated. I knew I was giving things that I didn't want to give. I knew I wasn't speaking my truth. I was unhappy but, as usual, I allowed something to happen that I was not okay with. Also not unusual, I had played a very active role in letting this all happen. While I had made great progress since beginning to see My Guy, some things would take much more time and courage to change.

I waited a few days into the new year before approaching Bob again. I had decided that I needed to divorce, but I couldn't get my constant need to accommodate others' behavior to change to match this. So, the conversation stretched out over the next two months, and during this time, I at least managed to get Bob to move from the guest room and into the studio apartment over our detached garage. Bob kept saying that he did not want a divorce, yet he was unwilling to make any changes to allow our relationship to work for both of us, nor would he talk to me about anything. He did, however, find a way to get me to delay the divorce discussion yet again.

Over and over for two months, I had heard him say things like, "How can you do this now? My son is getting married in May. Why can't we wait until after then? You do remember that they asked us to host their rehearsal dinner here at the house, don't you? How can we disappoint them and make changes now?" On and on he went. He kept at me and finally wore me down to the point where I felt compelled to do what he wanted, even though I wanted to say no. I was going to allow the conversation to be delayed again, but that wasn't sitting well with me. I wanted a different decision but, instead of using my voice to speak up for myself, I decided to try to control things instead. To avoid the confrontation that saying no directly would bring, I came up with another solution.

I decided that we could have a conversation with his son and his fiancé. We would tell them we were having marital difficulties, that Bob was now living over the garage, and while we didn't know what was going to happen, we wanted to let them know. We would also tell them that while we would still like to host the rehearsal dinner, given the current uncertainty, we would gladly incur the expense of hosting it at a restaurant and make all the arrangements as well. The decision would be theirs to make, but what I was counting on, my ace in the hole or so I thought, was that I believed I knew the fiancé well enough. I thought that there was no way she was going to risk making a last-minute change from the house to a restaurant. There was also no way she would want to be in the middle of a marital issue at the time of her wedding. This was my solution to get what I wanted when I wasn't willing to just say no. Well, as they say, the best-laid plans.

Bob agreed to this, and we went to see them in March. We told them we would give them a few days to talk it through and asked that they get back to us. I felt good after the conversation and was sure I was out of hosting duty. Unfortunately, I had underestimated the draw of our large, spacious, completely remodeled house that sat on the water just 50 feet from the

Long Island Sound. They called a few days later to say that regardless of what may be happening, that they were fine with keeping the dinner at our house. 'What?!' I remember screaming to myself in my head. How selfish could they be? Did they not have any regard for what we were going through? Was I really going to have to host this dinner? I was so angry but, rightfully so, it was mostly directed at myself. This was just another instance, in a long list, when not speaking my truth had resulted in my feeling put out again. When was I going to learn? Bob, of course, was happy. The inevitable was delayed again.

I was numb, and I was angry, and I was distressed. I was feeling so much, and then again, nothing at all. The next few months were difficult. While I could have changed my mind, put my foot down, and said no to the rehearsal dinner, I didn't. I was still operating in my world of 'don't disappoint others, do what is expected, don't rock the boat, you are probably overreacting to the situation' and, the icing on the cake, delivered gleefully by my Inner Critic, 'you deserve to be used like this.'

27

I SNAPPED AT MY
FATHER

RIGHT IN THE MIDDLE OF THE DIFFICULT AND STRESSFUL TIME
I was having while trying to untangle myself from Bob, I went to visit my
dad. It was March of 2012. It wasn't unusual for me to visit my father, and
I typically went down two or three times each year for maybe three or four
days at a time. Sometimes during my visits, I would head out to run errands
or get a few things that I never seemed to have time to shop for when I was
at home and, to spend time with me, dad would come along. I enjoyed his
company, and we always managed to find something that was funny or
interesting that we could laugh at or talk about. I loved hanging out with
my dad. Just like in childhood, there was always something to learn.

Dad and I have many things in common, but there is one item in particular that we differ on. My dad is a perfectionist. He does everything with
150% effort, he never quits, and he pays attention to every little detail. I
have never seen myself this way. I always put 150% effort into the things
that I do. There are things, however, that I don't do that maybe need to be
done, and there are times that I am not fully committed and quit while
working on something. This is a difference I have noticed many times, especially during a shopping trip while on a previous visit.

Dad and I left his house and headed to the outlets, where we began to
tackle my list. New sneakers, check. New pajamas, check. Then, on to see
about a wallet I had been looking for. I was a bit frustrated that I had not
found it yet, as the one that I had been using for many years fell apart, and I
was now using a small clutch bag as a replacement. Ugh, how I hate those. I
have to be in the mood to shop, and I am less in the mood when in need of

something that I haven't found yet, despite having already looked. I was not in a shopping mood on this particular trip with my dad. The wallet I was looking for was not a traditional one with the change purse and the compartment where you can slide money in flat. Those were big and had too much space. I just wanted a wallet similar to the one that I had before. It should be about 2.5" x 3.5" and expandable to maybe 1½" wide. It should open on the long side and have a few slots to hold a credit card or two, my driver's license, the small religious medallion I carry, and if the bills were folded in half, cash.

Having searched a few other stores, we walked into Coach. Still not exactly sure what I was looking for, dad kept holding up different ones for me to look at.

"Like this?" he would ask.

"No, not quite," and I explained why it wasn't. As he was looking around, so was I. Toward the back of the store, I found a flat box-like table that was maybe three feet square. The sides came up a couple of inches, just enough to hold all of the wallets so they would not fall on the floor. It was at that box table that my dad and I came together, both having gone through the rest of the store separately. In my 'I am not fully committed, and I am sure I am not going to find it' way, I glanced through the wallets with no luck. I told my dad that there wasn't one like what I was looking for and wandered away from the table. My dad, however, was methodically going through each one, placing those that he looked at to one side as he picked up the next. As I watched him, I smiled, knowing that he would go through each and every one despite what I had said. Convinced my wallet was not in the store, I wandered around looking at all the other pretty items, waiting for my dad to be finished.

Not too long later, my dad walked over to me and held up a wallet. He asked, "Is this the type that you're looking for?" He had found it! In his perfectionist way, he had looked through each wallet individually, and there it was. A beautiful, mauve-colored wallet. It was, in a word, perfect. I was so happy. I was happy that I had the exact wallet I was looking for but more so because, as he had been doing my entire life, my dad had taught me a lesson. This one was about commitment and staying engaged.

* * *

WHILE I MAY HAVE HAD A FEW THINGS THAT I WANTED TO DO, most of my time was spent helping my dad with whatever he needed during my visits. Leading up to my arrival, he would call to tell me the projects that he had on his 'Heidi Do' list. I didn't mind. I loved helping him. The items on his list were usually related to technology and, while I know he would have figured out whatever the issue was, dad was so busy with his other around-the-house tasks and his business projects. He would just put them on my list and leave them for me. I tackled things like switching out their cable box, setting up Wi-Fi, installing a webcam, downloading pictures from their camera to their computer, as well as teaching him how to use his new flip phone. I know that besides getting these tasks completed, my dad assigned me these jobs so I would be near him during my visit.

Dad and Ann own a marine upholstery business which they run out of their converted one-car garage. Most of the space is occupied by a large worktable on which they lay out and cut canvas material to make boat covers and cushions and other related work for boats, trucks, or outside furniture.

Down the outside wall of the garage is a door to the outside, shelves with all his tools and hardware neatly arranged in bins by size, color, use, etc. Next to the shelves is the office desk where my dad sits and returns phone calls, does his billing, and places orders with his suppliers.

On the far side, next to this desk, in the corner at the front of the garage, is a small computer desk and chair. This is where I spend my time working on the computer or using a portion of the large worktable to complete the various items dad had assigned me. Dad's work would have him in and out of the shop all day, so being tucked down in the corner  worked well for me to not be in the way, yet I was there when he came and went.

In my home office, I have a picture of a big yellow smiley face and, when I see it, it brings a big smile to my face as it relates to my dad. During one of my trips, I set up his new color fax machine. I showed dad how to work it, and that was that. I was at work a week or so later when my father called. As it was unlike him to call me during the day, I picked up. He apologized for bothering me but said he wanted to be sure that the fax machine was working and asked if I would mind sending something to it so he could check. This was so like my dad. In many ways like my father, this was another area in which we differed. If someone told me that the fax machine was working, I would move forward with that understanding until I found that it wasn't the case. Not my dad. In dad fashion, he wanted to avoid any potential problems with an incoming fax he was expecting the next day. He also asked, of course, if it could be in color so he could not only be sure that the fax was working but that it would also print in color. I told him that I would send him something shortly.

Smiling as I got off the phone, I decided to send him a big yellow smiley face. The face took up about half of the page, and then I added text at the top which said, "Have a Great Day Dad!" and beneath it the words, "With Much Love, Your Daughter." I was still smiling when I faxed it. I then took the page and pinned it up on the small bulletin board in my office, just above the phone. I looked at it frequently throughout each day, and, reminding me of my dad, it always brought a smile. On my next visit to Florida, as I came into the shop and glanced around, I saw that dad had also posted what he had received from me next to his computer. Two minds, sometimes with different thinking, this time thinking alike.

* * *

AT THE TIME OF MY MARCH 2012 VISIT, MY DAD KNEW THAT I wasn't happy with Bob's drinking, but he did not know that I had asked for a divorce. I was feeling extremely stressed and took this trip to get away for a few days. As usual, there was a list of items for me to take care of, one of which was to put his logo on the invoices and business letterhead I had set up for him a couple of years prior. While I feel pretty savvy from a technical perspective, working with logos was not something I had ever done, and I was becoming frustrated trying to get it situated the way he wanted it on the invoices for his clients. He had a number to send out, and he had waited to send them knowing that I was coming down. Because of this, I was feeling added pressure.

After fiddling around with it for several hours, I finally came to understand what needed to be done to get it to where dad wanted it. I typically have a great deal of patience for working through things, but not that day. When I had it at a point where I was satisfied with it, I showed it to dad. He wasn't satisfied. He wanted just one piece of the logo moved so it lined up a bit differently with the rest of the logo. I went back and tried again. When I got it closer to what he wanted, even though it wasn't exactly what he had explained, I showed it to him anyway, hoping he would think it was good enough and that I would be done. No such luck. Dad was looking for perfection and, with my lack of patience, I didn't think it was necessary. It wasn't that what was there looked bad. It looked great, but he just wasn't satisfied.

I kept at it, but my frustration and impatience were growing. Many different pieces made up the logo so when I moved one, the others moved, or I needed to move them to have it look right. Attempt after attempt, and dad was still asking me to go back and work at it some more.

The hours continued to go by, and the frustration I was verbalizing in my head was getting louder. *Why did it have to be perfect? Why was what I was giving him not acceptable? Why do I have to do everything?* I was stressing, but dad kept telling me to keep at it. I finally hit a point where I couldn't take it anymore. I was at the computer and dad was sitting in his office chair next to me, looking at yet another sample that was still not good enough.

So out of character for me, I stood up from my chair and said to him, "I can't do this," in a tone that sounded mean and sharp and not at all how I had ever spoken to him. I don't recall ever snapping at my dad like that, and as I stood there, on top of what I had been feeling, I now felt cornered as I was at the end of the room, and dad and his chair were mostly blocking my exit. Half sitting on the worktable, standing on my tippy toes to work my way around dad and his chair, I mumbled, "Sorry."

I knew how I had just spoken with him was not nice, but I couldn't help myself. The tone and words came out exactly as I felt them, and it was more than just being frustrated over a logo. I knew that it was mainly stemming from what was happening at home with my marriage breaking up, along with my continued work to find peace in my life that didn't seem to be going that way even though I had been at it for about eighteen months. I headed toward the inside of the house, not sure where I was going. Dad got up and followed me.

"Where are you going?" he asked.

"I don't know," I replied without emotion.

"Just come back and finish this up. You're almost there," he said.

"No, I can't figure it out," I snipped back.

"Yes, you can," he calmly replied. I stopped in my tracks. Still within the shop, having not made it inside the house yet, I turned around to face him.

In a tone that sounded like it came from a defeated person, I replied quietly, "No, I can't. I can't do everything."

"Sure, you can," he immediately replied.

"Dad, I am at my breaking point. This will break me, and then I'll have to be committed."

I was so surprised by what had just come out of my mouth, but I knew it to be the truth and a reflection on where I was at this moment. I was unable to stifle myself, and I seemed to be resigned to the fact that I was headed for a real break-down. It was a scary moment for me.

Dad had obviously heard what I said and, without asking for more details or background on why I had said it, he answered me with, "And what then, have someone else take care of you and make decisions for you?" I don't recall answering. I really did feel like I was about to break.

There were not many opportunities to talk about anything of depth in our family. We mostly talked about what I would call surface things. Things that don't dip any deeper than what you see on the top.

In typical fashion, the conversation ended there. I went to take a break, knowing that in 'good girl, do what is expected fashion,' I would take a quick moment and, 180 degrees counter to what I was feeling on the inside, I would put a smile on my face, go back to the computer and not quit until the logo appeared in the document the way dad wanted it to.

The next day I apologized to my father for my outburst. I told him that I was just feeling stressed. He said that he understood. He didn't ask any questions, nor did he ask for any additional information or insights. We hugged. There was no further discussion. That was it. It was ending no differently than how I would have expected. I didn't know any better. It was how I had grown up. It was how my dad had raised me.

28

SYD, MY MOTHER

IT WAS AROUND THE TIME THAT I SNAPPED AT MY DAD THAT, when getting to know a new friend, she began asking questions about my childhood. I told her that I was raised by my father and that I did not know my mother. I explained that she moved out of our house in June 1971, just a few weeks before I finished kindergarten and as I was about to turn six. In a succession of statements and questions, which to the average person might seem logical, she jolted me.

She said, "Oh, so if you lived with your dad, then you must have seen your mother on the weekends."

"No, I never saw her."

"Not ever?"

"No," I replied.

"She must have called you?"

"No, she never called me," I responded.

"So," she went on, "When was this, in the early '70s?"

"Yes."

"In that era, it was unusual for children to be raised by the father. Were you taken away from your mother?" she probed.

"I don't know," I replied quietly.

"Did she give up custody?"

"I don't know that either."

"So did your dad have legal or full custody of you and your brothers, then?" she inquired.

Once again, I answered, "I don't know."

The jolt for me was not only that I didn't know the answer to these questions, but that I had never thought to ask them. They brought up so many other questions for me, and I did think that knowing the answers to them might be helpful. Had my mother given me up? Why did I not see her on the weekends? Why didn't she call me?

When I began to see My Guy, he brought up my relationship with my mother and used the word abandonment to describe it. The first time he said this, I disagreed with him shaking my head and saying, "No, I don't feel like she abandoned me." He gave me a few reasons why he thought this was the case, but none of them sat right with me. I just didn't feel any attachment to my mother, and the thought that she abandoned me was not something I felt I could take ownership of. My Guy brought this up on several occasions, and I reacted the same way every time, but the possibility lingered in my mind. I lived most of my life without any understanding of why things were the way they were when I was growing up. While time has provided me with answers to some, what I still do not know, and probably never will as my mother passed away in 2001, is why I never saw or spoke with her again during my childhood.

* * *

IT IS SAD TO ADMIT, BUT I ONLY HAVE TWO MEMORIES OF interactions with my mother, and they are both related to the same situation. The first memory is of her standing over me. I had fallen asleep in her bed, and she had just woken me up. It felt like it was the middle of the night, and the only light in the room was coming in from the hallway behind her. I was in kindergarten, and I felt so small in that big bed. I also did not feel well, and my skin was very scratchy. I didn't understand why I was feeling this way, but I did know that this was not something that was going to go away overnight.

My mother was talking to me, holding a beautiful wooden doll cradle, saying that she was sorry. I didn't understand why she was saying she was sorry, and as I couldn't get excited about the cradle because of how I felt, I started to cry. My mother laid the cradle on the far side of the bed and sat down next to me. For the longest time, she sat there and, over and over, she pushed my hair out of my face.

She was trying to get me to stop crying and kept saying, "Shh, it's okay, it's okay." Her hand felt so cold on my hot face. I was hoping she would never stop, but she did as soon as I stopped crying. Before I fell back to sleep, my mother told me that she had bought me the doll cradle, hoping it would make me feel better. It didn't. I felt so sick, and I just wanted to feel better.

It would be many days before I was feeling well again, and, as I recovered, my brothers kept teasing me that my mom must not like me very much if she made me get sick. So that was what she was trying to say. I wasn't dreaming that part, I thought. My mom *had* done this to me. It had all happened about a week or two prior when visiting a neighbor. This is the second and only other memory I have of an interaction with my mother when I was a child.

As she sat in the living room talking with my friend's mom, my mother told me to go in and play with my friend Debbie. When I went into Debbie's room, she was lying in bed, and she said she was sick. She told me that she had the measles and that I should not come near her unless I had already had them. All kids knew about the measles, and no one wanted to get them. I ran back out to the living room and asked my mom if I had ever had them. She said I had, so I went back into Debbie's room to play. Well, as it turns out, I had not had them. Having gone through the measles with my five older brothers at times that she could not control, my mother decided to take this opportunity to expose me, hoping that I would get them so she wouldn't have to deal with it at an unexpected time later.

I have often wondered why the only two memories of interactions with my mother are linked together by the measles. Was I mad at her for having purposefully exposed me? Was I mad because she wanted to make it all better by bribing me with the doll cradle? Why had she told me that she had purposefully done it? Was that something I needed to know? I was only five years old. Was it possible that I remembered these times as I thought she was selfish to have done what she did? Was I angry at her for having done it?

I never did play with the doll cradle. I have never forgotten, however, lying in my mother's bed those many days when I was sick, looking at it. It was dark brown and had rounded legs so you could rock your dolly back and forth. It was maybe eighteen inches long, and in it, there was a small baby doll with brown hair covered by a soft white blanket. It was so beautiful. It was a baby doll cradle that any little girl would want.

* * *

MY MOTHER MOVED OUT NOT TOO LONG AFTER I HAD THE measles, and it would be twelve years before I saw her again. It was the summer of 1983, and I was eighteen. I was in New York to visit before I went into the Marine Corps. I went to see Joan and the friends that I had not seen since I moved to Florida three years earlier.

Joan was now married to Chris, a nice guy. She was still teaching and had met him at her school, where he also worked. I enjoyed spending time with him and getting reacquainted with Joan. I was staying with them during this trip and, one evening, Joan let me know that my mother lived not too far away and that she wanted to see me. I didn't want to, but Joan kept insisting, and, as always, I agreed.

I would learn that Joan and Syd had become friends a few years earlier, and Syd had even attended Joan's wedding two years prior. Joan made the call and, while I thought I was just going for a short afternoon visit, she let me know that she had arranged for me to have an overnight visit with Syd. When I found this out, I really didn't want to go but, again, I did what was expected.

A day or two later, I found myself sitting in the passenger seat of Joan's car as she pulled up behind Syd, who was parked on the side of an exit ramp off a local highway. It was around noon, and I was minutes away from seeing a woman I had not seen in many years, a lifetime, in fact. I was a young child the last time she had seen me, and I was now a young adult. I don't recall Joan getting out of the car or making any introductions. The next thing I knew, I was sitting in the front seat of Syd's old car and off we drove. The car smelled disgusting. It reeked of cigarette smoke.

We had not been in the car more than maybe ten minutes when Syd made a stop, parking in front of a small local bar saying, "Come on. Let's go in, have a drink, and get acquainted." It was obvious from the way the bartender greeted her that Syd was a regular there. The bar was dark with only a few basement-size small windows, and the air smelled stale. The bartender brought her a beer and then looked at me.

"What'll you have?" he asked. I was feeling extremely uncomfortable. Not saying a word, I just pointed to Syd's beer. As the bartender went to get me a beer, Syd began to ask me questions about things that she should have already known. Was I a good student? Did I participate in sports? What were my friends like? I was feeling resentful, but I was taught to be respectful of adults, so I answered her with as short an answer as possible each time. It didn't feel like a conversation. It felt more like twenty questions to me, although she filled in the empty air between us with talk. I refrained from calling her anything during my visit as I didn't know what to call her. I had always just referred to her as my 'real mother' or, as was more common as I got older, just Syd.

As we left the bar, Syd told me that we were going to Kings Park Psychiatric Center to pick up her husband, Joe, as he would be coming home for the weekend. She went on to explain that Joe suffered from mental illness and spent a great deal of time in and out of treatment centers. If it were even possible, this made me even more uncomfortable, as did the fact that she had just had two beers in a matter of thirty minutes, and I was not sure she hadn't had more before I got in the car. We were now going to be driving forty minutes on the expressway to go pick up her husband. Raised to do what I was told; I didn't say a word and spent the rest of the time looking at the clock on the dashboard, willing time to go faster.

A few hours later, after picking up Joe, we arrived at her rental house, a small old bungalow located near Fire Island, an ocean beach on the eastern end of Long Island. I don't remember much of the rest of my time with Syd other than something I heard her say. I didn't know this, but my brother Robby, who I had not seen in maybe nine years, lived nearby and was close with Syd. She told me that he was stopping by and would be having dinner with us. I had only memories of chaos surrounding my brother and his time living at the house, so my level of discomfort was raised a bit more. I was inside the house, wasting as much time as I could in the room where I would be sleeping when a car pulled up. Suspecting it was my brother, I drew back the corner of the sheer curtains to peek at him.

Syd and Joe were outside sitting at a table smoking, and, as Robby got out of the car, she said to him, "Wait till you see your sister. She has boobs. I don't know where she got 'em, but I know she didn't get 'em from me." I was mortified to know that she had been checking out my body and now had made this crass comment to my brother, of all people. So inappropriate. So awkward. So unsettling. I just wanted time to speed up. I didn't feel good being with her. I wasn't at all comfortable. When she dropped me back with Joan, I was never so glad to have something come to an end.

That visit was the last time I saw my mother. I did speak with her a few times as Joan, without my permission, gave her the phone number to my barracks room after I joined the Marine Corps. While she called a couple of times early on during my service, we never established a relationship. I had no interest in one after my overnight visit, and one particular phone call cemented this for me. It was the beginning of July in 1984. I was stationed at Henderson Hall just up the street from the Pentagon in Washington D.C. While I didn't want to speak with her, I was polite when she called.

At some point during this call, she said, "I'll forgive you for forgetting my birthday if you could see your way to send me a Marine Corps sweatshirt and a pair of combat boots. I'll be able to brag to all my friends that my daughter is in the Marine Corps when I wear the sweatshirt, and the boots will come in handy as I love to fish. Those will be great for that." I was floored when she said that but had the presence of mind, as I didn't already know, to ask her when her birthday was. She said it was June 17.

"Oh, okay," I responded.

When the call ended, I was fuming. How dare she put guilt on me about her birthday when she had never once shown me that she remembered mine which, also in June, is just nine days after hers. I never did send her the items she asked for.

I don't recall speaking with Syd again while I was in the service, and I only recall speaking with her one other time in my life. It was on February 17, 1995. Joan had passed away in a car accident on Valentine's Day, and my brothers Keith and Chris were coming to stay with me for a day or two to take care of a few things related to her passing. I was taken aback when I answered the phone and realized that it was Syd. She was calling to speak with one of my brothers. She asked how I was, and we exchanged a few pleasantries. I was not happy that she had called. I didn't even know that she had my phone number. It turns out that one of my brothers had given it to her in case she needed to reach them while they were at my house. It was then that I demanded of the brothers who were in my life and who also spoke with her that she was not to be given my phone number ever again. I had no desire to have any type of relationship with her, and I never did.

29

TRYING TO MAKE PROGRESS

As the spring of 2012 continued, so did my stress. I also had a severe sense of heaviness within me. I was struggling to untangle myself from Bob and was feeling mostly defeated. While the announcement of our divorce was on hold, our conversations about it continued, and Bob was getting nastier and his words and tone belittling. He was incredulous about the divorce. He told me that he had not done anything to contribute to our marital issues, and he wasn't going to participate in the process. He kept telling me that the reasons I wanted a divorce made no sense to him. He also kept telling me that there was something wrong with me.

While I was certainly struggling, I was also trying to get my feet underneath me and not be influenced by what others said. Emails to My Guy helped me to get out what I was feeling inside, particularly as it related to issues with my husband, like this one:

I'm going to try to focus on how I feel about myself and not what he is saying. Going to an Alanon meeting today. I am not in a good place. I feel like I am right back to where I was a year and a half ago. I know this will pass. I need to have patience, and I need to just give myself time. I will be alright.

A<small>T THE SUGGESTION OF</small> M<small>Y</small> G<small>UY</small>, <small>WHILE DIFFICULT</small>, I approached Bob about the idea of going to a counselor to assist us through the divorce discussions and be an arbiter of sorts. I thought this a great idea, as it would certainly provide me with some much-needed support. Bob said he wouldn't go. I kept asking, and, in the end, he finally agreed, but only if we changed the focus of the discussion. He wanted the counselor to listen to the reasons why I wanted a divorce and for him to tell Bob, in his honest opinion, if I made any sense at all. *Yeah*, I thought, *nothing can go wrong with this idea*. As it had been so exhausting just getting to this point, I said yes, once again giving in to someone else's desires and putting them above my own.

We were both working in New York City, so we selected a counselor in the city and met at his office after we both got off work. Bob arrived defensive and resolved to prove, once and for all, that he was right and that there was nothing wrong in our marriage. I arrived exhausted and just wanted to get it over with. The session was scheduled for fifty minutes. It ended after about twenty-five. Upon arrival, Bob explained what he expected to be addressed. The counselor, a bit to my surprise, obliged this request and asked me to explain my reasons. I listed them in the same manner I had been stating them for months. Among other things, there was the fact that there was no intimacy between us. I said his drinking was getting worse, as he was having blackouts and wasn't acknowledging this. I also did not feel appreciated for all I was contributing in terms of time, effort, and money to our marriage, the house, and his family.

After I finished, Bob turned expectantly to the counselor and said, "Well?" The counselor answered him, stating that I appeared to have expressed my sincere feelings and I had provided valid and reasonable back-up for them.

Bob, usually containing his anger in public or in front of other people, always wanting to give the illusion that all was right in his world, exploded. He raised his voice as he stood up and said that he knew this was a set-up. He accused me, the counselor, and My Guy of setting up this meeting to embarrass him. There was nothing more that the counselor could do, so the meeting was ended. We left together headed for the train home to Long Island. He, of course, stopped at the bar cart on the train platform and purchased two double drinks for himself. It was a long train ride home.

Still struggling, I sent an email to My Guy:

I am trying to be strong, but it is not working very well. I am not certain I will get through this, but I am just trying to take it one moment at a time.

STILL TRYING TO WORK THROUGH ALL I WAS THINKING AND feeling and showing my lack of understanding of why things were the way they were, in April of 2012, I sat down at my computer and typed:

Why did my life turn out this way? This isn't what I wanted it to be. There is no one for me to rely on. I see people in relationships that look so good and loving. I want that. I want someone to hug me and I want to feel how much they care. I am scared that nothing is going to change. I remember way far back being in the same sad place. Coming home and flopping down on the bed and just lying in that position for a long time. I had no one to talk to. I had brothers but was an only child.

I used to put my dad on a pedestal. Why? He doesn't deserve to be there. I always thought I could rely on him. Problem was I couldn't. He didn't teach me to be a loving person. He showed me what I guess he learned – survival.

Why can't I say no to things I don't want to do. Why can't I say something when an uncomfortable situation comes up? I feel like I continue to let people abuse me.

I feel like I am not connected to the universe. I could not be here tomorrow, and it wouldn't matter. There isn't anyone, besides maybe my dad, that would be impacted. Bob would get the house and all my money, so he'd be happy.

I feel like I've been crying out for help for my entire life. No one has helped. I put a smile on, I try not to get in trouble, and I try to do the right thing (using other people's standards, of course).

I'm tired. Tired of feeling sad. Tired of feeling so lonely. Tired of feeling empty. Tired of feeling like I am a piece of shit because I can't get my life right.

I am not normal. There is something wrong with me. I don't have the patience to wait for me to be 'fixed.' I want to know what is wrong with me. I've been patient and haven't asked questions in trying to trust. Trust My Guy. Trust the process. On a logical level, I get what My Guy explains about why I am feeling the way I am feeling. He indicated that he knew I would go through this. What else does he know that he isn't telling me?

I can't continue to be in the air without a direction. Just saying I am working toward a more peaceful place where I can be happy isn't working anymore. I'm not convinced that I will get there. Sure, as in the past, I feel better for a while, but it always comes back. The feeling of failure, loneliness, and unhappiness. I don't want this life. I just want someone to care for me. To take care of me. To step in when I can't take care of myself, and to know that they will do it for me, even if for just a moment, as I like to be tough and in charge.

Yes, Alanon helped. I don't want to go there for the rest of my life. Someone said I could find friends there. I don't want Alanon friends. I want a life. Not one made up with people who have had the same difficulties I've had. I don't want to deal with it every day. I want to deal with my 'life issues' and move on. I don't want to take any drugs for depression. If I take them, it will further confirm of what I already know – that there is something wrong with me. If anyone finds out, they'll know I'm not right.

Nineteen months I've been at this. I started by saying I had become a bitter, nasty, and unhappy person and didn't know how I got there. I'm now not nasty, and I'm not unhappy (not happy, either), but I think I may still be bitter. I just don't show it as I have in the past. So, I've become a better person to the outside world. Still feel like a piece of shit inside.

IT DIDN'T MATTER WHAT I WAS FEELING OR GOING THROUGH, AS there was always something to do, as was the case when I wrote this piece. We were just a couple of weeks away from the wedding and, no matter what I was feeling, there was lots of work that needed to be done, and that is where I put my focus. It was also during this time that I went to see a lawyer about preparing the necessary paperwork to get the divorce process started. I had finally had enough of trying to work with Bob to come to an amicable divorce arrangement. I fully expected that he would fight me, but I couldn't wait any longer as I knew he would just continue to drag it out as long as possible. The next number of weeks were difficult given all the events that were coming up and now, on top of it, I was trying to move the divorce forward. Why did I always have to put something else on an already full plate? When would I learn? Bob began to shower me with guilt about how selfish I was to have gone to the attorney when he had not yet agreed to the divorce, and that we had his family coming in, the upcoming wedding, and all the surrounding events. I was miserable and feeling defeated.

* * *

Bob's brother and his family would be staying at our house for the wedding, so Bob moved back into the house and the master suite the day before they arrived. We had not lived in the same house since February and had not slept in the same bed since March of last year. I was feeling cornered and highly stressed. Of course, all that was happening was on top of my commute, my executive-level job, and teaching on the weekends. Also, in addition to all of this, as I had been doing for several years, I was serving as parade chair and organizing the largest Memorial Day parade in our township. There was certainly a lot going on. I had thought that getting the divorce papers in order and presenting them to Bob would be helpful, but I was not feeling any relief. By the time his family arrived, all I was focusing on was surviving and getting through to Monday afternoon of this long Memorial Day weekend when his family would be gone, the wedding over, and the parade chair duties completed. By then, as we had agreed, Bob would have moved back out to the apartment above the garage.

I barely survived the weekend, getting through it with my head down and not making eye contact for fear that I would start crying over all the pain I was feeling inside. Being with Bob and his family had become a very lonely existence for me, and I was feeling the weight of this despite the happy occasion. I arrived home on Monday afternoon, and, still in my Marine Corps League uniform, I poured myself a glass of water and sat down in the living room to take a big breath and relax for a moment.

I am sure that I had not even taken a full breath in when Bob emerged from somewhere and sat down on the ottoman in front of me. He had agreed to the plan that while I was at the parade, he would move his things. Bob, as usual, without asking how I was or even how the parade went and having it be all about him, said defiantly, "I am not going to move out of the bedroom." I stopped breathing and froze. I had come so far, and now here we were. I felt like I was right back to the beginning when I initially asked for a divorce some seven months prior. I don't usually curse and, when I do, it is a sign that I am mad. I had a lot of pent-up emotions which came up and out of me in a rage at that moment.

I showed this to Bob when I stood up from my chair and sort of growled at him in a low and slow cadence, "No fucking way are you not moving out of my room. If you don't get your stuff out of there now, I will throw it out of this house myself. Try me!" I was livid. How dare he. Not a thank you for all I had done. Not a thank you for not showing anyone the pain that I was enduring. Not a thank you for supporting him in front of his family. No recognition that he was going back on what he had previously agreed to.

I was tired of being used. I was tired of feeling like I didn't matter. I was tired of being taken advantage of. I was tired of letting people take advantage of me. I was tired of saying yes to whatever anyone else asked of me, no matter how I felt, and knowing that how I felt was just incidental and of no consequence to anyone else. I was so very tired of always doing for everyone else and giving in to others. I was tired of falling for what Bob had to say, then allowing him to not live up to what he agreed to. This was not going to happen this time. I am sure that my never-before-seen reaction to Bob is what made him realize that he couldn't manipulate me into agreeing that he didn't have to move back to the apartment as there wasn't anything more said between us before he went upstairs and began moving his things.

* * *

I HAD MADE IT THROUGH THE PAST FEW MONTHS, AND NOW I was ready to get Bob to sign the papers and to let our families and friends know about the divorce. I waited a few days and then called him and, getting his voicemail, I left him a message asking if we could get together on Sunday morning to talk.

Bob stopped into the house on Sunday morning.

"So," I said. "I wanted to see if you had looked at the papers I gave you and, if so, would you sign them."

He simply replied, "I'm not going to sign them. I told you that I don't want to get a divorce, and I will fight you."

I calmly replied, "Bob, you can fight me all you want, but in the end, I will be granted a divorce. You can't stop that. It will just take longer and cost more money if you fight it."

"I don't care," he said. "I don't want a divorce."

I just wanted peace. I didn't want to fight. I didn't want a divorce. I just wanted him to stop drinking and for some things to change. Maybe, I thought, he had finally woken up and understood that I was willing to walk away now that I was pushing for him to sign the papers. Perhaps he was realizing how much I meant to him. Perhaps things would change. There was nothing in Bob's words, tone, or demeanor that led me to this conclusion, however. These were thoughts that I made up in my mind. It was how my mind had been working for my whole life, and how I had gotten to the destructive place where I found myself. That day, perhaps because I was just so tired, I held that door of hope open, and, not unexpectedly, Bob (figuratively) kicked it wide open. He took the opportunity and worked hard over the next couple of weeks to avoid the divorce conversation and talked a lot about how things were for us at the beginning. There was no talk, however, about any changes or work that he was willing to do to help our marriage. It was just another delay tactic.

* * *

We had been hosting a large July 4ᵀᴴ party for the past number of years. We lived on the water, and our back deck was front and center for the annual fireworks display our village put on. Bob's father was born on July 4ᵗʰ, and the whole family and lots of other people we called friends, but most of whom I would not even consider acquaintances, were invited each year. My world, I had come to recognize, was mostly filled with shallow, mean, negative, and/or alcohol-addicted individuals. We were now in mid-June, and Bob convinced me that it was too late to cancel the party. Always focused on the optics and how he would look, Bob said, "Everyone will know that there is a problem, and we can't disappoint everyone." On and on, Bob went. Not surprisingly, I gave in once again. My stress was continuing to rise, as was my disgust with myself. The end, which I thought was in sight back in November, continued to be a moving target.

I woke up a few days after the party knowing that I was at my end. While I would have liked to believe that my newfound resolve was because I had finally decided to honor what I had known for a long time was the right course of action, but I know that that was not it. The only reason I was finally going to put my foot down was that there was nothing else that Bob would be able to come up with to delay this any longer. There were no upcoming weddings, holidays, or birthdays. There were also no planned family events within the immediate family. It was only in this knowledge that I found the courage to sit down with Bob that afternoon and bravely, calmly, and with sadness inform him, "It's time." While it still took a few weeks, Bob finally went over and told his parents that we were divorcing, and then he called each of his adult children. I would meet with his parents and his children later, but Bob had wanted to tell them himself.

The months following the filing of the divorce papers were not any easier on me in terms of dealing with Bob. While he signed the papers, he did not give up trying to change my mind. I allowed things to happen on many occasions and went along with what he wanted. I was still trying to find my voice, but it was clearly still missing. One of the things I did but did not want to do included having dinner with him on several occasions as he said he needed to talk with me. The dinners, however, were just an opportunity for him to continue to dump guilt on me. He asked me to come to his house on another occasion as he said he needed to speak with me about something serious. It was in this conversation that he accused me of being a lesbian. Still in denial over the reasons I had wanted the divorce in the first place, he told me that this was the only thing that made sense to him. As I would find out, this is what he told all his drinking buddies downtown when finally forced to acknowledge our divorce. I guess it was easier for him to think this than to admit to any of his own failings.

30
OCTOBER 2012

It was mid-October of 2012, just a couple of months after the divorce papers were signed, when I called My Guy late one evening. In the two years, I had been seeing him, this was the first time I was reaching out outside of our scheduled appointments. While one might have expected that I would have been feeling better with all of the recent developments, this was not the case. Before he even had a chance to return the call, I sent him an email early the next morning:

Good Morning, I left you a message last night. I am ok. No need to return the call. We can talk next Tuesday. I am trying to work through your continued recommendation to go on depression medication. Again, we can talk next week. Thx.

His response was:

Ok. Please feel free to use my cell. If you call, I know you really need to talk. Ok? You okay?

173

My response was:

Ok. No, not ok but same not ok as the other day. Working on being ok.

While we discussed going on the medication at our next session, I was still highly resistant and made no arrangements to do so.

October was turning out to be a busy and stressful month. Around this time, I was finalizing the paperwork to transfer the house Bob and I owned together into my name. After deciding not to run anymore, I had purchased it in the divorce. I had been running my whole life. Reflecting back, I had used many things to avoid dealing with any difficulties I faced including making major life changes, starting and ending relationships, moving houses, and sometimes changing employers. I did these things to cover up the inadequacies and pain I was experiencing, and that I had carried with me since childhood. No more band-aids. It was time to figure me out. I knew I needed to change my behaviors if I wanted my life to be different. Staying put in the house until I knew what I should do next was a good start. I also made a decision about dating. In the past, I had gone from one relationship to another. Not anymore. I was going to date, but not someone else. I was going to date myself. I needed to know and get comfortable with myself before I moved on to another relationship.

As October continued, life again showed that just when I thought things would calm down, they don't. Hurricane Sandy hit New York in late October, and, by this time, the house was fully in my name. I felt very vulnerable having to take care of the house all by myself and, when the hurricane hit, I regretted the decision to purchase it and my decision to stay in it during the storm. The storm was fierce, and it was scary. Living so close to the vast openness of the Long Island Sound, I had a close-up view of the churning water and the large, violent waves crashing against the back of the house. I was without power for seven days, and there was damage to the siding, back deck, and a couple of the windows and doors. While I fared reasonably well, considering more than 650,000 homes were destroyed in that storm, more stress descended upon me as I worked to deal with the clean-up, my insurance company, the National Flood Insurance Program, and contractors. It was a long and difficult process for many reasons, but mostly because I felt so alone.

It was also October when my dad let me know that he had gone to his annual physical, and the doctor was a bit concerned about some of the numbers from his blood work. My father didn't say that he was worried, but I felt a heightened need to know precisely when his next appointment was.

With all that October was delivering, I was surprised that I finally wrote the letter to the Universe that My Guy had been suggesting for almost two years. It was an exercise that I had allowed myself to avoid for too long.

It turned out to be less a letter and more a series of separate, unfocused paragraphs. I was still struggling to understand what I was truly feeling. I had been describing my emotions as anger for a good long while, so I decided that I needed to focus on that and a few other concepts I had been discussing with My Guy. For example, feelings of resentment and abandonment. Interesting, and so like me, I looked up their definitions so I could be sure I understood them.

Anger: Feeling or showing resentment

Resentment: Persistent ill will or displeasure at something regarded as wrong

Abandon: Leave somebody behind; to leave somebody or something behind for others to look after, especially somebody or something meant to be a personal responsibility

So, a letter to the universe. Why am I angry? Who am I angry at? I think about things, times, and people I may be angry at, and I discount them as unimportant. Not being as bad as I perceive them to be. I tell myself that the people who have hurt me or made me angry didn't know any better, so how can I be mad at them? Should I look at this by person?

My Dad – He did not show me a healthy way of living or having relationships. He showed me how to be angry. To cut people off and out of my life if you don't like what they have to say.

Joan – Why wouldn't she let me go live with her? She knew the house where I was growing up. She knew what my dad was like.

My Mother – What really happened that I ended up living with my dad, without her in my life? Do I think it had anything to do with me? No, honestly, I don't. I believe exactly what I have been told, which is that she was an alcoholic. Did she abandon me? I guess that is right. Am I angry about that? Why do I not think so? I know that not having her in my life impacted who I am ... but so many other things impacted who I am as well. I do need/want to find out what she was like and why she wasn't in my life. I honestly feel I was better off without her. Well, maybe not better off — but sure that I should not have been with her.

I was told not to focus on myself but that is where it makes the most sense to start. I am sad and angry and disappointed in myself. I know that I am stronger than I live up to at times. I let people walk all over me and cross boundaries that I set. On many occasions, I haven't behaved honorably, ethically, or compassionately. I hurt people along the way in my life.

I am angry now because with Bob and most of the alcoholics and people that created chaos for me out of my life, I'm left with me. I now have to face that my life has been unmanageable for a long time. My relationships haven't worked for a LONG time. Somehow, I never saw the patterns and have relived the same destruction over and over again.

What goes through my head? I don't think I am a burden on others or that the world would be better off without me. What I do think is that I am tired. I don't know how to fix me. I am broken. No one is convincing me otherwise. Am I depressed? Yes, I am sure of it. Do I want to stop being depressed? Yes. Do I have the energy to get out of this depression? Not yet. But I want to, and I am going to try. I am feeling like a person who weighs 600 lbs., but wants to get healthy, so they start walking and can only go 10 feet, then they have to sit down. I am trying to find the courage to get up and go even just 2 feet. Went to an Alanon meeting today. 1 step. Maybe the gym tomorrow? Go easy on myself.

THIS LETTER WAS A TELLING SIGN OF MY CONTINUED FEELINGS of despair. While I now had some tools for coping with life in more constructive ways, and I was feeling a bit better, stress was building again and had been for the last year. I had been focusing on and working toward understanding myself and changing the parts of who I was that I didn't like. I had also spent a great deal of time thinking about my marriage and then the needed divorce. All the while, I had also been withdrawing from people who were not good for me, those who created chaos, and who did not have my best interest at heart. A lot was going on within and around me which is why, perhaps, I didn't see the darker times that were coming. The day when a new rock bottom came calling.

31

THE BOTTOM

It was Sunday, December 1, 2012, at around 9 a.m., on the bleakest of mornings, when I sent out a cry for help which, for me, was like no other. This cry had been building for years, probably my entire life. At that moment, despite the handful of times I had felt like the world was closed to the possibility of freeing myself from the pain and anguish of my past, I just knew that I was at the bottom. Well, thankfully, I was just slightly above the bottom. I was aware enough to understand that if I didn't act, the bottom would arrive, and I might just find myself in a place of no return. Although it had never previously found its way into my conscious mind, I truly believed that I could find myself in a place where I might just consider or, worse yet, act on some impulse to take my own life.

It was Thanksgiving weekend. While I had several invitations, I decided to spend the holiday by myself. I spent the morning happily watching the Macy's Thanksgiving Day Parade, then football in the afternoon. Having thought ahead and picked up a turkey dinner with all the trimmings the night before, I had a delicious holiday meal during half-time of the late afternoon game. All-in-all, it was a lovely day.

It was a long weekend, and a girlfriend had offered me the use of her vacation home in upstate New York. I decided to take her up on this offer. It was a five-hour drive, and I was excited as I just adore road trips. I was feeling good when I woke up Friday and drove through the day, and arrived in mid-afternoon. I had stopped along the way to pick up groceries for breakfast and so that I could cook myself dinner during the two nights that I would be there. After getting settled, I turned on the gas fireplace and looked through the DVDs she had, selecting Castaway as my evening movie. I sent a quick video showing my girlfriend just how comfortable I had made myself, and then, after a delicious home-cooked meal, I sat down to watch the movie in front of the comforting fire.

I woke up Saturday morning looking forward to what the day would bring. I had no specific plans other than to go out exploring. As I made my way downstairs toward the coffee, I glanced outside and stopped in my tracks. There was snow on the ground. Normally snow would make me happy, and I would instantly want to go make a snow angel. Not today. The sight immediately made me unhappy. My car does not drive well in the snow. I had checked the forecast, and snow was not called for, so this was a complete surprise. With absolutely no other trigger than the sight of a little snow, I started to sob. It was as if all that I had been going through, all that I was trying to address and change, and all that I had been trying to hold at bay was descending upon me and it was happening all at once. I was in the middle of the woods by myself. I was feeling anxious and very vulnerable — like a loser and a failure. I was feeling unlovable, lonely, and completely alone. I had to get out of here. I had to go home. The need was immediate, and I couldn't fight it.

As I would have to wait until I knew the roads were clear, I set about putting the house back in order, including washing the sheets and putting them back on the bed. A few hours later, I was on the road headed home. I was a mess, but holding it together enough to drive safely. I arrived home by late afternoon, feeling a bit more protected being in my own surroundings.

What had been in the back of my thoughts for most of the year as I worked toward a divorce from Bob was now fully present in the front of my mind. Deep feelings of disappointment with my life. I never expected to be forty-seven, not have any children, and not be married. I see how I got there, but I did not like it. I sat crying for most of the day. I wasn't able to sleep that night and, by early Sunday morning, I sent out that cry for help. Even with the direness of what I was feeling, I wrapped it all up in what I felt was a somewhat innocent, "Hey, how are you? If you have a minute, could we chat? I am having a bit of a tough time," email to a friend.

* * *

I HAD KNOWN AOIFA O'DONNELL FOR A COUPLE OF YEARS, AND, on top of being a friend, she was a licensed social worker. She was also the CEO, soon to be owner and president of National EAP an organization who, among other services, provides support to individuals in crisis. While I had been seeing My Guy for over two years, I didn't reach out to him. My logical brain rationalized it by saying it was a Sunday, and there was no reason to bother him with what could just be over-reacting. Perhaps this was just a momentary stumble into a darker place that would pass, so there was no sense in letting him in on it if this were the case. I was having a hard enough time coming to terms with all that My Guy pushed me to deal with, and I didn't need another example to analyze with him about whether how I felt now was any different than the moment I had begun seeing him. I was, however, at a dark point. A place that was darker and deeper than I had ever experienced before, despite the work I had been doing.

I guess my cry for help wasn't masked as well as I thought. Aoifa replied within a few minutes, saying that she would call me in half an hour. I started crying again. I cried out of fear. Fear of the unknown that I had opened up by reaching out for help. I also cried with relief. I had not previously known the pain I was now feeling, and it was coming from an overwhelmingly scary place. I was feeling raw and more vulnerable than I had ever felt before. I knew I was at my bottommest point. I also knew that I had to do something different than I had been doing. I had been resisting, and I knew I needed to fully surrender. I had to allow myself to give in to the process and this journey I found myself on but, I wondered, did I have the courage to do that? Would I surrender myself to the unknown future which, up until this point, seemed scarier than where I was? When the phone rang, I knew the answer was yes, but I was terrified. I still did not know if the pain of the place I was in was more bearable than the scariness of letting someone see the depth of despair that I was feeling. I answered the phone, however, and stepped forward to truly begin my journey away from my past.

After I told her why I was reaching out, my friend did what one would expect a therapist to do upon hearing that the person on the other end of the phone was in the pit of despair. She asked me questions to assess whether I may be suicidal. I was not offended or embarrassed by the questions. I was quite resigned to the fact that it was totally appropriate and necessary given how I was feeling. The questions also confirmed for me that I was, indeed, in a seriously troubled state. I answered truthfully and, as I expected, she concluded that I was not suicidal. I went on to say, "No, you are right. I am not suicidal, but if someone told me that life was going to end tomorrow, I would be okay with that. In fact," I told her, "I would welcome it, and this is not the first time that I've felt this way."

I explained that I had been working with a therapist for a couple of years to come to terms with all the terrible things I felt that life had thrown my way. I said, "I am beginning to be convinced, based on where I was and feel I am now, that I am never going to be able to get past them ... so an end to life would just put me out of my misery, as the saying goes." I then added, "I am reaching out as I need help. I guess more help than I have been getting." I was even brave enough to tell her that I was at a point that if someone told me that I would have to be admitted somewhere for 30-days, I would be okay with that.

"Is that what you want?" she asked gently.

"No, I don't, but I will admit that I feel like I am crazy, and perhaps I belong there."

I felt like I was deep within the earth in a dark, scary, and small cramped space with no way out. One might say that the way out was up, but I could not even tell if there was light coming from above and up seemed, as I would come to realize I had been thinking all along, impossible. I was out of gas. I was out of, 'I'll pick myself up by my bootstraps, put a smile on my face, and just carry on.' I was out of ways to work around all that had happened and the many emotions I had buried deep inside of me, which were now making themselves known. I was, quite frankly, all out of ways to move forward, yet still driven by the voice inside of me that I was running from. The voice that told me, "You're not worthy. You are a loser. You don't matter. You are not loveable ... and nothing will ever change these things."

Aoifa and I talked a bit, then she recommended that I meet with a colleague of hers, also a licensed social worker. She thought they could help me assess the assistance I had been getting to see if she had any additional thoughts on what could be helpful. This sounded like a sensible option, so I allowed her to set up an appointment.

One of the first things that the other therapist, Bonnie, asked me the next day was why I had not reached out to My Guy. While I conveyed to her the excuses I had already thought about, I knew that they weren't the real reasons, so I then added, "I'm not quite sure." After exploring this a bit, avoidance was the conclusion we arrived at. I have called myself a procrastinator for as far back as I can remember. This was something I did even during my childhood. The reason for this, at least what I would tell myself, was that this was just how I was. This was how I handled things. I would also tell myself it was because I spent a lot of time thinking about something in my mind first, before I started doing whatever I was procrastinating on. I thought this was helpful to the process of getting whatever it was done. I also said it was because I was good under pressure, and I liked to feel the adrenaline as it helped me to have a better outcome. While I do procrastinate, these were mostly just excuses for what the real issue was and, as evidenced by that moment, continued to be. She was right. What I was doing was avoidance.

I had been avoiding things for so long that I even had a name for it. I refer to how I deal with things as employing the extinction method: Avoid something long enough, and it goes away. Avoidance was also another way that I didn't use my voice. My avoidance is based on fear and also the impact of the words spoken by my very vocal and insistent Inner Critic. He would certainly need to be addressed as he turned out an overwhelming number of negative and self-defeating thoughts and this voice, solidly situated inside my head, talked at me all the time. He never stopped talking, in fact. He was relentless. There wasn't anything I could do for which he didn't have an opinion. If I worked out, the criticism was that I hadn't put 100% effort into it. If I ate something that was unhealthy, he'd say I shouldn't have eaten it. If I was rushing to get to the train, I was lazy and had not gotten out of bed early enough. I could not remember a time in my life when that voice was not there voicing negativity. He had been at work as far back into my childhood as I could remember.

As I continued to talk with Bonnie, several things became evident. First, I needed to go back and speak with My Guy. Next, I needed to seriously consider his ongoing recommendation to go on depression medication, and, last, that I needed to consider going to Alanon again. I had stopped going after the divorce was final, but Bonnie made me realize that just because I was divorced from Bob didn't mean that I was free from him or his alcoholic spell.

My time with Bonnie was helpful, but I was embarrassed on top of all that I was feeling and thinking. I felt that I should have been in a much better place by now and was just shocked to find myself at an even lower point than when I began seeing My Guy.

32
LEARNING ABOUT DAD

"**Ten days, God, ten days**. That's all I asked for." I said these words, in an angry and accusatory tone, as I stood in the bathroom of my stateroom on a cruise ship bound for the Panama Canal. I was looking up at the ceiling when I said this. Then, I quietly bowed my head, ashamed that I had spoken in such a way to God. I shook my head from side to side and said, "Yeah, I know. I can handle this too."

I had just heard the news through an e-mail from Ann that my father had been diagnosed with stage four prostate cancer. It was January 2013, and I was seven days into a ten-day cruise with my girlfriend, Diane. I had been looking forward to this trip for several months. The last few years had been extremely difficult, and plans for this trip were made in late summer after the paperwork for my divorce from Bob had been filed.

My father's health had been floating beneath the surface of everyday life for the past few months after blood work showed elevated numbers related to the prostate. More blood work and additional tests and biopsies were ordered, and we were told that more would be known after his next appointment, which was scheduled for January 9.

A few days before Christmas, my dad had told me that the latest development was that the doctor was putting him on an antibiotic, thinking, perhaps, there was some type of infection and that the medication would fix it or rule that out.

He lowered his voice a bit and quietly said, "I don't think that's what the issue is." I was scared hearing him say this, but as was typical in our relationship, I did not ask any questions and tried to pretend that all would be okay. Something inside of me, however, had a feeling that it wasn't. I would be on the cruise the day of my dad's big appointment, but he promised to e-mail right away.

The morning of Tuesday, January 9th, I was very nervous and waited all day to log onto the ship's internet to see if I had received an email from my dad yet. There wasn't one, but I didn't think much of it, figuring he was busy getting his tasks of the day done. By the next morning, I still had not heard from him, and I was feeling extremely anxious and was very concerned. It would be more than 24-hours before I received an email — and it was from Ann. The sentence that immediately caught my focus said, "It wasn't a good day on Tuesday, and your dad's biopsies came back as cancerous."

It would be another excruciating day-and-a-half before I heard from my dad. His email was classic dad. A little humor, only a short amount of time focusing on him, details provided as factual information only, no feelings discussed, and a hint of being unhappy with something someone had done. In this case, he was unhappy with Ann for sending me an email before he had. While the content was difficult, it was comforting to hear my dad's voice in my mind as I read:

My Dearest Heidi,

I'm sorry the news isn't any better than it is, but that's how the river of life is - you never know what's around the next bend. Damn the torpedoes! Full speed ahead! I played John Paul Jones in a play a long time ago. It was my best line. I love it. Seems appropriate right now.

Today I met my oncology doctor, Dr. Michael J. Katin, 21st Century Oncology (Leading-Edge Technology for a Better Tomorrow) - let's hope so. He's easy to like and spent a great deal of time explaining the program. Looks like my father. We left feeling good about him and what is about to unfold.

Next Tuesday is the CAT scan and bone scan, which determines if the cancer is confined to the prostate (good) or it has escaped to other parts of the body (bad).

We left with a positive feeling about being in good hands for the future.

Other news - Patti is arriving this Sunday to take me out for my birthday. Eve's sister is arriving next week for a visit.

Long day! Didn't e-mail you earlier, wanted to have some information for you. Being first doesn't impress.

Enough about me. How's the cruise going? Anxious to hear how much fun it is. Seems strange not to be able to talk with you.

Miss you!
Love,
Your Dad

IT WAS AFTER ANN'S EMAIL THAT I WAS IN THE BATHROOM yelling at God. When I received the email from dad, I was just numb. There was so much to process. Hearing it from him made it real. I didn't know how I was going to deal with this. I didn't like that I was so far away. I wished that I could have been with him and not on this ship. As I just didn't know what to say, it took me a full day to respond. My equally matter-of-fact response was:

Dad,

I am sorry the news is not any better either. Yes, your line does seem appropriate now. Please know that I am thinking of you, and I am always available (or will be when I get back to shore) if you want to talk. Tuesday is a big day, and I guess a lot of questions will be answered. I am glad I will be home Monday. I hope you have a happy birthday tomorrow and that you are focused on the good and the today.

With much love, your daughter, Heidi

EVEN WITH THE HEAVINESS THAT I WAS FEELING, I SMILED deeply when I received another email from my father just a day later. The subject was 'Prepare to Smile: I'm Smiling.' So like my dad. He thanked me for the birthday gift that I sent to him that had just arrived. Dad always has a way of making me feel so special, even when I am doing something for him. He always makes a big deal out of the things that I do for him or for him and Ann. He makes a point to say thank you and to comment on whatever it is. Take the regular occurrence of sending flowers down, usually from me, my sister Patti, and our respective husbands, for holidays. He calls to tell me they arrived, gushes over how beautiful they are, and then he describes them for me. He also takes numerous pictures and sends them to me with a little note about how long they lasted and what they smelled like. The email that made me smile read:

Good morning at Sea, Heidi,
    Thought I knew Mr. Brown had my marine supply order when he pulled up. Boy, what a surprise to find out Mr. Omaha was on board. Couldn't have been more surprised! Great menu choices. The wine is ready to go and so are we. Thank you for your thoughtfulness. You are always right there with the right thought at the right time.
    Sea Day + Sea Day! What a nice way to relax a little from going ashore. Anxious to hear all about it when we can talk again.
    Thank you again for making it happen.

Love,
    Your Dad

---

* * *

AS THE CRUISE CONTINUED, I WAS BEGINNING TO REALIZE THAT the depression medication that I had begun taking only a few weeks prior must now be in full effect. Despite what I had learned about my father, I still felt quite relaxed. It had just gradually changed my demeanor, and I had not noticed. The follow-up appointment with the PA at my doctor's office happened about one week after my return from the cruise and, during this visit, I discussed with the PA how I was getting along on it. I discussed the 'I don't care what happens' feeling that I had. I was feeling somewhat numb to the world, which, I must say, helped in dealing with the news of my dad's cancer. What I was unsure about was if this was how I was supposed to be feeling. I told the PA that, perhaps, the dosage was just too high. As I was feeling very lethargic and laidback, we decided to cut the dosage to 10 mg. Understandably, I felt a bit nervous doing this, but I

188

hoped it would be a happy medium between not taking it and how I had started feeling on it. I was still focused on the fact that it was only two months prior when I had felt that I was in a place darker than any I had ever experienced before. I was desperate not to go back there.

* * *

WHEN I RETURNED TO PORT AT THE END OF THE CRUISE, I WAS so glad to speak with my dad. We were both still very matter-of-fact about the diagnosis. My dad did not say so, but I could sense that he was scared. I also knew he didn't want to scare me, and I, of course, didn't want to say anything that would upset him, which, I am sure, is why we were both reserved, and we just focused on the facts. As was my dad's nature, and as is mine, we change the subject when something difficult is going on, if we are uncomfortable, and definitely when the focus is on us.

It wasn't too long after my return that it was confirmed that the cancer had spread to dad's bones. I went into action mode, trying to do all I could to find information that might be helpful to him. I researched cancer centers and worked behind the scenes to get him in more quickly to see the doctors he needed to see. With dad so far away, I was feeling pretty helpless so the things I *could* do were a welcomed distraction and made me feel, at least a little bit, like I was contributing.

* * *

GETTING TO KNOW WHO MY DAD REALLY WAS WAS A LONG HELD desire and this was evident from early adulthood. When I was in the Marine Corps, I attended classes off-base at a local college. While I haven't saved many things over the years, I did save an assignment from one particular class. It was all about goals, and it was written in April 1987, about 5 months before my discharge. I was answering several pre-written questions and, in response to one of them asking what my long-term goals were, I wrote that I wanted to be closer to my father and understand him better. While I do not recall what prompted me to write this, I know that this significantly influenced our relationship going forward. I know I went into the service as a child and came out a more confident person — with a mind that was beginning to question more and had a desire to understand things, including my dad.

Sadly, I didn't make any extraordinary effort to get to know my dad. I found that certain events in my life, like my divorces, opened me up to talking more about my inner feelings and thoughts with him. One such conversation happened in July of 2012 when I called to tell my father that Bob and I were divorcing. It was during this call that I said, "Dad, one of the things in life I regret is not having had children, as I would have loved to see you playing with your grandchildren and teaching them all the things I know you would have."

Perhaps my admission allowed my father to open up a bit as well. As he began to tell me about things from his childhood that were meaningful and that I had not previously heard, I jotted them down on a scrap piece of paper using just a few words. We didn't have conversations like this frequently, and I didn't want to forget anything. My biggest regret from that conversation was that after it ended, I did not go back to what I had jotted down and expand on them by writing down the additional details that he had mentioned. My second regret was that I had just listened. When dad provided insights into his past or explained his thinking about any serious or important item, I never asked questions. It was so unusual for him to speak about such things that I was just grateful to hear whatever he was willing to tell me. How much more could I have learned had I just asked him for more information?

My father told me during the call that when he was growing up, he thought he had a normal life. Dad was an only child, and he said that he was happy, played by himself or with kids in the neighborhood, and was good in school. He said that it wasn't until later in life that he realized that he hadn't had a normal life. He went on to say that his father left the house every morning to catch the 6 a.m. train into New York City and did not return home until 6 p.m. Dad would sometimes walk down the street and meet his father at the train station, and, as they walked back home, they would talk for just those few minutes. Dinner was always on the table when his father walked in, and by 7 p.m. each evening, his father disappeared to the attic. A hobby my father would also pick up in his teens and continue into his early 30's, his father was an amateur ham radio operator, which he spent his evenings during the week doing. Dad went to bed without having the chance to say goodnight to his father, and his mother was alone until eleven when his father would come down and have coffee and cake with her and then go to bed.

Dad explained that weekends, like weekdays, were also a routine. Friday night, his parents played cards with friends in a nearby town, then Saturday was what he called a 'house day' when household chores were done. Things like touch-up paint and changing storm windows. His dad was mechanical and took care of those types of chores and, of course, the heavier chores like changing the storm windows to screens in the spring then back in the fall. His mother cut the grass and did the painting, both inside and outside the house. On Sunday, like it was for me, dad attended church alone. His parents did not go with him. There was a family dinner, usually with his father's family, then he and his father might work together in the afternoon on a model airplane or use the portable ham radio to connect to the local tower, Beacon Hill, and talk to people. He told me that this routine rarely varied.

* * *

Funny what knowing that a life will soon be coming to an end does for communication. I would tell people that my dad and I were close, and we certainly had grown closer over the last number of years. What we usually discussed, however, only dipped slightly below the surface of everyday life. After his diagnosis, however, my dad began to open up about more. It was mostly new territory for both of us, so it didn't occur to me to ask many questions and I usually just waited for him to share. I could see that my dad was trying to come to terms with all he was and perceived he could be facing, and he began to share his inner thoughts with me. One particular occasion was during my drive to the college to teach a Saturday morning class. It was just a few weeks after his diagnosis.

Sometimes, on my drive, I would call my dad's work number and leave him a message when he wasn't yet in his garage workshop. I loved hearing his voice on the answering machine, and I knew it would make him smile when he heard mine. When I called on this particular day, however, he answered the phone. I was surprised but happy and, as I continued my drive toward the college, he said he wanted to tell me something.

Dad began by telling me a story about someone he knew who had recently died by suicide. He told me that this person had found out that he was terminally ill and decided that this was the best way to deal with it as he did not want to be a burden on his family. My dad explained that the issue was that he had not discussed it with his family at all, and that had left them in despair. My dad told me that suicide was something that had already crossed his mind, but he wanted me to know that if he ever decided it was what he wanted to do, he planned to speak with Ann and me about it first.

"I wouldn't do it without you knowing," he said. It was a very surreal moment. My dad, in his style, was direct and came across as dispassionate. My response to him was somewhat the same. I told him, "Dad, I am not surprised by the thought of suicide being an out and I will support you in whatever you feel is right for you."

When I hung up the phone, I said out loud to myself, "Did I just have that conversation?" Yep, I did, and never in a million years would I have ever thought we would have discussed something like that, and certainly not at this hour of the day. I must say that it felt good to be talking with him about something that serious and meaningful to him. Despite what he was facing, I smiled as I realized that this is what is meant by a silver lining. I now had these types of conversations and learned things that I may not have otherwise. I was still, however, operating under all the restrictive rules that I had learned in childhood, so it didn't dawn on me that I should do anything more afterward like, perhaps, get on a plane to go check on him.

33

STATE OF DEPRESSION

As I MADE MY WAY TOWARD MY GUY'S OFFICE FOR OUR weekly session a few days later, I was trying to work through how I was going to tell him that I had reached a new low. I wondered how I could possibly explain to him that I had made a conscious decision not to reach out to him and speak with someone else instead. I was concerned about his feelings and what he would think about me, and the decision I had made. These thoughts, I would come to realize, were part of the reason I was where I was. My focus was always on everyone else. On their feelings and their ideas of what I should or should not do. To move on from where I was, I would need to focus my thoughts and feelings only on things that impacted my life.

As I should have expected, My Guy took the news in stride. I filled him in on the conversation with my friend as well as with the other therapist. This included the thought I had expressed that if someone said that I should be committed to some type of inpatient program for 30 days, that I would go.

"Are you still feeling this way?" he asked.

"Yes," I answered honestly. "But I don't feel the acute pressure and pain that I was feeling over the weekend. I guess the benefit of time has lightened me a little bit. Also, when discussing the possibility of attending some type of immersive program, Bonnie explained to me that if I did go, much more would be brought up in a very short period and that, perhaps, I was not in a position at this time to deal with all of that." I even admitted to My Guy that I was scared in talking with Aoifa and Bonnie because I did believe that they had the power, given their credentials, to commit me. It is certainly a telling sign of the depth of my despair that, despite this belief, I told them anyway. I went on to say, "I know that this lighter feeling is also because they expressed that they did not believe that I needed to do that."

He smiled and said, "I can understand how that would bring you some relief." I went on to tell him that the possibility of attending some type of outpatient program was something I wanted to continue to think about. He agreed, and we moved to the topic of depression medication.

We had been talking about this for an extended period and, just as I was resistant to going to Alanon because of the stigma I was attaching to it, I resisted the medication. In truth, I was much more forcefully opposed to it than anything else My Guy had recommended. I felt that if I went on an antidepressant, it was proof that I am not alright, that I am not normal, and that there is something wrong with me. I had, stubbornly, been unwilling to face all of that on top of what I was already actively trying to address.

During this visit, however, I asked My Guy, "It looks like I am at a place where I might not be able to resist it anymore, so if I decided to do this, how would we go about it?" He went on to explain that the medication would need to be prescribed by a doctor, so I would have to schedule an appointment with my primary care physician. Still resisting, I asked, "What if I don't want them to know?"

My Guy let me know that there was another alternative. "You could go through a psychiatrist," he explained. We would need to find one, schedule an appointment, and they would probably need to see me for a few visits before they would write the prescription. I asked if he could find me someone to talk with, and he said he would do so by our next meeting.

It was the first item we spoke about the following week. He had a name for me and said if I was ready, I should make an appointment. I agreed to do so, but was still feeling apprehensive. I didn't even know what it would feel like to be on the medication or how it actually worked, so I decided it was time to do my own research. I called the Employee Assistance Program, which is a benefit provided by my employer. Among other things, they handle crisis management, and the individuals that answer the phone are all licensed clinical therapists with, usually, two or more years of experience working directly in the mental health field. I called late that evening and asked if I could discuss what depression medication actually did. Thankfully, the woman I spoke with was simply wonderful, and I immediately felt safe speaking with her. She was calm, informative, understanding, and nonjudgmental. What I especially liked about our conversation was that she asked me, "If this is something that is being recommended by your therapist, what is holding you back?" She wanted to understand what my concerns were, and then she talked through those.

I told her, "My concern is that I don't know what it would be like to be on the medication. I imagine that I will feel lethargic and have no energy, and I would not like that feeling."

As we talked, the phrase she kept using repeatedly was that it would just take the edge off. She explained, "It would take the edge off of the pain and discomfort and, with that gone, you would be better able to focus your attention on the issues you need to address without constantly feeling the pain, anxiousness, and doom and gloom feeling you say you are carrying with you now." It was this conversation that helped me.

Having come to terms with the need to do this and with my concerns answered, I called my primary care doctor's office the next day. I scheduled an appointment for the following week, December 13, 2012. Having made the decision and then the appointment, I felt lighter and somewhat more hopeful.

When I arrived at the doctor's office, I was told that I would be seeing the new Physician's Assistant (PA) and not my doctor. Still living in the future and always planning out conversations ahead of time, I had prepared for the conversation that I was going to have with the doctor I had been seeing for 10 years. I felt uncomfortable having to see the PA, but I could no longer tolerate the pain I was feeling.

The PA, as it turned out, was comforting and informative. We talked through the different options, settled on Prozac, and started at 20 mg. He told me that 10 mg was the lowest dosage but based on how I described my feelings, 20 mg sounded like the right level to start with. I felt good, but felt even more secure in all we had decided when he informed me that my doctor would be coming in to talk with me. He explained that, as a PA, he was not authorized to write prescriptions. My doctor would consult with me and, if he agreed with what we had decided upon, he would sign the prescription. If it hadn't been about this important situation, I am sure I would have been annoyed having to explain everything a second time, but, at that moment, I was grateful for the extra step.

I left the office and headed to the pharmacy to pick up the prescription they had called in, holding a small card noting the date of my follow-up appointment, which would be about a month later. I was still feeling a bit uneasy, but I was settled in all that I had done to make the decision.

34
THE BUCKET LIST

I BELIEVE MY FATHER WAS TOLD THAT HE COULD EXPECT TO BE around another two to three years. As he was the first person I was that close with to have been given such a diagnosis, I was unsure what to expect and felt rather anxious. I discussed my dad, his diagnosis, and his current health during most visits with My Guy. I wanted to be sure I could do what was needed for my dad in a way that I would feel good about and not derail my ongoing journey to a peaceful place. With all the instances I had to reflect on in my life, I was quite aware that stressful situations bring out the worst in people, including myself. I set my mind to ensure that I did not have any regrets about my behavior or actions as they related to my dad and his diagnosis.

My dad and I began to talk much more frequently and, as usual, I was always thinking about him and what I could do to support him. He called while I was at Staples one day, picking up some office supplies. It was early in the year, as I recall, and I had my winter coat on. Given his diagnosis, I never rushed our conversations, so I took a seat in one of the office chairs that were on display while we continued to chat.

It was during this call that I asked, "Hey, dad, do you have a bucket list? It would be nice for us to do the things that are on there."

To my surprise, my father asked, "What's a bucket list?"

I explained it, and he said, "Oh, like going to see the Grand Canyon?"

"Yes, exactly," I said.

"I don't have one," he answered. "What's on your bucket list? We can just do those things."

I thought this was funny and also predictable for him and told him so. We both laughed. I explained to him that it would be great if he could create a list that we could work through and, to help him, I told him about the movie *The Bucket List*. He had not heard of it, so I picked it up that day and sent it along. I waited a week or so and then asked him if he had watched it. He said he had. "And ..." I asked.

"It was too emotional," he said and then added, "And it isn't realistic because if you had that much money then, of course, you could do all of those things."

"Yes, of course," I replied, ending the conversation knowing that my dad did not have any interest in discussing this topic further.

* * *

THE REALITY OF HIS DIAGNOSIS HELPED ME FOCUS A BIT differently on improving my own situation. It was obvious by the email I sent My Guy on April 3, 2013, that I was feeling much more confident and hopeful. I also knew that my focus for the foreseeable future would be on my dad, so continued visits with My Guy would not be as productive. By this time, I had been seeing My Guy regularly for over two and a half years. There was more work to be done, and down the road, I would get back to focusing on me and my needed transition. The email read:

It certainly has taken me a great deal of time to get to a point where I feel I can handle life in a way that makes me happy about myself, proud of the life I am living, and to feel as if there is some purpose to my life (not that I think I know what it is yet). I want to thank you for all that you have done to get me to this point. I know I would not have been able to get to this place without your help. I am glad that I reached out to you and that I found the trust and faith to stick to working with you. Thank you.

So, the other reason for my email. I have been talking about and thinking about this for a while, but waited until I was sure I was fully comfortable with this. I am going to end my weekly sessions. I understand it will/may be helpful to visit with you again in the future. While I understand it is my decision to make, I would like to have your

*support. I am planning for next Tuesday to be our last regularly sched-
uled session.*

LATER THAT DAY MY GUY RESPONDED, AND HIS MESSAGE WAS:

*I am touched by your expression of appreciation. I am thrilled to see you
feeling well and moving forward. Yes, I will support whatever decision
you make. See you Tuesday.*

* * *

MY DAD TURNED 79 THE WEEK HE RECEIVED HIS DIAGNOSIS. I HAD
been thinking about his 80th birthday for a bit and had decided that I wanted to
take him on a cruise. He and Ann did not really go on vacations. Their big
getaway occurred once a year, when they stayed in Myrtle Beach for a week,
then came up to New York for a couple of weeks. I spoke with my sister Patti to
see if she wanted to go with us. She immediately said yes and even offered to
split the cost with me. The idea was presented, and dad and Ann loved it.

We set sail on May 17, 2013, and, as we were boarding, one of the most
special moments of the trip happened. My father looked at me, told me that
he was happy we were on the boat, then he leaned over and kissed me on
the top of my head. I felt such joy from having made him so happy. Once
we settled in, my dad and I went on what we referred to as a walk-about
adventure to see where the dining room, pool, and other amenities were.
Dad and I spent a lot of time together, just the two of us, on the trip.

On the first full day, we stopped at the cruise line's private island and,
when we returned to the ship later that day, I told dad I wanted to take him
someplace special. We met in the hallway just outside our adjoining state-
rooms, and he was surprised when I turned toward the back of the ship as
all of the common areas were the other way. "Trust me," I said. It took a
few tries to find the door that I was looking for but, when I did, my dad
smiled.

"I know where we are," he said. We were at the very back of the ship.

The engines had been shut down for the day, but they would be started up again soon.

"From here," I said, "we will have a front-row seat to see the water begin churning as the engines start and the wake forming behind us as the ship begins to move."

He loved this and, as we stood there leaning on the ship's railing, just taking in the sights and sounds, dad said, "This reminds me of being on the ship when I was in the Navy. I loved my time in the Navy. I was best in my company in all of the drills." It was so much fun finding out these little details from him.

* * *

DAD HAS ALWAYS HAD A SPECIAL relationship with food, and he has a method for getting it ready to eat. Take his sandwiches. Dad is famous for them. It is a big process, and they look like a masterpiece when he gets done. It starts with a piece of bread — rye is his favorite — then mustard, liverwurst cut to fit on the bread, tomato, onion, another slice of liverwurst, then another slice of tomato and onion, more mustard, and then he tops it off with another piece of bread. While liverwurst is his favorite, dad also makes unique sandwiches like potato salad ... which is potato salad on bread. Sometimes he adds baked beans to this sandwich.

Growing up, one of our daily chores was to make our lunch for the next school day. On a couple of occasions, dad surprised us and made them for us. I was always excited that I didn't have to do that chore. That was until I opened my lunch the next day. I was still in grade school, so I was younger than 12. Sitting with my class at our assigned table in the large, loud, and crowded lunchroom, I open my bag in anticipation of what dad had made me. Maybe it was peanut butter and banana or, perhaps, peanut butter and fluffernutter. Those were my favorites. Unfortunately, it was neither of those. Nor was it anything else I would expect him to have given me, a child, for lunch. It was a cream cheese and fresh green pepper sandwich. I didn't eat it, and when he ask how I liked my lunch, I am sure the word 'eww' might have come out of my mouth. Dad was quite matter-of-fact with his response when he said he could not understand why I did not like it and that he felt it was a special and appropriate lunch.

Dad's approach to food did not change while on the ship. He is a creature of habit, and he has his way of doing things. For breakfast, dad would order two eggs, an English muffin, and tomatoes. When it arrived, he did the same thing he did at home. He cut each of those items into six pieces. I sat watching him, smiling. He looked up and saw me watching him. Thinking he needed to explain what he was doing, he said, "I cut each of them into the same number of pieces, so I have one of everything in each bite."

"Yes, I know," I said happily. "I have watched you do this same thing for many years."

During the cruise, we went to the beach one day. Dad and I opted for a picnic table in the shade of a tall palm tree while Ann and Patti went down to sit near the water in the sun. My dad was known for taking a lot of pictures when he was away. The first time he came to my new home, he must have taken at least 300 of them, taking several shots in each room from different angles. As we sat there, relaxing in the shade, I heard my father begin fiddling with his camera. I didn't, however, hear him taking any pictures. Always his tech support, I asked him if I could help with anything. He said, "I just need for you to turn around," and when I did, I realized that he was trying to take a selfie of the two of us. I loved that he was taking it. It was a great shot of the two of us and one I treasure to this day.

What is especially interesting about the photo is the photo number. It ended in 711. I didn't notice this for a long time, and it was only after copying the image into a document I was working on that the number was shown as the photo caption. It stopped me in my tracks and made me smile. For as long as I can remember, I have known that my father's favorite time of the day was  7:11. When asked why he liked it, he would say there were several reasons for this. One of them was that it is a time of the day that you usually see in the morning and the evening — you were usually awake for both. Another, he would explain, is that it looks good in digital form when you see it on a clock. Also, this time was quiet, both in the morning and in the evening. It was before work started in the morning, and he was usually having break-fast and coffee. In the evening, dinner and dishes were usually done, so it was also another quiet time. This time was such a known thing about my dad that, to keep him close, I had '7:11' tattooed on the inside of my left wrist.

* * *

ABOUT A MONTH AFTER THE CRUISE, DAD WAS ADMITTED TO the hospital. I was on a business trip to Chicago, and I immediately flew down to see him. My dad seemed a bit weak, and I was grateful when he was released a few days later. After this time, I began visiting Florida every few weeks, staying for a handful of days. I went back down to visit around July 4 and, upon my arrival, I found my dad resting in the living room. This was not at all like my dad, who rarely sat down to relax and was always on the go. It was very concerning. During my visit, he mostly rested, but he said he wanted to finish up a job for a customer on one particular day. He said they wanted a canvas cover fitted on the bed of a pick-up truck and they had been waiting too long for it. The truck was parked on the side of the house and, while I didn't feel he was physically up to it, there was no arguing with my dad. As a compromise, we agreed to work on it together, and I so enjoyed that time with him.

It was during this July visit that I had another idea to bounce off my dad. "Dad," I said. "Do you remember a few months ago when we talked about a bucket list?"

"Yes," he answered, a bit hesitantly, and I immediately recalled his reaction to the movie and felt a stab of pain in my heart. Perhaps I had gotten him emotional over his diagnosis when I sent him the movie, and here I was bringing it up again.

"Well," I continued anyway, "I have another idea. Since you don't have a bucket list and I don't like the idea of us doing what is on my bucket list, I thought that I would make a bucket list of things I want to do with you, and we could work on that list." Dad immediately smiled and said he liked the idea.

"What would be on it?" he inquired.

"Well," I replied. "One thing could be that we get a pizza and go down to the Sanibel Bridge Causeway and eat it while watching the sunset." Dad smiled again, saying that he thought this idea was pretty neat.

35

ALICE SPRINGS
CHICKEN

By the middle of August, dad was in and out of the hospital, so my visits with him were different. One such visit began on Wednesday, September 18. I flew in early morning and went straight to the rehab center to see him. Dad had just been released from another hospital stay, and I was now well versed in the routine that a stay in the hospital would always mean a stay at the rehab center before returning home.

I was with my father the next morning when a new doctor came to visit with him. She discussed my dad's pain, and he indicated that he was in significant pain and discomfort, so she said she would prescribe a different medication for him. It was administered shortly thereafter, and it was not too much later when my father, mid-sentence, began to fall asleep in his wheelchair. He said he couldn't keep his eyes open. I spent the next few hours sitting with him as he slept in his chair. He was totally out of it, and I felt bad as I assumed it was my visit that was tuckering him out. They helped my father to bed that evening, and the nurse told me that it was probably the new medication and that he should be better by the morning. I left feeling uneasy.

When I returned on Thursday, my dad had been moved back into his wheelchair, but he was still not with it. You could get his attention with a little bit of effort, but he couldn't speak much at all before falling back asleep. I immediately went looking for the doctor, and, in talking with her, she explained that what my dad was experiencing was expected as she had prescribed a sedative type of pain medication, and he would mostly be out of it while he was on it. I recall knowing that the doctor was a palliative care doctor, and either she knew more than we did or, perhaps, we were avoiding the reality of how badly my dad was doing. The doctor agreed to change the medication and, by the end of the day on Thursday, my dad was doing much better.

* * *

Ann and I had established a routine when dad was in the hospital or rehab center. If I was allowed to spend the night in dad's room, I would. Sometime later in the morning, Ann would come in for several hours while I went back to their house to take a break and shower before I returned later in the afternoon to relieve Ann. While I had usually eaten before I got back to dad, on Friday of this particular visit, my dad was doing so much better that I told him I was going to make him dinner — the one he always requested that I make.

I was going to make him my version of the Outback Steakhouse dish Alice Springs Chicken. I grill chicken tenders, place them on a cookie sheet, and spoon sauteed mushrooms and cooked bacon pieces over them. Then, I pour honey mustard sauce and sprinkle Monterey and cheddar cheese on them. These then go under the broiler until the cheese is melted. Dad loved this dish, and I was so happy to be cooking it. Ann decided that she would join her friends at the real Outback for a few cocktails, which meant that I had dad all to myself for dinner. He didn't eat much, but I know he was happy just spending time with me.

It was during our time that evening that my dad told me two things that made me smile. First, referring to my thought to go home and cook him dinner, he said that he likes my ideas. He also told me that he thought of me every day at five o'clock. He said this was when he watched the Fox News show, which is broadcast from New York. He explained that while watching, he pictures me commuting home. He told me that it made him feel closer to me for that one hour each day. That is so my dad. He was always thinking of those types of things, even though he didn't usually tell you about it.

I was not surprised that dad thought of me each afternoon, as he called me quite often around six o'clock when I was usually on my way home from work, and he was winding things down in his shop. When he called, if he didn't reach me, he would leave me a voicemail message.

The messages dad left were always fairly short, maybe ten or twelve seconds, and were usually about routine life things. Sometimes it was about something he heard on the news, while others, it was to wish me a happy whatever-holiday-it-was. Another message was him checking to see how the mid-term exam I had given my students in the college class I was teaching went. Sometimes his message was that he had called to hear my voice and to tell me that he loved me.

After dinner that evening, I asked my dad if we could go out and see the sunset. "Yes, that would be great," he answered. We got him situated in the wheelchair and headed out. During this outing, somewhere in the hallway between the front door of the facility and his room, I took a picture of the two of us. It would be the last photo of us.

Before heading to the airport on Saturday morning, I visited with my dad, and he was back to his old self. He was even in the bathroom brushing his teeth and shaving. I was elated watching him do his morning routine and, as my plane took off, I waved in the direction of his rehab center and smiled, knowing he was doing well. This feeling was very short-lived.

* * *

EARLY THE NEXT DAY, SUNDAY, SEPTEMBER 22, 2013, MY PHONE rang, and I saw it was my dad calling. While I was surprised to see his name come up, I was excited that it was him. I answered the phone saying something like, "Well, look at you up and at 'em early this morning," and expected to hear my dad's laughter. Instead, there was silence, and then I heard a voice, it was Ann's. She let me know that my father had been admitted back to the hospital very early that morning. She said he was in the ICU with some type of infection, and she wasn't sure how he was doing yet. I asked her to call me later that day.

When she called that evening, she didn't have much news other than to say that he was doing okay and that he may have to be in the hospital for a few days. I asked if she would call me the next day and, when she did, she said that he had been moved out of the ICU, but that he was not up for talking. When we spoke on Tuesday, she told me essentially the same thing she had said the day before — also letting me know that dad had pneumonia, a urinary tract infection, and a fever. I was beginning to worry. I so wanted to hear my dad's voice firsthand to know he was okay.

36

A DNR

EARLY WEDNESDAY MORNING, I WAS IN A CONFERENCE ROOM in my employer's New York City offices, holding a meeting with my staff. My cell phone rang and, while I didn't recognize the phone number, I knew the area code was Ft. Myers. I answered the call to find that it was a palliative care doctor who was treating my father. I asked if she could hold for a minute, and I excused myself from the meeting.

As I made my way to the hallway, my hands began to shake, not knowing what I was going to be told. As soon as I told her to go ahead, she told me that my father was all right. *Oh, thank goodness,* I thought, collapsing against the wall I was standing near to. She told me that my dad wanted her to call me and see what I knew.

"Know about what?" I asked.

"Do you know that your dad wishes to have a DNR?" she inquired.

"Yes, of course," I replied. "That was discussed last week, and I thought all of that was in order."

"Okay," she said. "Now that I understand that from you, I want to go back into your father's room and put you on speaker." She did this and mentioned that two nurses were in the room. Once on speaker, the doctor explained that she had come in to check on my dad, and he had told her a few things that she thought I should know. In her words, things had become dire as of yesterday.

I then heard my dad's voice for the first time since I had left him the previous Saturday. He proceeded to talk in a steady voice, which clearly showed he was irritated. What surprised me most was how strong he sounded, given that just the day before, I had been told by Ann that he was not up for speaking with me.

My dad proceeded to say all of the following without prompting from anyone, "She has allowed her basic control factor to take over me. She is shoving food down my throat, and she is making me say things I don't want to say and making decisions for me that I don't want to make. She is out of control, and I no longer feel that she can make good health care decisions on my behalf." I was stunned by what he had just said. The doctor then said that my dad wanted to switch his Health Care Power of Attorney from Ann to me and asked me whether I would agree that.

"Yes, of course," I replied immediately.

Dad then said, "I want to talk about a DNR. I want one, and Ann is not allowing it." I knew what a DNR was, and the three of us had spoken about it during my last visit. A DNR was a Do Not Resuscitate directive, which means that the patient does not want any extraordinary means to be used to keep him or her alive.

I told him, "This is your decision, dad, and if this is what you want, then I support it."

"So," I asked the doctor, "what do we need to do to make the changes he is requesting?" She explained that the nurses were serving as the witnesses to this requested change and that my dad's chart would be updated to list me as the Health Care Power of Attorney. She explained that the DNR would also be registered in the chart and a wristlet placed on my dad's arm so anyone coming to care for him would know his wishes.

The doctor then asked, "Should I call your stepmother to tell her?"

"No," I said. "I'll do that." I honestly didn't want to do it, but I felt that that was not the best use of the doctor's time. I also did not expect Ann to handle this news well. The doctor was ready to hang up the phone, so I didn't get a chance to speak with my dad except to say that I would see him soon. He told me he loved me, and then the phone disconnected.

I leaned back against the wall to steady myself. What had just happened? What was Ann doing that would cause my father to speak the way he had spoken and request this change? It would take me a while, but once I had a chance to digest what he had said, my thought was that perhaps Ann was scared. She was scared of my father dying, and by forcing him to eat and not allowing the DNR, he might be around longer. If this was what she was thinking, I could understand it.

* * *

DAD AND ANN HAD BEEN TOGETHER FOR MORE THAN THIRTY-four years, and they had been living in Florida for virtually all of them. When we moved to Ft. Myers at the end of my freshman year of high school, it wasn't long before I began to notice that people thought that they were married. I wondered how this could be and, after focusing on it, I came to see that they sort of presented themselves that way. If someone commented on them being married, they wouldn't correct them. If someone commented on my being Ann's daughter, that was also not corrected. When asked how many children they had, they said combined they had nine. This was especially interesting as Ann had not met four of my brothers.

Over time, I began to see items coming into the house through the mail that listed Ann's last name as Hayden. This was my father's last name and not hers. The documents were not junk mail but items like utility bills, mortgage statements, and the like. My curiosity got the best of me, and I began to snoop in the meticulous files that Ann kept. I was shocked to find a marriage certificate showing that my father and Ann had married in April of 1955. I knew that was not correct and soon pieced together that this was a falsified version of my father and mother's actual marriage certificate.

The topic of when they would get married was discussed periodically after I had been out of the house for a good number of years. Dad and Ann explained that they had wanted to get married after their respective divorces were final. Still, they decided not to, as marriage licenses were published in the local paper, and all of their friends already thought that they were married. These discussions always brought the knowledge of the falsified marriage certificate to my mind, but I never said a word. Another secret held within the family.

How sad it must have been for them to have had to live a lie for so long. It would take them more than twenty-four years, but they did finally marry in September of 2003. As they weren't willing to give up the lie, they married in Myrtle Beach, South Carolina, during one of their yearly visits. Patti and I traveled from New York to be with them for the civil ceremony held in the living room of the condo they had rented.

While it would be in my nature to acknowledge a wedding anniversary, given the circumstances of how they got together, the impact it had on me, and the fact that I couldn't openly celebrate it given their secret, I chose not to recognize it, and I never did. Not in my words or actions.

As for my dad and what Ann was doing now, or how my dad perceived her actions, my father's wishes were now in order. My next thought was that I would need to get down there. As it was almost mid-day, even if I could get on a flight that night, I would get in too late to stop into the hospital. I decided to work another few hours to get things in order, then fly down early tomorrow morning. I booked myself on a 6 a.m. flight and was comforted in knowing that I would be at the hospital by 9 a.m.

While I have no interest in rehashing all that transpired when Ann learned of the changes the next morning, I will just say it went as I expected it would — and it did not go well. None of that matters, however. I knew back when my father was diagnosed that I needed to be mindful of the personal journey that I was on so as not to derail it. Despite all the chaos that transpired, I feel that I conducted myself in a respectful, loving, and straightforward way, honoring what was important for me and keeping my father as the focus.

37
STORY TIME

MY FATHER'S FIRST WORDS TO ME WHEN I ARRIVED AT THE
hospital early on Thursday were, "What took you so long?" I joked about it
being a long way to there from New York and left it at that. When he said
it, I did feel a quick sharp pang of guilt and the feeling that I was in trouble.
I happily realized, however, that I wasn't absorbing that statement into me.
This was progress for me, as previously, my mind would have been spinning
out of control with guilt and should-have's. I had done what I had done
and, having thought it out rationally and knowing that I couldn't change it
now, I was okay with it. I felt so grateful for all the work I had done to be
able to handle situations such as these more easily.

It took me only a few moments to look at my dad and know that he was
not going to be around too much longer. I guess being okay to a palliative
care doctor is different from what I thought it meant. My father was not
okay. The next few days were a blur, and I spent virtually every moment
with him. By the next morning, Ann and I decided to place my dad in
hospice care, and he was to be moved the next day to their facility.

While he slept most of the time; and by Friday afternoon he was not
talking more than a few words. I played music, and my dad and I talked.

I wish I could recall what it was that I said, but my father responded to
it by saying, "For such a smart woman, you are very silly." He said he didn't
agree with a question I chose to ask, and he then called me stupid.

I laughed and, in a kidding manner, said, "Did you just call me stupid
after you just said I was smart?"

He said, "Yes, I did, and it was because of the question you asked."

Direct and sometimes cutting. Same as he had been my entire life. This same day, my father told me that I had pretty eyes. I would realize, later, that these were the last words that he said to me.

On Friday, while Ann was visiting with dad, I sat on the floor outside his room and took a moment to reflect. I realized how well I was doing and felt the need to send an email of thanks to My Guy:

My father's health declined very quickly. As I sit here outside my dad's hospital room, keeping vigil until he passes, I am reflecting on a number of things. I am doing well in handling this, and I wanted to say thank you to you. Without the work you helped me with, I would not be doing so well. So, thank you.

ON SATURDAY MORNING, WHILE ANN STAYED BACK IN HIS hospital room to gather all his personal items, I rode with dad over to the hospice house. She joined us a little bit later. He was settled into his beautiful room by 12:30 p.m. and, after being examined, the doctor told us that she expected dad would be around for another two to three weeks. Dad was put on morphine for his pain, and, as had been the case since the previous evening, he was non-verbal.

Once he was settled, I left Ann to spend time with him, and I went back to his house and packed my bag. I intended to stay with him as long as he was around. By 9 p.m., it was just the two of us in his comfortable, spacious room.

While he moaned periodically, dad had not opened his eyes since Friday evening. As I had done in the hospital on Thursday and Friday, I played music. I was also talking with, well, to, him for several hours that night. Interestingly, my dad's eyes were open from about 11:30 p.m. until about 1 a.m. He was moaning, and I could tell he was trying to tell me something, but it was unintelligible. I told him that I loved him. I told him that I knew he loved me. I told him I would continue to make him proud. I also told him that I liked being with him and talking with him.

As he was moaning loudly and was so restless, the nurse came to the door to remind me that I could push the morphine button to settle my dad down. I smiled and said, "Oh no, my dad and I are talking."

She continued into the room and, upon seeing that my dad's eyes were open, said, "Well, yes, and I see you have beautiful blue eyes." She walked out shaking her head and seemed genuinely surprised that he did have them open.

After a while, I got tired of music and felt like I had run out of things to say, so I decided I would read him a book. I was reading the Harry Potter series on my Kindle and had been making my way through all of the books since early that year. I found it a great way to detach from the world and the reality of my father's diagnosis. As Harry Potter was not something that would make sense to read to him, I decided to read a Dr. Seuss book. I had just seen an art exhibit in a local gallery, and there was this beautiful print of a drawing from one of his books, which had Seuss throwing books over his shoulder to his little friend behind him. I couldn't remember the full name, so I went online and just typed 'Oh by Seuss' as I knew it started with that. Up popped *Oh, the Places You'll Go*, and I quickly downloaded it. I thought dad, a former schoolteacher, and an inquisitive individual, would like it based on what I perceived it was about.

As I made my way through the first couple of pages, I kept thinking that it was not what I expected it to be. I thought it would be about reading and all the places where it could transport you. Figuring I had interpreted the print incorrectly, I kept reading. When I got to the end of the book, which goes, "Be you Buxbaum, Bixby or Bray, Mordechai Ali Van Allen O'Shea, today is your day, so climb the mountain and be on your way," my first thought, and it was startling, was that I had just given my dad permission to die. This was all too overwhelming, so I decided that we should go to bed. It was about 1:30 a.m. I moved the sleeper chair up close to dad's bed and, before curling up in the chair, I opened the curtains so we could both sleep under the glow of the moon and the beautiful palm tree just outside. We both slept well.

* * *

WHEN WE REALIZED THAT MY DAD WOULD BE PASSING SOON, I called my sister and told her she should come down. She made the arrangements to arrive early on Sunday. Ann arrived around 10 a.m. and Patti and her husband, Sam, at about 11:30 a.m. It was just before noon when we all received a beautiful surprise. Ann Niner, a long-time friend of my dad and Ann's, had driven several hours to come to see us. After seeing my dad, Patti and Sam stepped out to go get breakfast, and I left Ann and Ann

Niner in dad's room to catch up. I went down the hall to sit in the common area.

About an hour later, I heard Ann's voice and got up to look around the corner and down toward my dad's room. Ann saw me and motioned for me to come down. As I approached her, she told me that she thought he had passed, and she had come out to get the nurse. We walked into his room together. She told me that she and Ann were over by the sliding door talking, not next to dad, when they realized they could no longer hear his breathing.

I was shocked that my dad was gone. I didn't know how to react. It wasn't supposed to be this quick, but it would be just like dad to take his leave when no one was looking. While his time of death was marked at 1:20 p.m., I believe that his actual time of death was 1:17.

* * *

THE DAY AFTER HIS PASSING, AS THE WORLD STOOD STILL AND we waited to meet with the funeral home staff, I contacted the gallery that had hosted the Seuss exhibit. I told them I wanted to purchase the print, *Oh, the Places You'll Go*, that I had seen on display. They responded that they did not have that print and that the print on display was, *Oh, the Things You Will Learn*. Ah, now that makes more sense, I thought.

They tracked down the print of the book I had read to my father, and I purchased both of them. In reflecting on how and why it happened that it was that particular book I read to my dad, I know that it was God stepping in to help us both deal with his transition a bit easier.

In responding to a friend who had heard of his passing, I wrote:

Yes, you are correct. I certainly didn't expect this. I arrived mid-day on Thursday, and it was evident by Friday morning what was happening. I had some very precious and special moments with him the last few days, even though he was unable to speak from late Friday evening on. If I could have scripted something peaceful and "perfect," I could not have even imagined something as perfect and peaceful as it was. I will look back on this time with the sadness of the event, but with the happiness of his easy transition at the end and the time I had with him.

IN THOSE FIRST DAYS AFTER HIS PASSING, I FOUND VERY comforting the voicemail messages that he had left me. I hadn't deleted them off of my phone in quite a while, so I was grateful I still had them. How helpful those bright, cheery messages from him were, and I knew they would continue to be as time went on. In total, I had saved fifty-four messages that he had left me, and I treasure each one. They have kept his voice and laugh fresh in my mind. I do not believe that there is such a thing as a coincidence. I do, however, believe in signs, symbols, and synchronicities. The number of messages that he left me, fifty-four, adds up to 9 if you add the digits, and, in numerology, that number means completion. Also, knowing that my dad's favorite time of the day was 7:11, it wasn't surprising at all to discover that the last message he had left me was on 7/11. I am filled with gratitude for the messages as well as the signs my dad has provided in these numbers.

* * *

THE NEXT FEW MONTHS WERE DIFFICULT. DAD'S PASSING WAS devastating, and I had a hard time coming to terms with it. I felt like I was in a fog and tried to keep my mind occupied with many things. Ann, now his widow, hosted a celebration of life gathering at their home a week after his passing, and it was such a lovely event. So many people came, and I enjoyed hearing the stories of their memories with my dad.

Those last months of 2013 were also occupied with making plans to scatter dad's ashes. Dad did not want a wake or a funeral. He wanted to be cremated and his ashes scattered in the waters near his home. After much discussion, Ann, Patti, and I jointly decided that we would scatter his ashes on January 12, 2014, the day before what would have been his 80th birthday. So, three-and-a-half months after his passing, we boarded a boat owned by their friends who had graciously agreed to take us out. Dad had such a love of lighthouses, so we scattered his ashes near the Sanibel Island Lighthouse, not too far from where he had lived. It was a beautiful tribute and, unexpectedly, it brought me a sense of closure.

PART THREE
GETTING TO NOW

"The future depends on what you do today."

—— *Mahatma Gandhi*

38

STRESS AND
SOLUTIONS

WHILE DAD'S ILLNESS AND HIS PASSING HAD BEEN A
distraction from my personal journey to a better place, I was still experiencing much stress. A month or so before his passing, I began seeing My Guy again after a four-month break. As with most other times in my life, just when I think that things will calm down, they don't. Less than two weeks after scattering dad's ashes, I developed shingles. At age forty-eight, I was a few years too young to have this, technically, but was not surprised to learn that stress was a contributing factor. It was an extremely painful experience that affected my nerves, and the following forty-five days were rather unpleasant.

Knowing that the past leaves clues, I began reflecting on my health and realized that all that was going on within and around me had impacted my health and manifested itself physically. I had a very bad cold at least once a year for about twenty years. Beginning as far back as I can remember in my adulthood, I developed large, ugly fever sores on my upper lip. They were unsightly and embarrassing. They began appearing more often and became much more severe, leading me to finally ask my doctor for a prescription to help control them. The pill helped lessen the outbreak and shorten the recovery period, but they continued. These persisted on a regular and frequent basis up until around 2014, then stopped almost altogether.

I have always known that I held my stress in my jaw, neck, and upper shoulders, so it is not surprising that another physical manifestation was my jaw-locking. In the 1990s, my jaw would make a clicking sound when I ate, but I was told it was just part of how my jaw was sitting, and it was nothing to worry about. By the early 2000s, however, my jaw had begun to lock. The dentist said I had TMJ, and there wasn't much that could be done short of having surgery. As it wasn't intolerable, I just dealt with it. Over time, I would learn that my issue was related to stress and clenching my jaw when I was sleeping and during the day.

When the locking began, it would lock for an hour or two every few months and then ease up, but, over time, the frequency and length increased to the point that, when it did happen, it would be locked for at least three or four weeks. Thankfully, it locked in a somewhat opened position, usually with enough room to get my toothbrush in and to eat small bites of food. I began to recognize when it was going to happen, and I would do everything I could to prevent it. It may have delayed it, but it always ended up locking.

In April of 2018, my niece and I were on a cruise to Alaska when I heard that there was an acupuncturist on board. I had never been to one, nor had I ever thought of doing so. I am not sure what made me decide to go see this one, and on a cruise ship of all places, but I did. What a fabulous decision. I had two sessions with the beautiful soul of a woman named Crystal. Based on the research I hurriedly did before I met with her, if she got to the heart of the issue, I would feel a painful explosion as the needle penetrated the right spot.

The pain was momentarily excruciating when that happened to me, but I was convinced that it had worked. I left the ship feeling great overall and secure in the fact that it wouldn't happen again. Much to my surprise and dismay, it locked a couple of weeks later. I was so tired of dealing with this but decided that I had to somewhat resign myself to the fact that it was going to be staying around. About a day later, however, much to my surprise and delight, it unlocked — and it has never locked again.

Sleep is also something that was impacted by my stress. There were periods when I would wake up in the middle of the night and not be able to go back to sleep. More typical, however, was that it would take a very long time for me to get to sleep. I began taking Advil to combat this, which brought a sense of calm to my body. It helped the spinning that happened within my mind and the consistent feeling of a dull, painful vibration within my body. I took two tablets, and even took three for a brief period. I did this virtually every night of the week for twelve or thirteen years starting around 2002. Back then, I would purchase the large bottle of 250 capsules and always had a spare bottle on hand.

To combat my stress, I have always tried to use food. I am thankful for the good metabolism that I inherited from my parents because I know I would be much heavier without it. While I am a petite person standing at 5'2" and usually weighing around 120 pounds, I eat a ton of calories. Many more than is recommended for someone of my size. I like food, and junk food, carbohydrates, and sweets have always been my go-to comfort foods. Eating between meals is common, and ice cream, donuts, candy bars, brownies, pancakes, cookies, and milk are just some of what I will eat. At mealtime, I eat a lot of pizza, pasta, bread, and grilled cheese for comfort. I have never had any willpower, for other than a couple of days, to not eat these things or to only eat them in small quantities. Using food for comfort is something that continues to this day, but I am getting a bit better, especially at not eating a whole tray of brownies within twenty-four hours of baking them.

39
I MEDITATE

I HAD LIVED MUCH OF MY LIFE FEELING STRESSED AND ON
overload. I had the constant feeling that I was spinning around and around
and, as the years went past, the spinning became faster and faster.

I am thankful that, at times, I took a bit of time for myself. These times
were, however, infrequent. While I would now term it as self-care, at that
time, I looked at it as self-preservation. One such time was a trip I took in
October of 2011 when I decided to go to Mohonk Mountain House in
upstate New York, just a couple of hours' drive from my home.

Mohonk is an all-inclusive resort with a beautiful old hotel tucked away
in the mountains. It is a quiet and serene place with no TVs in the rooms or
common areas. I spent that trip just being by myself. I turned off my phone
so there were no calls or emails, and I had no connection to the outside
world. I hiked, read, and spent time at the award-winning spa. It was on
this trip that I tried meditation for the first time booking the private guided
meditation option at the spa.

I had never tried it, but at this time in my life, with my brain stuck in a
constant spinning motion that was becoming too painful to endure, I
thought it would be a good time to try it. As was my nature, I was focused
on the session even though it wasn't until the next day. I didn't like going
into something without some sense of what to expect and what would be
expected of me, so, to try to calm my nervousness, I stopped at the spa desk
to inquire.

The woman at the counter was an inch or two taller than I am, with
straight brown hair and an approachable face. She wore a tank top, and her

toned arms told me that she spent a lot of time working out. I told her that I was scheduled for a private meditation the next day and had some questions.

She smiled warmly and asked, "Are you, Heidi?"

"Yes, I am," I replied.

"It's nice to meet you," she said. "I will be doing your meditation. What can I help you with?"

"Well," I replied, "I should probably tell you that I have never meditated before, so I was wondering what I should expect."

She pointed to what I would have called a workout room, which had mats covering the floor and mirrors on two sides of it, and said, "This is where we will be." She then went on to explain the process she follows for a meditation.

"Ok, great," I said. "Now, one last thing. I should tell you that I would describe myself as a Type-A personality."

"Ah, I see," she responded and then added, "Well, then it sounds like this is something that will be helpful to you."

"Yes, I am sure you are right. Thank you," I said. "See you tomorrow."

* * *

WHEN I ARRIVED THE NEXT DAY, SHE GREETED ME LIKE I WAS AN old friend. She indicated that there was a slight change of plans and that someone had scheduled a class for the room we were supposed to use. Instead, we would be going into an empty hotel room to conduct the session. I was nervous just to be there, and I dislike changes at times when I am already feeling uncertain. I think she could sense my body tighten a bit as I tried to retain my composure to look like it was all fine.

She just said, "Have no worries." I followed her down the hall, wondering if I should just cancel. I know a change of room doesn't sound like much, but I was very tightly wound at this point in my life, and I just needed things to go according to what and how I expected. In typical 'always do what is expected of me fashion', I continued to follow her.

The hotel was one large building, but several additions had been added to the original building which was built before 1869. We entered a room that was in one of the older sections. It was so beautiful with its big, long, old windows, dark wood, and original fireplace. But for a tall wooden antique wardrobe, there was no other furniture.

She positioned a small hard plastic chair-like item on the floor, which had no legs but had a base to sit on and a short back to lean on. She gestured for me to sit down on it. It didn't look very comfortable, and I was sure it wasn't going to be. I was also sure that these thoughts were written on my face. Doing as I was asked, I got situated on the floor and was quite surprised at how comfortable the contraption was, even with my legs straight out in front of me.

She put on some calming music and turned off the overhead light. My tension eased a bit, but my body still felt tight, and thoughts were racing through my mind. She told me that she was going to begin the meditation, and all I had to do was to concentrate on my breath. Sounded easy, but it wasn't. My brain kept thinking of other things, and after maybe ten minutes, I still did not feel calm. *This isn't working*, I thought. In the next moment, however, I remembered that this was something I had willingly scheduled and that I thought could be helpful. I needed to get serious about the simple task of just focusing on my breath. Once I committed myself, I quickly found my brain calming, and my body began to feel like it was melting. I did have to keep reminding myself to focus on my breath but, in time, it was as if the world faded.

The next thing I knew I was opening my eyes and raising my head that had, unbeknownst to me, fallen just a bit forward. I didn't feel like I had been asleep, but I couldn't place a thought around where I had been. As I began to focus my eyes, I saw that my guide was leaning down in front of me. She asked me softly, "So, how was it?"

My response was something I would never have expected, "I feel like I just had a massage."

She smiled deeply and then said, "When I met you yesterday, I wasn't sure what would happen today, but I am thrilled that you found this relaxing."

It was this experience that taught me that meditation could help to calm me. I would come to try it a little bit here and there over the next few years, but never on a regular or consistent basis. That is until, a significant issue arose that I was particularly angry about.

* * *

I DON'T CURSE, EXCEPT WHEN I AM ANGRY. AN ISSUE CAME TO light that made me so mad that, over the next two days, I cursed a lot during any conversation I was having that was related to this issue. One person I was talking with was my brother, Robin. On the morning of day three, he called to see how I was doing. I was still mad and, as I answered his question, with curse words still interspersed, he said, "Yep, I can see that you're still mad."

Not feeling like I could help myself, I asked, "Are you tired of listening to me?"

"No," he said, "but perhaps you could change the first word of every other sentence, just to make it a bit more interesting for the listener."

"Oh," I said, feeling bad. "Am I saying the F-word too much?"

"Well, if I'm being honest," he said, "it's beginning to sound like you have Tourette's."

I realized that he was right. I had been so angry and upset that I had been cursing for several days straight. I knew I had to change this. I vowed that I would get control of my anger over this issue by not allowing myself to talk about it until I could calmly articulate the reason or reasons that I was so angry. This worked during the day but, at night, my mind was spinning. I couldn't sleep, and I was on day four of literal eyes wide-open and no-sleep nights. That night I pulled out my phone and opened the meditation app called Insight Timer. I had kept it on my phone for a few years but had used it only a handful of times.

I was determined to get some sleep, and, using their awesome search function, I found a sleep meditation that was thirty-seven minutes long. I listened to the full meditation, but I don't recall hearing a word of it. My focus was still on the thoughts that continued to race through my mind. I put it on again, and the same thing happened. I then put it on a third time, and, at some point, I fell asleep. Success. Every night I did the same thing. I played the meditation, and if I wasn't asleep by the end, I put it on again. I recall telling someone that I had begun meditation due to something particularly stressful and that I had meditated a total of eighty-seven times since January 6. It had been forty-one nights since I started listening to this one particular meditation, and, on average, I had played the same 37-minute meditation more than two times each day.

As I had learned back in 2011, this was another reminder that meditation could help me calm my mind and overcome the spinning within it. Even now, I fall asleep almost every night with a meditation playing softly in the background.

40
RECONNECTING

After I joined the Marine Corps, I felt free to make decisions regarding whether to have relationships with my brothers or not. As we had done after I moved to Florida, Chris and I continued to keep in contact via letters and phone calls for a few years. Through Chris, I reconnected with Keith, my second oldest brother, in about 1984. While there were times that life kept us busy and we would go a few months without talking, Keith and I have had an ongoing relationship since that time and talk just about every day.

The oldest, Ronnie Bill, would connect a little bit with my dad and me after he joined the Navy, which was around the time he turned eighteen in November 1973. While I am not aware of what caused it, Ronnie Bill had another falling out with my father and, in December 1980, he wrote a letter to dad making it clear that he would never speak with my father again. He never did. I would have a regular connection with Ron through about 2005 and then, after a difficult visit when he came to New York to see me, we also had a falling out. It hurt and saddened me, and I did try to connect with him after my father passed in 2013. Unfortunately, that did not go well, and I made the difficult choice to not contact him again. Perhaps one day I will change my mind or, perhaps he will decide to reach out to me. I leave that possibility open and would welcome the opportunity to try to have him in my life, even in a small way.

Once my brother Robby left the house, other than seeing him when I visited with Syd when I was eighteen, I never saw him again. Sometime in the mid-1990s, I did speak with him on the phone when he tried to establish a relationship with me. We all knew that Robby had anger issues and general mental unrest and, based on his behavior and frame of mind at the time he reached out to me, I felt it best not to have a relationship with him.

What had prompted this decision was that after just one conversation, he began getting possessive of me. If I didn't answer the phone when he called, he would leave a message demanding to know where I was. This escalated and was particularly concerning when he left a message on Christmas Eve. I received it when I returned home after a lovely evening out with my husband, John, and his family, celebrating the holiday with a big traditional Christmas Eve dinner. As it was well after midnight, I did not return his call. Robby, however, called back around 3:00 a.m. That conversation didn't go well, and it was within the next few weeks that he began to call, always late at night, and say he was going to kill himself. I understood from Keith and Robin that Robby had been doing this same thing to them regularly and had been saying it for years. It wasn't something that I wanted to deal with, so I asked him not to call me.

Sadly, Robby did die by suicide in November of 2001. He was close with my mother and, after her passing in July and the understanding that he was facing serious jail time for yet another assault charge, this was what he chose to do. None of us were surprised.

As for Robin, after he left the house in 1973, I had not seen him other than a quick visit with him, courtesy of my brother Keith, around 1985. The advent of Facebook, however, brought us together when his wife connected us in 2013, just a few months before our father passed away. It was nice to reconnect, and we have both worked to establish a beautiful relationship in which we can talk about almost anything.

41

UNLEARNING LESSONS

THE LAST FEW YEARS AND THE LOSS OF MY DAD PUT MANY things into perspective for me, and I was finding that I was able to incorporate and use the tools that My Guy had been providing to me more easily. I was also beginning to peel back the cover on certain things and to see them differently. In essence, I was unlearning lessons I had learned in childhood.

One of the lessons my father instilled in me was that I could only count on myself. This saying, along with it being reinforced through childhood experiences, played over and over in my actions long into adulthood. One particular memory of dad that reinforces this took place in my junior year of high school.

"Dad," I whispered softly. No answer. "Dad," I whispered again. He was still asleep. I whispered again, a little louder, "Hey, dad."

"Huh, what?" he said.

"I have a flat tire," I replied.

"So, go change it," he answered as he rolled over and went back to sleep. When I bought my own car, my dad taught me basic car maintenance as he had done with my older brothers. I was not even allowed to drive it until I could show him that I could change a tire. So, while I knew how to change one, this was different. It was 5 a.m. and pitch-black outside. I was already running late to pick up my friend ahead of a several-hour drive to spend the day at an amusement park. As dad drifted back to sleep, I made my way back outside, rolling my eyes as I went and quietly wondering why he was being so selfish. Why couldn't he just get out of bed and help me? As he had, essentially, ordered me to change it, I had no other option, because if I stayed home, I was still going to have to change it myself, as well as answer why I had stood up my friend and not just changed it in the first place.

I rummaged around in the glove compartment for the flashlight dad always insisted I keep in there and used it to find the lock on the trunk and open it. After struggling to remove the trunk floor liner that was covering the spare tire, I placed it on the ground somewhere behind me. The spare tire was extremely heavy and I maneuvered it up and out of the trunk with great effort, but it slipped out of my hands. I wished I had thought to take my flip-flopped foot out of the way. It bounced off my nearly bare foot, and I cried in pain. Ignoring the pain, I was onto the next step, which was to place the jack under the car. As I stepped back to shine the flashlight on the ground to find where I had put it, the heel of my foot took another hit when it connected with the sharp edge of the jack. *Ouch! Again?* I thought, grimacing.

Continuing on, I laid down on the ground to find the right spot to insert the jack. It took me forever. Once I had it seated correctly, I began to pump the lever, and the car began to rise. I had always thought that jacking up the car was fun. Not so much, I was thinking, when it is so dark, and there is no one to help shine the flashlight. I knew that I had to raise the car high enough so that the spare tire could spin without coming in contact with the ground. While it wasn't hard to pump the lever, I was never one for putting in any more effort than was needed, so I kept stopping and checking to see if the flat tire was off the ground yet. Nope, still touching. More pumping. Still touching? Yes, more pumping. Finally, raising it enough to get the flat tire off and allow for the fully inflated spare to be easily put on, I was ready for the next phase of the operation. I just needed to loosen the lug-nuts, take the tire off, put the spare tire on, tighten the lug-nuts, put the flat tire in the trunk, and then I'm off to the park.

My sense of accomplishment quickly ended when it then hit me that you can't drive too far on a spare tire so, not only did I have to change it, but I would also need to find an open gas station to have it repaired. I felt as deflated as the flat tire, but I had to keep at it.

It took a minute, but I found the tire iron that I had put haphazardly on the ground and placed one of the four sides on one of the six lug nuts. Saying 'righty tighty, lefty loosey' in my head, I began pushing down on the left side of the iron with my left palm down, then pulled up on the right side with my right palm facing up. It didn't budge. I reset my grip and tried again. No luck. After my third failed attempt, I stood up to regroup. I was a junior in high school and, at this time, weighed maybe 90 pounds. *I am never going to get these off*, I thought. Back into the house I went.

I quietly approached my dad again, who was still sound asleep.

"Dad, dad?" I whispered.

"What?" he said, not moving anything or opening his eyes.

"I can't get the lug-nuts off." As I said this to him, I was convinced that he would get up and help me. I was so wrong, and I had no reason to be surprised by this as my father had taught me that I could only rely on myself.

He simply said, "I'm not getting out of bed. You're going to have to figure it out."

Dejected and mad, I walked back outside and stood staring at my car for a very long time. How was I going to do this? It was a rhetorical question. I wasn't. I stood there sulking for a while and then bent down to try again. I exerted all my energy, but it still did not budge. I needed to be stronger. Hmmm, I thought, maybe there was a way. I went back inside and put my sneakers on. I then climbed up on the tire iron as I held onto the roof of the car. I proceeded to jump a little with my left foot on the left side of the tire iron. Had it moved, I wondered? I could only jump a time or two before I lost my balance and my feet ended up back on the ground, but, finally, after a little more umpf, it began to loosen. I kept at it until the nut finally loosened to a point where I could get down and loosen it by hand. With one off, I knew I could do the rest. It was just a matter of perseverance.

It took me more than an hour and a half to change the tire. I recall it being around 6:30 a.m., and the sun was finally coming up. I put everything back in the trunk and closed it before going into the house to wash my hands and put my flip-flops back on. With the tire changed, off I went to find a gas station. When I pulled in, I told the man that I needed help with a flat. He walked around the car and then looked at me like I was a silly girl.

"You don't have a flat tire," he stated.

I smiled and said, "Yes, I do. It's in the trunk." About 2 ½ hours late, I was off to the park.

I was unhappy about how my dad handled my flat tire for a long time. It took me years, but I finally decided to look at this differently. I now choose to look at this as my dad taking the opportunity, knowing I was in a safe location, to teach me that I could count on myself — which is a great deal different than thinking I can *only* count on myself. With this new view, I have come to appreciate this experience as a gift from my dad. When I think back now, I picture him peeking out the front window, smiling with pride, watching me take care of the flat all by myself.

* * *

ALONG THE WAY, MY FATHER ALSO TAUGHT ME NOT TO TRUST other people. Unlike most other husbands in the neighborhood, dad was home much earlier in the afternoon as a schoolteacher. Dad graduated college with a degree in industrial arts, and to say he was handy was an understatement. Because of his skills, neighbors would come over and ask for help.

One day, a woman came over because an issue in her house needed somewhat urgent attention and her husband was at work. Dad was not willing to go help, telling me after she left that it was not a good idea to go to a woman's home without her husband present. That was just asking for trouble, he said. This instance, and others like it, left me with the impression that people couldn't be trusted, so it was necessary to always be on guard.

Another saying that I used or, perhaps, that became a mantra, like so many other negative influences that controlled my thinking was, 'I'll always be okay.' When I would say or think this, it was always from a stance of defensiveness, and, given what I perceived of others based on what I was taught, I had no other choice than to take care of myself. I used the saying as a protective shield for far too many years.

The concepts of not being able to count on others, not trusting, and always putting up the façade that I was and would always be okay brought me a bit of strength. Sadly, however, they became a strong pillar to a life of not trusting people, shutting others out, and never asking for help. These, along with the many other negative lessons from childhood, hardened me and made it virtually impossible for me to connect with others in a healthy way or to express myself in a meaningful or deep way. I had been using these sayings as a way to survive and navigate life, but it wasn't sustainable, so, inevitably and not surprisingly, my life began to crumble.

After a couple of years working with My Guy and developing tools to overcome the negativity, anger, and defensiveness I had always felt, I was facing a situation. I heard the voice in my head say, 'you can only count on yourself.' While I may have said this a million times before, for whatever reason, it no longer felt right. The words tasted bitter, and I could no longer say them without thinking how wrong I had been to believe this for so long. I wondered how I could have gone so many years, decades, in fact, thinking that this was the right way to live. Cracks were developing, finally, in the thick armor that enveloped me.

42

A NEEDED PUSH

WHILE I WAS BEGINNING TO LEARN TO TRUST AND LET PEOPLE in, it wasn't easy for me. I had struggled most of my life with establishing and maintaining genuine and loving relationships. There was one relationship that I believed I was on the right track with, however. This was with my girlfriend, Diane. We had been best friends for fourteen years. We were in the same profession, and we knew each other's families. We shared many of the same friends, and we had dinner together almost every Sunday. Diane and I talked virtually every day, and I felt comfortable telling her anything. I could be myself with her.

My dad's illness and passing were difficult for me. Diane had been through something similar with her mother, who had passed just about a year before my dad. We were both close with our respective parents, and it was comforting to know that she understood what I was going through and would be there to help me.

It was Diane that I was with on the cruise when I received the email telling me about my dad's cancer. She also provided a reference so I could adopt a cat from the local shelter. Jennie, an almost all-black cat with just a few tufts of white on her underbelly that make it look like she is wearing a bikini, has the sweetest temperament. I was appreciative when Diane visited me the day Jennie came home. As she had several cats, and I had not had any for many years, she helped me get Jennie settled.

I was in a fog during the last couple of months of 2013. Things seemed busier than usual for both of us, and I didn't see Diane very much at all. By late January 2014, I had not seen her since before Christmas, so I stopped by her house to say hello and drop off a gift that I made for her. It was a frame with a picture of her, her sister, and her brother-in-law that I had taken the previous fall. I thought she would like it. Her brother-in-law had been recently diagnosed with stage four cancer, and this was the last picture that had been taken before this diagnosis.

I looked down the driveway and saw her car. Oh, good, I thought, she's home. I went to the door and knocked. No answer. As she worked from her home, she must be on a call with a client, I thought. Getting back into my car, I called her. It went directly to voicemail which, for me, was proof that she was on a call. I left a message and drove off, knowing that I would talk to her soon.

The next day, however, everything changed when I received an email from Diane. In my critical hour of need, after losing my father just four months ago and having scattered his ashes just twelve days ago, it appeared that our friendship was over. I was confused and I was devastated. As I never imagined that there would be an end, I guess it is not surprising that I never saw it coming.

The email began with, "I guess you are wondering why I have been avoiding you." What? She's been avoiding me? I was stunned but kept reading. She had been home the previous day, but she did not want to see me. Diane's email said that she was upset about a couple of incidents that had transpired over the last months of 2013. In the email, she provided a few examples of things I had done or said which she felt were out of line and hurtful. The examples that she gave were all within a month or so of my dad's passing. I felt so foolish. How had I not known that my best friend was upset and that I was the one who had upset her?

I thought that a true friend would understand that I was not exactly myself these days and, if they were hurt, they would let me know. I also felt that a true friend would tell me if my behavior was out of line or not what it usually was. I knew that I had been on edge and that I had been snappy with her on a couple of occasions. While I recognized this, I did not apologize or discuss any specific instance that had happened directly with her. Instead, I had chosen to acknowledge my behavior by giving her a card the night we met for dinner just before Thanksgiving. I thanked her for her friendship and support during an obviously difficult time and let her know how much I valued our relationship.

As evidenced by her email, Diane's thinking was not in line with mine. Diane had not approached me, and this email was the first time that I was being made aware of how she felt. I was feeling so much as I read and reread the email. I was mad, sad, bewildered, and devastated. I also felt stupid for not having known. While I sent a note of apology and reached out to Diane to try to repair our friendship, it was obvious that it was over.

Having finalized my divorce and experienced my dad's death all within about a year, the additional loss of Diane was huge, and I was feeling pretty sorry for myself. No matter how much I tried to see my behavior as being okay, I knew it wasn't, so I took and felt the total weight of responsibility for this precious friendship ending upon myself. I felt such guilt and was so ashamed. I had really screwed up this time. It was my fault. Wasn't it always me? I had to face the reality that I was the common denominator in a long string of failed relationships, and this was just one more example of my inability to manage and appropriately express my thoughts and emotions. Despite all the work I had been doing with My Guy over the past three-plus years, something was still wrong with me. This, to me, was abundantly clear.

Even now, I continue to mourn this loss. Thankfully, time and distance have helped me to heal the hurt and the sadness somewhat. I will always miss Diane and, even though I do not know how she is, I always imagine that she is well and living a life that makes her completely happy. I also have so much gratitude for Diane, not just for all that she contributed to my life, but that the end of our relationship became the push I needed to move my journey to peace forward in a bigger way.

43

DREADED HOMEWORK

I SPOKE WITH MY GUY QUITE EXTENSIVELY ABOUT THE situation with Diane and what I felt led to it. We decided that this might be a good opportunity to regroup on my goals and progress. Despite how I was feeling from this loss, I acknowledged that I had accomplished a great deal. I had cleared many hurdles and I had many tools and techniques, developed over the last couple of years, that I was actively and successfully using. We also took the time to revisit the previous recommendations and conversations we had had about other actions I could take. It was this conversation that resurfaced the talk about attending some type of outpatient program. This had been discussed when I hit my lowest point, some fifteen months earlier, but dad became my primary focus shortly thereafter. My Guy said he knew of a few programs, and he would do a bit of research. I knew it was time to take another leap and felt that finding and attending the right program could be helpful.

A couple of weeks later, My Guy presented me with a brochure on a program called Breakthrough. It was specifically designed for adults who had been impacted by family or relationship dysfunction in childhood or adult life. It was meant to address many issues, including the difficulty of overcoming loss or pain from the past that are having a negative impact on present-day living, trouble maintaining healthy relationships, feeling bad about oneself, as well as being preoccupied with worry. As I was experiencing all of these issues, I knew immediately that it was the right program.

When I called Breakthrough the next day, the woman who answered the phone was informative and emailed me some documents to help me to understand the program more fully. After reviewing them, I logged onto their online registration portal. I checked the upcoming program dates and saw that sessions were happening every few weeks, with each one beginning on a Sunday at 4 p.m. and ending at noon on Friday. The next session was happening in less than two weeks and, while my instant reaction was to think, great, I'm going to that one, I then hesitated. Why am I hesitating? It was because things with me were that bad — I knew it — and I was scared. I didn't want to face what the program would uncover.

As My Guy was expecting me to register, I now felt accountable to him, so I began the application process. As I worked my way through the different screens, I came to the section which spoke about pre-workshop work. It was here that I discovered that there was homework. I clicked the link and up came a document. The short instructions at the top explained that my answers to the questions presented would give the program therapist a brief history of my background.

Curious, I scrolled through the questions. I immediately panicked just reading the first one. No one has ever asked me such a direct question — and not only was I being asked to answer it, but I was also being asked to write the information down on paper. The question asked me to describe my current home situation, listing those I live with, my intimate partners, and also telling me to discuss my feelings about those relations. It went on to ask what my stresses or concerns were about these relationships. This question was a deep one for me, and already I didn't like the feelings I was experiencing within me. My heart was racing, my stomach was churning, and I could feel my shoulders sag a wee bit more than they already were.

While I wanted to close the document and run the other way, I scrolled down thinking, surely, the next couldn't be as intense as this one. I was wrong. That one asked me to discuss any addictions or abuse, past or present, in my family. I could feel the weight of my family and my past continuing to come down upon my shoulders. Scrolling a bit further, I found several more equally intense and invasive questions, including one that asked me to describe my major relationships outside the home and the feelings or concerns about each, to describe my family of origin — including birth order — noting who you were close to as a child, who you were distant from, and any significant events. Another heavy question was about significant life events, and I was asked to list the dates and a brief description of major events from childhood to present, including trauma to self or family, illnesses, deaths, marriages, divorces, moves, etc. Thankfully, there were a few questions that didn't seem so bad — like the one asking me to discuss my occupation and whether it is a good match for me.

Breakthrough was looking to understand so much about so many different aspects of my life. I had tried to bury much of this deep inside of me and I preferred not to think about these things, let alone put them down in one place and on paper for all to see. I wasn't sure I had the strength to answer them and, if I did, could I find the courage to answer them honestly and fully, providing the necessary depth and details? I was feeling invaded, and I was also petrified. My hands were cold, and my legs were numb. There were snippets of items I would have to disclose running through my head. These included the sexual abuse, my mother abandoning me, my brother Robby dying by suicide, and being hit by my father. I was also thinking about all of the people who had been there, then left, during my childhood.

These were just some of the things that happened when I was young. What about those that happened in my adult years? It looked like I was going to have to disclose the embarrassment of having been married three times, driving my best friend away at a time when I needed her the most, and, my biggest shame, being punished by God by not being able to get pregnant. I had always said out loud that it was because I had said too many times when I was younger that I was never having children. What I was hiding inside, and what I really believed, was that I was not worthy of having them.

That evil Inner Critic. He was enjoying this. He was making these memories go round and round in my head and he kept repeating what I already knew. I was a piece of shit, and now everyone else was going to know it. He encouraged me to avoid these disclosures and made that option look so welcoming that I closed the browser on my computer. *Nope, I can't do it*, I thought as I got up from my office chair and walked out of the little cubby office just off the kitchen. How could I be honest and let someone in on all of these things?! I was feeling alone and scared, as usual. I crumbled onto the couch sobbing as my Inner Critic called me weak and a coward.

* * *

Mid-day on Tuesday, I walked into My Guy's office, dreading him asking if I had registered. Not surprising, it was his first question as we settled in for our 50-minute conversation.

"So, tell me, did you register? When will you be going?" he asked.

I bowed my head, not wanting to look him in the eye, as I answered truthfully, "I haven't registered yet."

"Why not," he asked, sounding surprised.

"There is homework," I replied. "And it is too intense for me."
"What do you mean?" he asked.

"They want me to write down everything about my life," I replied.
"Who I am intimate with, have I been abused, is there addiction in my
family, significant events in my life, and to discuss my relationships with my
family members. It is just all too much," I said as I began to cry. I continued
on, saying, "My story is embarrassing. How could so much have possibly
happened in one life? Putting it all in one place and having to face it isn't
something I can do. This is what is finally going to break me," I cried.

My Guy gently stated, "You've said this several times over the last few
years. You've also said that you already feel like you are broken." He was
right. His words were a jolt of reality while said out of kindness and
support. I was already broken, and I did need the help. If I wanted to
change everything I was thinking and feeling, I had to register, pick a date,
and do the homework. I left his office resigned to this reality but still
dreading the homework.

That feeling of dread and not having a choice sat with me for several
days. I am not sure how my thoughts changed, but I believe it was that my
preference has always been to stay in the lead position and not be a
follower. Having to do the homework made me a follower, but there was a
different way to view this.

So many ugly and difficult things *had* happened to and around me. I
had learned to soften out the roughness of an event and make it feel
smoother, and to take the cold hard reality of a situation, and warm it a bit.
I had learned to smooth out the good and the bad that had happened to
make everything seem more middle-of-the-road. I had also learned to keep
my thoughts to myself and to not develop my own opinions, which made
me compliant and a rule follower. While all these lessons I had learned had
made me very successful in my career, this was not working for me in my
personal life.

What I realized was that I held the key to telling the world, at least the
world of this workshop, all that I had been through. I was going to write
everything down so that they would have no choice but to agree that I had
been handed a bad hand and had a rough go of it. I was going to let
someone see my entire story and seek the confirmation that was so clear to
me now that I needed — the confirmation from someone else that my life
had, at least up until now, been crappy.

I sent My Guy an email letting him know I would be registering. In the
email, I told him, "I am scared, but since I am tired of being scared and
holding myself back, I might as well start now."

* * *

Feeling determined, I registered and selected the latest date that was open, May 18, 2014, as I would need time to complete the homework. If I had been honest with myself, which I wasn't, picking the absolute furthest date away was just another act of avoidance. I was truly scared of the unknowns involved in this intensive workshop and putting it off was natural to me, especially since I had what I thought was a good solid reason for doing so.

I would be almost forty-nine years old at the time of the workshop and had been working with My Guy for almost four years. It was time to let these tendencies and unhealthy ways of dealing with life go, along with all that I was holding onto that was holding me back from achieving the life I wanted.

I spent a good deal of time working on the homework over the next couple of months, finalizing it just a few days before the workshop. When it was completed, I felt accomplished and strong. It was eight solid pages, single-spaced, adhering to all of their requests to keep things brief and bulleted only. It held lots of information, including all the secrets I had tried, throughout my life, to keep hidden.

44
BREAKTHROUGH

I ARRIVED MID-AFTERNOON ON SUNDAY, TAKING A DEEP nervous breath before entering the large two-story building located amongst the rural farms and gently rolling hills of Pennsylvania. I knew from the website that this building is called the Mansion and that it was built especially for this program. From the outside, it looked like it could have been someone's home. As I entered, just in front of me was a long set of stairs leading up toward a second-floor balcony area, surrounded by a dark wooden railing with white spindles. The door on my right was closed, and the hallway to the left had an opening not too far down before it disappeared into the darkness. I headed to the left toward the sound of people and entered into what looked and felt like a living room.

I was greeted by the sound of a young, chipper, and friendly female voice coming from across the room. As I made my way past the others, I quickly assessed that they must also be there for the program. Most were looking down and avoiding eye contact. By quick count, there were eight people, and I wondered how many more of us there would be. When I made it to the thirty-something-year-old woman, she cheerfully welcomed me again, asked for my name, and checked it off the list on her clipboard. She then asked me for my homework and, with a little bit of trepidation, I parted ways with my precious document. My story was now in their hands.

I took my seat among the others, trying to look relaxed but remaining anxious. I am not good with new experiences, especially when I have no idea what to expect. All I had to go on is what I had conjured up in my mind about what this week would be like based on the little insight provided by the program description.

Once all twelve participants had arrived, a one-hour orientation began. The young lady that had greeted us disappeared and five counselors, all licensed social workers, arrived in the room. They told us their names and then provided us with a general overview of what it would be like between then and our late-morning departure on Friday. They read a list of six names and told us that those individuals were in group one and the remaining six in group two. I wondered how they made the determination of which people to include in each group. I imagined it meant that the people in my group were the most similar to me. I never did figure this out.

The counselors went on to explain that during the program day, we would be doing everything together in these groups. As the program day ran from 7:30 a.m., when breakfast is served, until 9 p.m., lunch and dinner would also be eaten together — as well as all of the planned daytime activities, including any free time during the program day. After breakfast, the morning session started at 9 a.m. and ran until around 12:30 p.m. There was a meal break, then an afternoon session, including group recreation, which lasted until around 5 p.m. We then had a dinner break before an evening session which ran from 6:30 until about 9 p.m. Except for Friday, which was our day of departure, this was the schedule for each day of the four-day program. We hadn't even started yet, and I was feeling overwhelmed. They explained that two counselors were assigned to each group, and the fifth counselor was to bring our two groups together for the evening session.

The next order of business was introductions. The counselors provided us with a depth of information about their education and experience and the training they took to facilitate the program. Then, it was our turn. We were asked to introduce ourselves by providing our first name only, along with our home state. We were also asked to tell the group, in a few sentences, why we were attending the program. I must say that I found it surprising to learn that a few of the participants were recovering alcoholics who felt this program would further their recovery, while others discussed having family members who are alcoholics. A good portion of the participants used the same type of language that I used, including that my life had become unmanageable and, while I was taking other steps to get to a better place, I thought I needed this to help get me to a place I am not sure I would otherwise reach.

As I listened, I found myself feeling a great deal of compassion and empathy for each person. While their stories, even with the very limited information they shared, were significantly different than mine, we were all in a place we didn't want to be and wanted to get to a different place that was better. While still extremely nervous about what the upcoming days would bring, I was comforted knowing that I was in the company of participants like me.

The counselors went on to explain the three buildings that we would be using during our time at the program. Our morning and afternoon sessions were to be held in the Mansion, upstairs in the various rooms and other available areas. They explained that the dining hall is located just a short walk up the grassy hill and is a cafeteria-style facility with different choices, including hot meals, sandwiches, and salads. Breakfast and our rooms were in a third building, Harmony House, located just down the hill from the Mansion in a three-story building that looked older and had the feel of a space used for lodging during summer camp with entry to our individual rooms from the outside. Breakfast was held in the main area on the first floor, which housed our evening sessions when both groups came together.

The last order of business was the assignment of rooms. We were all to have one roommate, and while I knew this before I arrived, I felt myself getting defensive about why we weren't allowed to have some alone time after such long days. In some ways, the structure of the program reminded me of Bootcamp where there was no time for yourself. There was someone with you at all times, and there were rules and expectations that everyone was required to follow. The schedule in the Breakthrough program was packed each morning, afternoon, and evening as if they wanted to keep us on our toes and a bit off-kilter. My introverted self was already beginning to realize that the week was going to be challenging beyond what I had previously imagined — and having my own space to decompress would have been so helpful.

My assigned roommate was a woman named Noreen and, like me, she was from Long Island. Once the assignments were made, we were released to find our rooms. We would meet next for dinner and our first evening session. As I got up and made my way outside with everyone else, I was still feeling anxious, so I took the opportunity for a bit of a breather by walking ever-so-slowly to my car to get my luggage. As I walked, I wondered how I was ever going to get through the week. It already seemed like too much for me to handle and we hadn't even started yet. The program was a hurdle that I had not yet convinced myself that I would be able to get over, yet so much was riding on this being successful in transforming my life. I had to find and keep my determination to make it so.

When I finally made it to my room, Noreen was already there. We said hello, nervously reintroduced ourselves, and then gratefully distracted ourselves with the mundane task of checking out the room and choosing beds. Given that the building looked old from the outside, it wasn't surprising to find that the room was large, adorned with dark paneling on the walls and heavy wooden furniture. There were a few tall and deep box-type windows set along one side, which allowed one to sit in them and look outside. The furnishings were sparse and the room was clean. There were a couple more beds than we needed, and Noreen and I quickly chose the ones that we would use during each of the next five nights to rest our tired and emotionally drained bodies and brains.

* * *

I summed Noreen up visually, figuring that she was maybe a few years older than my age of almost forty-nine. Her short, spiky, brown hair gelled in place framed her beautiful, freckled skin which was adorned with perfect make-up. She wore a perfume I couldn't quite place. I had smelled it before, but it had been many years. While my first impression of Noreen was that she was a constrained and tightly wound individual, as soon as we started talking I could see that she was down to earth, and an extremely warm and caring person who, like me, was in a tough place and looking for some peace within. I considered myself very lucky to have been assigned to bunk with her. She made me feel at ease immediately.

In addition to Noreen and myself, the rest of our group of six included Jay, Athena, Denise, and Terry. While all unique individuals, one of the common threads that ran between us was difficulty coping with the messiness of our lives in ways that don't further hurt our fragile hearts and minds. Another common thread was a sincere desire to help our fellow group members in a kind, loving, and supportive way.

Perhaps a few years older than me, Denise was in an unhappy marriage with almost fully grown children. Looking to find her voice and place in the world, her bright and kind face, along with her beautiful laugh and loving nature brought me instant comfort.

Jay was somewhere in his late 30's. With a slight build and hunched over shoulders, it was evident that he struggled to carry the weight of a world he did not trust.

Athena was around forty with an exotic look and a beautiful oval face, framed by long brown hair. She gave the impression of a free and loving spirit who had traveled extensively and did not have a care in the world. This could not be further from her truth.

Terry, in his early forties, had just completed another in-patient stint in rehab for drug and alcohol addiction. He had struggled his entire life with these addictions, and, unlike the previous times, he felt that if he didn't get a handle on his life this time that all would be lost. He was so tightly hanging onto this program as his saving grace.

Our time was filled with tears and laughter, sharing and resistance, hugs and encouragement, emotions and feeling deeply, old thinking giving way to revelations, games and songs, along with lots of serious work and light moments of healing release. Each of us came in guarded and with our own pains and struggles and, through each interaction and exercise, we were letting go and joining together to become an extremely tight group, rooting and fighting for each other.

As we hadn't been given an agenda, each session was a surprise, and we had no advanced knowledge as to what we would be doing. While I typically hold back a little in situations like this — where I am not leading, and I have no idea what is going to be happening — I consciously made the decision that I am all in for this experience. I vowed to do my best to be and stay open, regardless of the fear that I had for the unknown that I was walking into. I needed this program to make a difference. I needed to make a change.

* * *

THE FIRST SESSION ON SUNDAY EVENING WAS WHAT I WOULD describe as an icebreaker and team-building session designed to get everyone comfortable and to begin to build trust in ourselves and in each other. Monday and Tuesday were filled with various exercises and new ways of thinking and behaving. We were asked to fill out forms, talk about feelings, begin to understand the behaviors and thinking that were holding us back, along with learning different vocabulary and ways to view circumstances and spot issues within situations.

We focused on grief and letting go and, in one exercise, we held a funeral. A large, rectangular, black piece of sheer tooling material was placed on the floor and we sat on chairs placed around it, two on each side and one on either end, so close in that our toes almost touched the black material. We were each given a 4" by 4" napkin and asked to think about something that we had been holding onto that we needed to let go. The napkin, we were told, represented it, and we would each take a turn giving it up by placing it onto the material as if it were a coffin. We were allowed to grieve for it, but then needed to let it go and leave it in the past. While we were given a few minutes to think, I knew immediately what mine was. I needed to release my hold on the life that I wanted and didn't get. The illusion of a life that I created for myself that never materialized. I have said that a life I did not choose chose me and, when I said it, I was not saying it with gratitude. It was with resentment and hurt.

During one of the evening sessions, the counselor told us that every day she gets up, goes over to the full-length mirrors on her closet doors, raises her hands high over her head, and says, "Touch down." This, she explained, was her way of starting her day on a positive note and reminding herself to focus on those things that are important to her. While she didn't ask us to come up with a similar ritual, I thought this was a really neat idea and began thinking of something similar that I could do. I love football and would have loved to use her touchdown gesture, but that would have just been copying her. I wanted mine to be original. I considered what I wanted the gesture to symbolize and decided that I wanted to stay focused on keeping a light feeling in my heart and not to take everything so seriously. What better way to accomplish this than to do something that I loved to do as a little girl? My gesture would be a twirl. As a little girl, the sensation of freedom and a feeling of being carefree would come over me when I would put my arms out to the side, lift my head up to look toward the sky, and just spin myself around and around. I loved this idea as just thinking of twirling brought a smile to my face and I knew the desired feeling of lightness would always follow.

One exercise had us talking with a partner about how we behave and whether we avoid or deny any of our feelings. We identified our feelings by name and described how they impact us. One of the outcomes of this exercise was learning to listen and provide feedback so the individual speaking knows that they have been heard. It was also about learning how to validate their views and feelings without judging theirs or sacrificing our own. The concept of affirmation was also developed. This is the ability to express one's honest acceptance in a way that honors the other's worth, feelings, and thoughts without requiring agreement with those views or perfection from the other person.

Generally, the exercises were centered on effective and honest communication, defining and expressing feelings, having and maintaining healthy relationships with self and others, letting go of the past, self-care, exhibiting loving behavior toward self and others, and, all the while, building our identities. The exercises were not centered on any specific past instance but presented in a way that allowed us to get to the core of what was causing the overarching difficulties in our lives as it related to each concept that was discussed. As I told myself I would be, I was usually the first to raise my hand to answer a question or volunteer for an exercise.

It was not surprising that a number of the exercises focused on how we were when we were young. One that I found particularly insightful was where we circle traits that we feel described us when we were no more than ten years old. There were thirty-six traits listed in total, and I circled nine of them. Those I circled were introvert, sweet, kind, active, cautious, busy, shy, helpful, and quiet. To give a sense of the broadness of the list, some of the other traits listed but that I did not pick included curious, fearless, smiley, enthusiastic, smart, passionate, and pretty. We were also asked to underline the words that we use as a way of coping. I underlined cautious, busy, shy, introvert, and quiet. It was an interesting exercise to see the traits that define how I coped with the world I found myself living in as a child. Very enlightening.

Also enlightening were some of the answers I put down on a short fill-in-the-blank questionnaire which, again, focused on the time before we were ten years old. The ones that I found sad and which I know I carried with me well into adulthood were:

- I often felt ... *detached*
- I was afraid of ... *being in trouble*
- I sometimes struggled with ... *self-confidence*
- I always wished that I could ... *be like other people*

ALL OF THE EXERCISES WERE EYE-OPENING, AND I FOUND THEM to be immediately and positively impactful not just on my thought process, but also my behavior. It was as if someone was giving me a new rule book that I could operate under. I slept soundly the first couple of nights, after days filled with sharing, listening, contributing, emotions, tears, laughter, compassion, trust, and getting to know myself.

45
IT'S TIME

By the time I woke on Wednesday morning, I was pretty exhausted, and I made the decision that I would just sit back for today and allow others to take the lead. That, unfortunately, was not meant to be. As the six of us entered the room, having made our way together, as required, from breakfast to the first session, we were greeted by our two counselors. They told us that we were going to do some individual targeted exercises and that, over the next two days, each of us would have a turn to be the focus. We were also told that while the focus would be on one person, we would all be involved in the exercise. I sat back and got comfortable, reminding myself that I was not going to volunteer to go first.

This time, however, they didn't ask for a volunteer. My counselor simply said, "Okay, Heidi, let's start with you."

I was surprised and immediately thought the only reason that she had called on me was because I had always been the first to volunteer, so I said, "Oh, no, that's okay. Somebody else can go first."

"No," she replied. "We're going to start with you."

I was immediately nervous and unsure. I had walked into the day thinking that the first two days had been the worst and most difficult that we would face and that it would be all downhill from here. This assumption could not have been farther from the truth, and I had no way of knowing just how difficult the next number of hours would be for me. Those hours turned out to be physically, mentally, and emotionally depleting. They were filled with tears, sobs, and discoveries of pain and fear that came up from the depths of me. They were also filled with healing and a sense of having released a large burden from within. As I would be told later, they started with me because they felt that I would be the easiest to crack open given my tendencies, like my go-along and people-pleasing approach, which go back to my childhood.

My individual exercise started simply enough. On the blackboard at the front of the room, the counselor drew the outline of a body. She then turned around and asked me to come up front, and, as I did, she handed me the chalk.

She said, "Now Heidi, in the last couple of days, you've talked about your feelings. I would like you to tell me where you feel those feelings within your body." I wasn't sure what she meant, so I asked her to repeat it. "The question," she said. "Is ... when you experience things like anger, sadness, and grief, where do you feel them in your body? What part of your body feels that emotion, and what does that body part feel like?"

I immediately began talking about the mouth. I told her, "My mouth always feels very, very heavy."

She probed, "Please explain that a bit more."

"It feels like individual weights are hanging on either side of it, dragging down the corners into a huge frown." I then describe the feeling that I have in my jaw. "It always feels so tight and tense and set in place as if in a defensive position. Like a stance of self-preservation, constantly happening, before anything bad even presents itself." As I talk, she encourages me to draw what I feel on the body she has drawn so, on the mouth, I put a wide and upside-down U and, at the end of the lines on either side, I drew a dumbbell as best I could.

At some point, the conversation took a shift that I didn't even realize had happened. I found myself talking about fear and that I always feel fear around me. She asked me to look at my five groupmates and to pick one of them to play fear for me. I did as I was asked, and the counselor gave them a piece of very sheer black material to hold up, then asked me to show her where fear is in relation to my physical body. I told her that fear is all around me, not just in front or behind, and that it is always just out of my reach. What I found extraordinary as I said this to her was that I didn't even realize what I was saying until I had already said it. I mean, come on, who really thinks about where fear resides in relation to oneself. My groupmate was then asked by the counselor to hold the black material up and in front of her and to float around me, just out of arms reach, as we continued the exercise.

Another interesting turn was when she asked me something, and I gave an answer that is, to me, a mistake, and I immediately told her, "I'm sorry, that's not right."

She responded by asking me, "Who said that?"

A bit slow on the uptake sometimes, I looked at her confused and slowly responded, "Me."

"No ... What made you say that what you had said wasn't right? What made you apologize?"

"Oh, that's my Inner Critic," I responded.

"You have an Inner Critic?"

"Doesn't everyone?" I said, as more of a statement than a question.

"No," she replied.

"Oh," I responded, clearly surprised by her answer.

"Tell me about your Inner Critic," she asked.

"Well, he is with me all the time. He has been with me since I was a child, so I guess you can say he's been a life-long companion."

"He?"

"Yes," I said. "My Inner Critic is a he."

"And how often does he chime in."

"All the time," I replied. "If I wear the wrong thing, if I say the wrong thing, if I trip over something, or if I say something stupid. When I start a project, he tells me that I won't be successful. When I start a course or class, he tells me that I will fail. He chimes in all the time."

"Ah," she said. Looking at my four remaining groupmates, she asked me to pick someone to play my Inner Critic. I did and they stood up in front of me.

"Where does your Inner Critic reside?" the counselor asked.

"Well, I hear him in my ears as if he is standing right next to me," I answered. She then instructed my group member to stand very close to my left side and to move with me as if they were attached to me.

Things were getting a bit weird and uncomfortable, and I was struggling to remain open and receptive. But I kept saying to myself, *It is now or never*. I knew that this experience, being in the program, was something that I desperately needed. The exercise lasted about two and a half hours. I was asked lots of questions about my feelings, thoughts, and behaviors, and, as I answered them, it felt like another layer of understanding was added, while at the same time, a layer of pain came off of me. The exercise moved fluidly from one thing to another and, once it was over, I couldn't fathom that it had been going as long as it had. I couldn't even remember much of what had happened besides the beginning and then the end.

Having no clue how I got there, I was kneeling on the ground in front of a square foam cube that was maybe 2'x2'x2'. I had a plastic blow-up bat in my hand, and I was slamming the bat as hard as I could onto the cube. My Inner Critic was still attached to me at my left shoulder, I saw the black material of fear dancing in front of me just out of reach, and my remaining groupmates were all leaning over or kneeling next to and around me, providing me a feeling of safety at a moment in which I felt stripped of privacy and secrets. The female counselor leading me in this exercise was standing over me, and her voice seemed to be booming in my ears and, every once in a while, I heard the stern tone of the male counselor telling me that I'm not giving all that I can.

Large streams of tears fell as I gasped for breath through my sobs and yelling. I was screaming out all that I was angry about from my childhood and my adult life. I was yelling out all the hurt that I had endured and my feelings of shame, guilt, abandonment, fear, worthlessness, and unlovability that I had always felt and had been carrying with me. Things like, "Why did you leave me, mom? I was only five years old, and you never came to see me after you left. Why did you let that man take me to the church? Didn't you know he would do something bad? Dad, why did you get angry so easily? Why couldn't you find a way to have a relationship with the boys? Why did you have to cut all of those people out of our lives? What did I do that was so bad that I deserved not to have been given any children? Why couldn't I get one of my marriages to work? Why am I always so afraid? Why can't I be like everyone else? Why do I feel like such a loser?"

This was all pouring out of me. I was scared by all that I was saying. I also knew that I was still resisting a bit and not fully releasing everything, but still knew that what was happening was huge. Fear was still in front of me and was something I would have to continue to work on.

The words stopped flowing first, even as I continued to beat the cube and the tears still streamed down my face. I felt raw both inside and out. Slowly, the bat blows lightened and then stopped altogether. I began to really sob, letting out the last of what had been loosened up from somewhere deep down inside of me. I had released so much and, surprisingly, I could feel that I was so much lighter.

When my sobbing calmed, only then did the counselor ask my groupmates to get up and move away from me. She helped me to my feet, sat me in my chair, and gave me some water. I couldn't process what she was saying to me, but whatever it was, it felt comforting and calming. By the time she asked all of us to stand, form a circle, and hold hands, my breathing had returned to normal, and I felt like I was present in the room. She then informed us that they were going to play a song. The song, she told us, was for me and they had specifically chosen it for me. They hoped it would provide me the confidence I needed to continue to move forward and away from the pain of my past.

The song was "It's Time" by Imagine Dragons. Such great lyrics, including the few lines, "...*and now it's time to build from the bottom of the pit, right to the top, don't hold back* ...." I must have played this song a thousand times over the next few months, claiming it into my soul as a motivator to keep moving forward to the place of peace I so desired.

46

A FUTURE VIEW

AFTER MY PERSONALIZED SESSION, I STOPPED WONDERING when I was going to meet with my counselor to go over my story, those eight pages of homework I so diligently prepared. I wasn't told that this was going to happen, but it just made sense as I was sure the revelations I provided them could be incorporated into my experience this week. What became clear was that they weren't going to talk with me about my story. This, I had finally realized, wasn't what the week was about. It was not about rehashing the past or taking the opportunity to further wallow in what did or didn't happen in my life. It was also not about placing blame or giving any more power to my story. It was about putting it in a neat package, then leaving it in the past and moving beyond it.

The stories from my life, all of those individual instances and circumstances and items that have happened over time, aren't who I was. I am not what happened to me. While I am who I am because of all that happened, I am not those individual experiences. I had been dragging all of this along with me and it felt like a heavy and restricting yolk around my neck.

I realized that I had been tying my being and who I am so tightly to my past that it was not surprising, inevitable really, that I had been living a somewhat self-fulfilling prophecy that repeated the same issues and patterns. My story was simply what happened in the past. Knowing this is truly life-changing, and I could feel it have an immediate and positive impact on my entire life. I had been feeling worthless, ashamed, guilty, embarrassed, and so many other things about all that I have endured from others' actions and also from my own. I was now free of it. My past had

257

almost instantly become something that I no longer felt the need to hide from people, and I no longer felt tethered to it.

I was beyond exhausted by the time Wednesday evening came. I was still feeling raw from my morning session, and I was a bit cranky. I needed some alone time to recharge, but, as required, I gathered with the others for our evening session.

The exercise that the counselor gave us that evening was to write a letter to ourselves from five years in the future. She asked us to consider all that we have learned about ourselves and what we want our lives to look like. I didn't know what to write and I was sure I won't write anything meaningful. Those were my first thoughts. My next thought was that this exercise is important and that I need to buckle down and do it. I excused myself and went back to the quiet of my room to complete it. I sat down in the window box, putting my notepad on my bent knees. Taking a moment to look out through the distorted old glass at a beautiful green tree that was in front of me, my mind began to calm.

Knowing that we had only 45 minutes and that time was ticking by, I moved my thoughts to the paper in front of me and picked up my pen. Words began to flow easily. *Where were these powerful and helpful thoughts coming from?* If I were writing it today, I would recognize them as coming from a guide, or my higher self. At that moment, however, I was just grateful that the words were flowing. In no time at all, my letter was complete and I rushed back to the room excited to share it with everyone else. I wrote:

Hey Heidi,

So, I am sitting here in 2019 reflecting back to you in 2014. What a ride the last five years have been. It is now comfortable sitting in my happy chair, and I rarely get comfortable in my ugly chair. In fact, I think it is gathering dust somewhere now. Oh, don't get me wrong, I still think about how comfortable that ugly chair was, and I still wonder how I stayed it in for those long periods of time before 2014.

I feel good that I rarely think now of the life I wanted and didn't get or achieve. The mourning was hard. I know you are just starting that process, so please hang onto the feeling you had during the exercise you did during this retreat when you put a tissue, representing grief, into that makeshift grave and began that healing process. Be sure to think about how just that action made you feel so much better. Keep working on leaving that feeling of mourning and despair behind.

Oh, and let me tell you that the relationships I now have are so wonderful. They are not perfect and not without difficulties and disagreements, but wonderful because they are with people who support me and love me; the me I am and not the illusion I created and showed back then. Please help me by being open to experiencing others. You have to trust without fear. So what if they all don't live up to your desires along the way? Each time you open up, you will be learning how to see people for who they are and also showing them the true you. Remember, life is a journey, and you need to experience it.

I want you to know that the work I did after this spiritual retreat on identifying and solidifying my values and what is important to me has paid off. I still teach as well as work in the human resources field, but for an organization that values me and fulfills my values at the same time. I am doing more community work, something you and I spoke about a great deal. Working with veterans has brought you so much fulfillment.

As for Fear, this is something that I don't see much of anymore. We made a deal, and we have both stuck to it. Fear got a much-needed vacation from working 24/7 for years and years and I finally got to bring that product idea to market. We both feel great having gotten what we both needed and wanted.

Know that it is now comfortable to laugh, and smiles come freely and easily. The weights that were holding down your smile took a hike. It was easy once I finally got your Inner Critic to stop pounding on me. Turns out it was easy to do ... just take the bat away from him and continue to say I matter, and I did great work today. To help me, I even put a gold star on the calendar every day I listened more to my heart and head than to the Inner Critic who wanted to keep me down. That visual, just like it does for a child, brought a smile to my face each time I gave myself one. Part of my smile was because I also envisioned your Inner Critic frowning. What fun that was shutting him down.

I caution you to not think so much. Also, sit with your feelings and identify them by name. Describe them and figure out what prompted them. This continuous process is what got me here to this peaceful and serene place.

You know, you have had that big serenity plaque in front of the house for 10 years now and your email even has the word serenity in it.

I feel so good now when I look upon both. I smile now instead of being reminded of how agitated and un-serene I felt back then.

Heidi, please do not lose sight of what I have written here because I like it where I am and if you mess with these things, you mess with your destiny, which is to be here in 2019, as I describe.

Know that I love you. You are a great person. Thank you for being too stubborn to give up on your happiness. You matter to me.

With love, your future Mighty Heidi

I WAS SO UPLIFTED BY THE LETTER, AND I WAS FEELING SO hopeful that the future could actually be what I had written. When we left at noon on Friday to head back to integrate our new selves into our existing lives, we were encouraged to keep things light for the first few days.

In support of this request, when I stopped at a Burger King to grab a bite to eat during my four-hour drive home, I asked the young lady behind the counter for one of the paper Burger King crowns that they give to children. Sure, she said, handing me one. I put it on my head and walked out smiling. I smiled as I was proud of myself for over-coming my fear and having attended the program. I smiled, knowing that I was already experiencing a lightness within me and an understanding of self I could have never imagined. I was also smiling because, for the first time since September of 2010, some three years and nine months ago, I felt like I was on the other side. I was cresting the top of the large deep hole I had been in, and I was also seeing large patches of daylight as I neared the end of the long dark tunnel I felt like I had been navigating.

While there is more work to be done, I knew, without a doubt, that I was solidly in a place far removed from my past, and there was no going back. As one last acknowledgment of how I was feeling, before I got in the car to finish my drive home to a life that I knew would never be like it was before, I twirled.

47
AN OVERDUE APOLOGY

It was a month or two after returning home from Breakthrough that I finally found the courage to apologize to the manager for how I had spoken to her during 'The Incident.' From the moment it happened, I was embarrassed by the way that I had behaved, and I avoided the manager as much as possible.

When I finally approached the manager, it was clear that she remembered the interaction. She tried to brush it off as no big deal, but I couldn't let her do that. I needed her to know how sorry I was to have behaved in a way that was just downright nasty and uncalled for. I told her that what happened was a big deal and that I had absolutely no right to have spoken with her that way. I told her, "I have been carrying this incident with me since it happened, and I can't continue to carry the guilt and shame." She was so gracious and supportive as I delivered the words that I needed to say.

The apology took way longer than it should have to come out. It had, in fact, taken me almost four years and it was as much for her as it was for me. Breakthrough had taught me many things and one of them was not to carry baggage into the future. The apology was just one of the many ways in which I was able to move forward and heal from not just 'The Incident,' but the many things that led to it happening in the first place.

48

NORMAL VS. REGULAR

When I began seeing My Guy in September 2010, I knew there was something wrong with me. I could not imagine that there were others in the world that felt like I did, and, on a frequent and consistent basis, I would say that I was not normal. Just as it had for my entire life, the word normal seemed so clearly defined to me. Normal was what I saw when I looked at other people. When I was younger, it was kids who seemed to have a good relationship with their parents, who easily moved through life and didn't fear it. It was parents who seemed to provide a life of stability for their families, and families who showed their love by being there to support each other. When I got older, normal was getting married and staying together. It was buying a house, having children, and then watching them grow. It was the enjoyment of life and settling into a routine. It was being loved and feeling supported. It was a feeling of being wanted and valued. It was a feeling of freedom and having a voice that others cared to listen to. These are not the things that I had experienced, even though normal was a label I so desperately wanted to pin on myself. I just wanted to feel like everyone else.

Normal, I was coming to understand, was the reflection I saw when comparing myself to others. All the work I had been doing was showing me that what I was seeing was not necessarily the reality of what was happening with and between others. Also, the lives that others were living were not necessarily better than mine; they were just different. As what I was experiencing in my life was just a perception that was based on my experiences, desires, and fears, I came to know that I should not define my life or myself as being 'not normal.'

It was a very long road to get me to the point where I could no longer sit in the pain and discomfort of feeling like I wasn't normal and thinking that something was wrong with me. Slowly but thankfully, I did begin to change how I referenced my life. It was a steady process of stopping the use of the word normal by not trying to be normal. I decided that I wanted to be 'regular.' I find comfort in this word.

My definition of regular is a place of peace within my heart, mind, and body. The place within me where I feel welcomed and comfortable with myself. It is a place that allows me to find the joy in each moment, regardless of what may be happening. Regular is a fabulous place to be, and I am no longer using something as arbitrary as others' views of what normal should be — or what my perception of others is.

Even after I started using the term regular instead of normal, I wasn't feeling it for a long time. I am grateful that I feel it now because I did finally arrive at the place that I define as regular. When deciding if I am feeling regular, I compare how things are at the particular moment against how I feel about what is happening within me. Even if there is external chaos, I can be regular. To use a word that I rarely utter now, regular is my 'normal' barometer and it is how I gauge how I am doing.

49
A MOMENTOUS
TRANSITION

It was mid-2017, and I had just turned fifty-two. I had been working as the Chief People Officer for the September 11 Memorial & Museum in downtown Manhattan for almost three years. It was time to take a break. It had been thirty years since I was discharged from the Marine Corps, thirty-seven years since I had started working, and, other than a very short break in between one or two jobs, I had been working non-stop and, most of that time, working two jobs. I was at a place where life had become peaceful, and I felt mostly settled into an easy flow of living without the crazy chaos and feeling of busyness that had consumed me for many years. Even though I was still uncertain about where I was heading and what my life would ultimately look like, I truly felt that my old way of living had been left solidly in the past, and I was navigating life in a way that I was happy with. Taking a break seemed like a good way to regroup, so I planned to take a year off.

As I stepped off the train after my last day of work, I smiled. I had been commuting into New York City since the spring of 2001, over sixteen years prior. I was feeling a sense of satisfaction along with an inner calm that came with knowing that a new adventure that I was fully ready to embrace lie just ahead.

I was right about a new adventure. It was only a nanosecond later that I received a call from an attorney with whom I had previously worked. We had kept in touch, and he knew that I was leaving my job. He told me that his yacht club on Long Island was looking for some human resources assistance and asked if I would consider doing some consulting work for them. This was not something I had ever thought about doing. It would mean having my own company and working for myself — and that was something, in the past, that would have been too scary to think about. A thought like that would have involved lots of input from my Inner Critic, who would convince me that it was not something I could do. I would have continued with this negativity, thinking through a million things that would have to be done, sure that I would never be able to do them successfully. On and on, my brain would have worked. Not anymore. Thankfully, the work that I had been doing to address my Inner Critic and negative thoughts along with tools, time, and an acknowledgment that I had all the work experience necessary to do this work, put me in a place much different than I would have been years before.

This opportunity was the possibility for a major change to my future and way of life, and it was also a great way to test my Inner Critic to see if he had taken that much-needed rest we had agreed to a few years prior. Amazingly and happily, he didn't show up. I was awarded the consulting contract, and, as the saying goes, I was in business. Literally!

I transitioned easily to working for myself and, without advertising or much effort, additional clients presented themselves within a few months. In early 2018, I decided that I would give this new business my entire focus for this calendar year, and then, in January 2019, I would decide whether I should continue or if I would go back to working for an employer. As I had also been toying with the idea of moving out of New York for several years, I would also use that point in time to consider if I should move. Once I knew that I wasn't going to make those decisions until a later date, I relaxed and allowed myself to thoroughly enjoy the year.

The consulting work kept me a little bit busy, but I also had time to do what I wanted, especially since I could arrange my schedule and I was doing most of the work remotely. It was not unusual for me to be working from a hotel room or lobby or a serene place, such as when I was sitting in a beautiful park overlooking a tranquil river. During this time, I traveled a good deal, taking another trip to Turkey, a cruise to Alaska, and went to Florida to visit with my brother. I also took many road trips to visit friends and, continuing with my ancestry work, to do what I came to call 'graveyard hopping,' which meant visiting cemeteries where my ancestors are buried. Things were going well for me, and the road I found myself on was finally smooth.

50
JUST CURIOUS

After attending the Breakthrough program in 2014, my life continued to change in positive ways and by 2018, I was solidly set on a course looking forward and finally living in a peaceful way. I also found myself embracing a spiritual journey that had taken me until then to even realize that I was on it. My journey is one of continued healing as well as the transformation, expansion and enlightenment of my heart, my mind, and my soul — and to discover and fully live my soul's purpose. It is also about developing my understanding of the capabilities we all have to communicate with other dimensions utilizing the energy and vibrations that are present in all things.

Since I was a child, I have believed in ghosts and the ability to communicate with the dead. I had not ever experienced anything that would lead me to believe that I had any such gifts or convince me that we all could develop them. I have long been curious about how psychic and mediumship gifts work, and my curiosity was heightened after my dad passed. He was the closest person to me who had passed away, and I missed him desperately. A year after his passing, I went to see Winter Brook Ryan, a psychic medium on Long Island. In the past, I had a few experiences with mediums as well as a palm reader, but each of those encounters had been random in how they occurred, and, while most of the information conveyed resonated fully with me, I viewed them as only for entertainment value. Seeing a medium for a reading to connect with my father would be an entirely different experience, and I had so much hope riding on it.

The reading didn't disappoint. Without a single doubt, I know that my father was present and conveying information through Winter. She was able to bring through evidential information that she would have no way of knowing. For example, she told me that my father was laughing and telling her that his shoe size was 9 ½. To her, it seemed random, and to others, it may seem like a lucky guess. To me, however, it provided me comfort that my dad was there. I was filled with such joy as I remembered that about ten days before he passed, still believing that he was going to be around for much more time, I asked him for his shoe size. We were in his rehab room, and I was online trying to order his favorite shoes as he would need them to do some walking and get his strength back. There was a funny exchange between us as my dad, slightly annoyed, asked me how it was that I did not know his shoe size given all the times I had previously purchased shoes for him.

It was such a comforting experience with Winter that I would come to visit her again in 2015 and late 2017. One unexpected piece of information came during the 2015 reading when Winter was able to validate, through her communication with my mother and grandmother on the other side, that my mother's sister, Aunt Claire, was still alive. I had never met her but had been searching through the work I was doing on my ancestors. As I had found no trace of her through any of the avenues that I had already explored, I had given up on the possibility that she was alive. After this reading, when I looked for her again, I found contact information for her within minutes. My mind was blown. I was thrilled to find that she was alive, and I connected with her shortly thereafter. She was eighty-two years old at the time and was, as Winter had conveyed, in almost perfect health and doing very well.

Along with my brother Keith, I traveled to South Carolina the following year to meet her in person. What a lovely, funny, and comfortable person to be around. Over the years since, I have shared with her information that I found through my ancestry work on our mutual ancestors, and she, in turn, has provided me first-hand information on my mother as well as her parents and grandparents. I have a loving and beautiful relationship with my Aunt Claire and, unexpectedly and gratefully, I have come to view her as a mother figure.

* * *

AS MY CURIOSITY OF HOW MEDIUMSHIP WORKED WAS ONLY heightened by my readings from Winter, I signed up when I happened upon an advertisement for a lecture she was giving in March 2018. When I arrived, I found it was a small gathering of eight people. Everyone was friendly and welcoming, and most of the group already knew each other. This became my first understanding that there were gatherings, workshops, and lectures given and attended by like-minded people who were all on their own individual and unique spiritual journeys.

The lecture began with Winter asking us to introduce ourselves and tell everyone where we were in our spiritual development. I had long considered myself spiritual and would tell people this when asked about my religious preferences. While the term was something I was comfortable with, I didn't understand how one developed it. We were arranged in a semi-circle in front of her, and I was glad she started on the other side of the room.

As each attendee spoke, they said things such as: "I'm at the beginning of my development and enrolled in classes"; "My modality is working with tarot cards"; and "I have studied at the Arthur Findley College." I didn't understand much of what anyone had said, and I was feeling overwhelmed and out of sorts.

When it came to my turn, I was a bit timid and simply said, "My name is Heidi, and I am just here because I'm curious." I then added, "Oh, and I should say that I didn't understand most of what you guys just said besides your names." Everyone laughed and nodded as if they understood this. I'm glad they did. I sure didn't.

If it wasn't for what happened at the end, I would not have recalled anything about the lecture. There were about thirty minutes left, and Winter told us that this was the time that everyone looked forward to. She said, "This is when there will be readings." My ears perked up. How wonderful, I thought. Winter was going to demonstrate the gift of mediumship by connecting someone in the room to a loved one that had passed. I imagined that not everyone would get a reading, so, to increase my odds, I put a smile on my face and sat up straighter in my chair. It worked.

Winter immediately said, "Heidi, let's start with you." Yeah! Maybe she will bring my dad through, I thought. I was so happy, but it only lasted for a brief moment. Confusion and then panic set in as she said, "Okay, Heidi, let me tell you how to do it." Do what? I thought. Did she mean that *I* was going to do the reading? I'm only here for a lecture. I don't have these gifts. I was feeling put on the spot but finally just resigned myself to what was happening. I was mostly anxious, but a small part of me was thinking, why not, give it a try.

She told me to look around at each person in the room and see if I felt connected to any of them. I took a deep breath and, nervously, scanned the faces of everyone in the group. I was feeling very self-conscious. I made my way around the semi-circle and I hesitated, oh so briefly, on a woman sitting two seats to my left. I didn't think much of this, chalking my hesitation up to her kind and welcoming face. After I looked at everyone, I looked back at Winter and just shrugged my shoulders.

"Go around again," she said with a smile of encouragement. "What do you see or feel?" What I was feeling was uncomfortable, but I did as she asked. I started again with the person across the room from me and spent a bit more time looking at the face of each person. It felt like an awkward eternity, and all the while I was still thinking that I had no clue what I was even supposed to be doing.

Surprisingly, though, something changed. When I came to the same woman I had stopped on previously and looked at her face, I lingered. I then lingered some more. I didn't look away. She certainly had a kind face, but even with the discomfort I had about staring at her, I felt incredibly comfortable looking at her. So, for a bit more time, I just looked her right in the eyes. Her eyes filled up with tears as did mine. I was unsure of what was happening, but knew that something was. I wasn't scared. I finally looked away and continued to the next two people and then looked back at Winter. Again, I shrugged my shoulders.

She said, "I saw you stop on this woman," pointing to the person whose face I had lingered on. "Why did you stop?"

My response was immediate and, I must say, it surprised me when I said, "I feel love. Well, don't get me wrong," I stuttered, "I don't feel love for her. I feel love surrounding her." I was absolutely sure of what I was feeling, yet it did not make any sense.

Winter then asked if I saw anyone standing behind the woman. *Like a dead person*? I thought to myself. I'm not crazy. "No, I don't see anyone," I replied quite defensively. I did feel compelled to add, "But I definitely feel love around her." I had no clue what was happening or how these feelings had formulated themselves into words and made their way out of my mouth. Winter then turned to the woman and told her that her deceased husband was with her. She then explained to me that while I could not see him, I was sensing his presence through the feeling of his love for his wife. While I would not fully appreciate it for a while, I had just had my first experience with the Spirit world.

More than curious now, after the session I asked Winter what she would suggest I do next with my curiosity. She suggested a spiritual assessment, and I scheduled it with her right away. So began my spiritual journey.

51
PRETTY ROCKS

I **OPENED MY HAND**, AND SHE PLACED A LARGE STONE IN MY palm. It was white and somewhat more jagged than smooth. It was maybe 3" by 4" wide and about 2" thick. Winter asked me to put my other hand on top of it and I did so, putting it directly in contact with the stone and almost encasing it within my hands.

She immediately reached over and, as she was raising my hand off of the stone about ½ inch, she said, "Now, don't put your hand directly on it. You need to leave some space in between so you can feel the energy." *Yeah, sure right*, my brain was thinking of the potential to feel anything. It's a pretty one, but it is still just a rock.

* * *

I HAD BEEN LOOKING FORWARD TO MY SPIRITUAL ASSESSMENT, but my excitement was mixed with a bit of apprehension as I had no idea what I was getting myself into. It was so unlike me to be blindly following along a path that I knew nothing about. I didn't even know what a spiritual assessment was. What type of questions would I have to answer? Would there be any questions? Would I be asked to take a test like the one I took in high school to determine the type of job I would be most suited for? I discounted every logical question I asked myself as not making sense about what this experience would be like. I didn't have anything, however, to replace these with — and this is where my apprehension originated from. It was the not knowing.

As I entered Winter's store-front office, she looked up from her desk at the back as the bells on the door rang, signaling my entrance. Her office, large and roomy with high ceilings, was bright and inviting. It was furnished with just the right number of chairs, side tables, bookshelves, and tasteful pictures on the walls. Winter greeted me with the usual pleasantries, inviting me to sit down at a large round table as she began the assessment. It took just a few minutes for me to realize that to conduct the assessment, she would be connecting with the spiritual world just as she does for mediumship readings. Essentially, it would be a reading just with a different focus and the involvement of different spiritual beings. She would be connecting with my spiritual guides. While I would come to learn that this made absolute sense, at that moment I didn't understand how it worked and was only thinking how great it was that someone could use their abilities to provide insight into another's.

Taking a moment to connect as she had in prior readings, Winter began to relay to me the information about where I should focus my attention in order to better understand and connect with the world of Spirit as well as certain steps I could take to help with the process. There were several areas we would cover, with the first being to form a connection with my guides. She explained that we all have a team in the spiritual realm that assists us in our journey. Winter explained that one way to connect was to make an appointment with them. She told me to just say out loud, or in my head, that I want to speak with them and give them a date and time. She then told me, at the time I appoint, to sit in a quiet space with a notebook and just write. She said not to analyze or to think about what I was writing. I was just to write. Once I was done, I could go back and read what I wrote. Over time, she said I would begin to see which writing had come from me and which was from a Spirit. She informed me that I could even ask questions or seek guidance, and that the response would appear in my writing. She explained that this exercise helps build a connection to our guides and will help me to understand how and where information from my guides and the spiritual world comes to me.

One area that Winter mentioned that I would naturally be inclined to is the ability to get out of my body and astral travel. She said that I have strong dreams, which I knew to be true. She also confirmed that she knows I go places, and I have the feeling of Deja-vu. Also, absolutely true. She said this happens because I have been there in a past life or a dream.

Winter mentioned that a color wheel was being shown to her and that I should look into colors. That's interesting, I thought. I didn't know colors had anything to do with the spiritual realm, but it seemed to make sense for me to look into this because as far back as I can remember, when I close my eyes, I see colors and geometric shapes. I had always assumed that what I was seeing had something to do with my eyes responding to the sudden change from light to dark when I closed them. I came to call them the "beetzies," having no clue how or why I started calling them this; it began way back when I was rather young.

One of the last areas that we discussed was crystals. The guides indicated that I would do well with them. They said I was going to be one of those people who bought four of them, then would have fifty just a short time later. When she mentioned them, it didn't resonate with me even though I mentioned to her that I still had a small stone from when I was a child. I had picked it up on the beach when my dad and I had taken a motorcycle ride out to Montauk and had held it ALL the time when I was young. While I have discarded virtually all of my physical memories of childhood, I still have that stone.

* * *

THE ASSESSMENT FLEW BY AND, AS IT ENDED AND WINTER busied herself with downloading me a copy of the recording she had made of our session, we engaged in some chitchat. I thanked her for everything, and, in typical fashion, I summed up the major points of our session and pointed out the areas that I believed I would focus on first.

As I outlined them, Winter quickly added, "And don't forget about the crystals."

"Yes, I know, but I'm going to start with these other areas first," I replied. In a way that was somewhat unlike her, and in a voice that was a bit of a demand more than an actual request, she asked me to put everything I was holding in my hands down. I did as she asked. She picked up a beautiful stone from the center of the table where we had been sitting. This was the stone that now sat in my hand.

As she looked on in anticipation, I stood there for a few moments. I didn't feel anything, nor did I expect to. I didn't want to appear rude toward her or the silliness of what she was saying. I was hoping she could not see my eyes rolling at the fact that she thought I was going to feel something from this rock. *Preposterous*, I thought quite adamantly. It felt like an eternity, especially with Winter staring at me, but at just about the time I was thinking *ok, enough of this*, I felt something. I felt it in the palm of the hand that was hovering over the stone. My hand felt like it was absorbing a vibration that was emanating from the stone below. I could feel a denseness in the air between my hand and the stone.

My eyes flew open wide, and I said to her, "You just blew my mind."

Excited, she asked, "You felt it?"

"Yes," I said, bewildered.

"Oh, good," she said, immediately taking the stone out of my hand and asking me to come with her.

She led me to a tall geode amethyst that had been broken open. She told me to put my hand into it and see what I felt. I was fully invested now, and I waited for the same feeling I had experienced with the first rock. It took a bit longer, but I felt it again. Except, it didn't actually feel the same.

"I feel something," I said. "But it feels different than how the other one felt."

"Yes," she said. "It would because of its properties."

My internal voice was questioning the term properties, but I never had the chance to ask about it as she was excitedly holding out yet another stone for me. I willingly obliged her excitement as I could feel my own, along with my confusion as to what I was actually feeling, growing.

The next one was a beautiful pink color and was maybe 2" by 3." It was oval and somewhat flat. Having held the two other stones from which I had felt what she called "energy" from, the sensation now felt different. I had something to compare this next stone to. When I felt the energy from this one, it was very soft and velvety. That sounds odd, but that is how it felt. Wow! This is awesome, I thought. She went on to explain that this crystal represents universal love, and it feels like you are getting a hug when you hold it. It was Rose Quartz.

My head was spinning when I walked out of my spiritual assessment. I had a list of items to go through and lots of learning that I wanted to pursue. I was overwhelmed, excited, feeling clueless, and, not surprisingly, still curious.

52
ENCOUNTER WITH
A DOG

AS THE FOREIGN SENSATION BEGAN TO MOVE UP THROUGH **my body**, I froze. What was happening? Should I be scared? What was this feeling? It was late summer 2018, and I was attending a workshop and trying the steps I had just been taught about how to connect with a loved one who has crossed over. Whatever this feeling that came over me was, it was not something I had ever experienced before.

I was at Lily Dale Assembly, commonly just referred to as Lily Dale, located in upstate New York. This was a place that, up until a month or so ago, I had not heard of. Lily Dale, I came to know, is a place where, among other things, those interested in learning or enhancing their abilities to connect with those in Spirit through mediumship can take classes.

I was sitting in a room with about 25 other workshop participants. The instructor was Winter Brook Ryan, the same woman with whom I had experienced my first encounter with the world of Spirits some five months prior — and the person who had done my spiritual assessment. I had not knowingly signed up for the workshop. I was there because I was helping someone who wanted to attend this workshop and, due to significant health issues, needed assistance while traveling. She had signed me up for the same events she would be attending. Once I was in the room and learned that this session focused on developing one's mediumship abilities, I became nervous. I wasn't planning to do this and, given the choice, I would probably not have.

Winter began by going over some concepts and then we were paired up for some exercises. I was paired with a lovely woman whom I believed to be in her seventies. I needed her to know that — other than the one occasion when I felt love surrounding a woman — I had no experience with mediumship, had not signed up for this workshop, and I was quite clueless about the entire subject. When she explained that she did not have much experience either, I was relieved and able to relax a little.

Before we could begin the exercise, we would need to connect with the Spirit world, and Winter explained that we should take a deep breath to calm ourselves first. We then focused on our feet and were to imagine roots growing out of the bottom of them into the ground and way down deep into the earth. Then, we would breathe up the energy from the earth, imagining it was passing up through our body, and connect, energetically, with the person sitting in front of us. We then were asked to open our hearts and invite the realm of Spirit to join us. It sounded like an easy enough process but, as I was trying to remember the steps and execute them, Winter was already beginning the exercise, and I missed half the instruction. I looked up at my partner, and she looked as lost as I felt.

I said to my partner, "I can't concentrate on doing the steps and keep up with her." She nodded in agreement.

I asked, "Would it be alright if I just ignored what Winter is saying and just see if I can connect and get anything?"

"Sure," she said.

I stood there in front of her and worked to tune her and the rest of the room out. I went back through the steps in my mind and began to carry them out. As I drew in my breath, imagining the energy from the earth coming up through the imaginary roots I had extended, this is when I began to feel the sensation. It was like nothing I had experienced before and, disappointingly, have not experienced since. It made its way up through my feet, feeling like a vibration of energy. It did not envelope my body. Feeling like a very thin flat plane of vibrating energy, it slowly began rising through the soles of my feet to my ankles, shins, knees and then continuing upwards.

It was an intense feeling, but not uncomfortable at all. My first instinct was to be afraid, but that was fleeting. A sense of calm and peace overcame me as it continued to move up my body. It stopped when it got to where I have always imagined the top of my heart is and, as it did, I put both of my hands over that spot. My mouth dropped open, and, all the while smiling and with a feeling of euphoria, I tried to explain to my partner what had just happened.

* * *

I DID KNOW THAT THIS WORK WAS ALL ABOUT ENERGY. I DID not recognize or understand that this energy was something that I would feel within my body. The feeling did not go away, but it became less intense after just a few moments. I was not sure what to make of it all, but I decided to just continue to see if there was anything that I could 'get' from Spirit for my partner.

It was then that a thought of the word April came into my consciousness. Not knowing where that information had come from, but somehow understanding it as the month of April, I said it out loud.

"April ..." I spoke.

She smiled and said, "My daughter's birthday is in April."

Wow! I thought. Had I just given her a piece of information that was correct?! In the next moment, I was saddened as I realized this meant that her daughter had passed away. As I am sure my face still conveyed happiness at having gotten this bit of information correct, I quickly gathered myself and said, "I am so sorry for your loss."

She responded, saying, "No, my daughter didn't pass. She's still here." Now I was confused and disappointed. I felt immediately defeated and told the woman she should take a turn. While she was practicing how to connect, I became focused on something else that I had seen at the time the month of April came to me. I hadn't told her about it, as once I knew her daughter had not passed away, it didn't seem relevant, but now I felt the need to tell her.

Once she had completed her turn, I said, "I am sure that this is nothing, but I saw a picture that I would like to describe to you to see if it means anything to you."

"Great. Yes, please," she replied enthusiastically, and so I began.

Holding out my hand to indicate the location I was talking about, I told her, "In my mind, on the right side of my body below my direct line of sight, I see a photograph. It has a white border and looks to be 3 inches by 3 inches. It looks older, and the photo is either black and white or is a colored photo that has significantly faded. In the picture, there is a girl, and she is maybe six or seven years old. She has hair down to her shoulders, and it is either a light brown or possibly blonde. It is parted in the middle. It is not straight, nor is it curly. It has some waviness to it. The girl is carrying an animal, and it looks to be a cat based on the coloring."

I then asked the woman, "Did you have a cat when your daughter was young?"

"No," she said.

My brain immediately came in again to say, See? You don't know what you're doing. Thankfully, I decided I was already halfway through so I would just continue. I looked back at the woman and said to her, "Well, I am saying it is a cat as the animal has longer hair that appears to be a little wiry, and it looks to be orange and white, so I was thinking it was a tabby cat." Again, the woman shook her head no. Pressing on, I said, "In any event, the girl is holding this animal under the front paws. The front paws are sticking up by her face and the rest of the body is just dangling in front of her. Have you seen something like that?" I asked, "When young children pick up an animal to hug it and then walk with them?"

"Oh, yes," she responded.

"So," I said, concluding my description, "that is what I saw."

The woman then said something I didn't expect. She said, "What you described is my daughter when she was a child. And it wasn't a cat you were describing; it was our dog. My daughter and that dog were inseparable. In fact," she continued, "she carried it around in a backpack at times."

This is amazing, I thought. I knew, however, that I didn't get it right because her daughter is still living. I was confused and felt like I failed in grasping the exercise. It was confirmation to me, of course, that I did not have this gift. When we brought our attention back to the rest of the group, Winter was announcing that we were going to be switching partners and there would be additional exercises. At that moment, I knew that was something I could not do. This all felt like too much. Thankfully, I was put in the one group that had three people. I really couldn't continue and was glad to make an easy exit without disrupting others.

As I headed to the door, I said to Winter, "I'm just going to step out." I never did go back. Between all of the new jargon, the experience with the energetic vibration through my body, seeing a picture in my brain, and then the woman telling me that it was her daughter and her dog, I was done. I felt like my energy had been zapped. I walked away confused and as expected, still curious.

* * *

TIME, FORTUNATELY, ALLOWS FOR REFLECTION AND understanding. After beating myself up about not being able to connect on a spiritual level with someone from the other side, I discovered that I had been successful. As a professional in the field pointed out, I had connected with someone. I had connected with the dog that was in Spirit and the dog had provided information that the woman recognized. I had provided the description, which resonated with her, and even a bit of the personality of the dog, which was allowing itself to be carried around in such a manner. Well, I'll be darned. One *could* talk to animals. I was truly amazed.

2018 was certainly providing me with much insight into the beautiful world of Spirit. Knowing that there is a world beyond the physical, brought me additional healing, much comfort and, something I had been searching for, a sense of true connection to life.

53
DECIDING

I AWOKE ON JANUARY 1, 2019, KNOWING THAT THE TIME HAD come for me to consider what I would do for work and where I would live going forward. I was excited to answer these questions, and it only took a few minutes to confirm for myself that I was enjoying the work and the flexibility of the Human Resources consulting that I was doing — and that I had no desire, ever again, to work for an employer. Now that I knew I was going to continue with the consulting, there was no reason for me to stay in New York as I could do that work from anywhere, and I was more than willing to travel to a client's location if needed. Now, for the fun part, it was time to decide where I wanted to move to.

In mid-January, I took a trip to the Virginia Beach area with my best friend Colleen. We were going to run a 5k race called the Freezer Burn, hang out together, as well as visit some houses that she was interested in seeing. She was also going to be moving and had been looking in this particular area for a while. After the run, we took a drive to explore different areas and stopped in to see a few houses she had found online and thought she might like. It was during our drive that I told her of my decision to also move out of New York. She was excited for me, suggested that I use Zillow to look for houses, and, of course, that I consider living in this area so we could be close together.

This last suggestion made me realize that while I knew I wanted to live on the East Coast. I also knew that I wanted to be close to or, better yet, *in* the mountains. I had always been drawn to them. The peace and serenity I found when visiting mountainous terrain always lingered long after I returned to my house in the heavily populated suburbs of Long Island and to my jobs in New York City. In addition to the necessity of mountains nearby, I also knew I wanted to be someplace south of New York and its surrounding states, but no further south than South Carolina. I had previously explored the possibility of moving to Georgia to be near my good friends, the beautiful Batcher family, but it didn't feel right.

As we continued to drive around, I pulled up a map of the East Coast on my phone and looked at it. I was immediately drawn to the Roanoke/Lynchburg, Virginia area, and I knew that this area was a possibility even though I didn't know the area at all and had only passed through on a couple of occasions.

I had once stayed overnight at a beautiful old place in downtown Roanoke and, on several occasions, stayed at a chain hotel just off the highway in Lynchburg. While the hotel was in a commercial area, the image that immediately popped into my mind was a beautiful grouping of trees across the street sitting back a bit from the highway. They were so beautiful that they caught my attention each time I stayed, and the image of them is etched in my mind. I knew I didn't want to live any further north than there, so I set about choosing a point as far south as I might be interested in living to begin to narrow my search area.

Knowing that I wanted to live near the mountains indicated by green coloring on the map, I followed the green on the map down from Roanoke/Lynchburg and came to Asheville, North Carolina. I also did not know anything about this area other than an overnight stop on a road trip. It seemed like a beautiful area. I had eaten fabulous barbeque ribs for dinner the night I stayed and was greeted by deer along the Blue Ridge Parkway the next morning as I continued my scenic drive back to New

York. That was it. I was set and it was that quick. I was going to live somewhere between Roanoke, Virginia, and Asheville, North Carolina.

Now that I knew this, I downloaded Zillow and began looking at houses. Over the next few weeks, I worked on Zillow. It was easy to use, but I quickly became lost as to where I was on the map as I just kept clicking on the blue dots that indicated a house for sale. I found a house that I liked, with its log cabin feel and open floor plan. What I didn't like about it was that the property was very small, and there was another house pretty close by. I decided to see if there were others in that same area that were similar, so I continued to click on the nearby blue dots. When I found another house that I liked, I tapped on the narrative description to get an understanding of what the house offered — and I loved what I read. Instead of talking about the house, it contained information about what was described as the quaint downtown area with friendly merchants. It also mentioned many places nearby to hike and a large music performance center that attracted top talent. Sounds great, but where was I? I had started looking in the Roanoke area but had expanded beyond the city limits at some point and had just been clicking on blue dots. I zoomed out and was quite surprised when I saw where I was. I wasn't near Roanoke at all. I was in an area a good hour south of Asheville.

This wasn't in my target zone, but I was so hooked by the description that I felt compelled to look into this town a bit more. It was Brevard, North Carolina, and it was located in a county called Transylvania, which, I came to learn, is known as the land of waterfalls. My quick research told me that it might be the perfect area. Great for young, old, couples, and singles. Right at the mountains, near the Blue Ridge Parkway, it had a downtown area, and was similar in size to the small town I lived in on Long Island for about eighteen years. This, I decided, would be where I started my search.

* * *

I CONNECTED WITH A CLOSE FRIEND OF MINE, FRANK MEARS, who had been in real estate for years. I had known Frank for many years, having worked for him after I got out of the Marine Corps when I was living in Irvine, California with John, before we moved back to New York and got married. While Frank lives in Augusta, Georgia, he knows lots of people, and I knew he could find me the right agent to assist me in the area that interested me. Within three weeks of choosing to move and two weeks of deciding on the area I wanted to explore, Frank introduced me to a top local agent from Brevard.

When I spoke with Nancy Witek of Beverly-Hanks Realtors, we immediately connected. Nancy is a beautiful soul with a great laugh, easy style, and an over-abundance of knowledge and experience in her field. Nancy and I decided to work together and scheduled the first weekend of March for me to come down to see Brevard and the surrounding areas with her as well as to see several houses. I called it my 'just looking' trip. As I wanted to be sure she understood what I was looking for, after the call, I sat down and created a document that she could use to prepare for our time together. I titled the document 'The Big Move for Love, Joy, and Adventure' and listed all that was important to me in my next home.

1. **House – Want**
   Log cabin / log cabin feel / cozy / country-ish feel
   Not an ordinary house
   View of mountains or lake
   2 bedrooms or 3 - they do not have to be too big
   1.5 or 2 bathrooms
   Office space or ability to take loft and make an office
   Porch – wrap-around or more than one side
   Sunset or sunrise view
   Do not want fixer-upper
   Master suite with a view of something and, perhaps a door to a porch
   Near mountains
   Not a huge house but room for guests
   Bright open layout on main floor
   Garage
   Kitchen just needs to be functional
2. **Location Must Have's**
   Fireplace is a must
   Hiking nearby
   Culture nearby
   Reasonably quick onto highway
   1 hour or less to an airport (international)
   20 – 25 minutes from shopping area
   Land / acreage around house
3. **Areas to consider**
   A few hours' drive to Simpsonville and Acworth GA
   Along the mountains
   If my house were in or near the "green" forest area on a map I would be happy

It was rainy and cold the day I found my new home. Almost from the moment I arrived on the property, my heart and soul knew it was where I was meant to be. It was my first day out with Nancy, and while I was just looking, the Universe had a different plan — and I am eternally grateful for that. I was literally only three steps inside the front door when I said to Nancy, "Wow, this place feels like a home." This was followed, only three steps later, by my heart saying, "Yes, this is *your* home." This feeling only strengthened as we toured the rest of the home and property. While I felt obligated to look at the additional houses Nancy had scheduled us to see, after doing a bit of due diligence, I put in an offer on the home that I would come to call The Haven.

It is not surprising that my new home fits virtually all of the criteria on my list. What it does not have, however, were some of the must-haves I had listed. While there is a big stone fireplace and I couldn't get any closer to the mountains as I would be living in them, the house is situated three hours from an international airport and the closest highway is just over an hour away. As a very wise friend told me, and I concur, those things turned out to be artifacts from my past and things I no longer need.

As if I didn't already know that I was supposed to be at The Haven, the house number is 117. From a spiritual perspective, I love this number as it signifies manifesting good things, that the angels are watching, and it reminds us to be grateful to the Universe for all the blessings we have. From a personal perspective, it connects me to my father, whose favorite time of the day was 7:11. All of this was additional confirmation and I know that my dad and the rest of the Universe have been hard at work.

54
MIGHTY HEIDI

I closed on The Haven in April of 2019, and I set my official move date out of New York toward the end of May. I was ahead of schedule on all that needed to be done to be ready for my move and was thankful that I was able to spend most of the month with good friends. One of those, Noreen, my precious friend with whom I went through Breakthrough, took a trip to the east end of Long Island with me. We spent the day laughing, eating, walking, and even being kids as we rode an old carousel. We also talked about attending the program, and she reminded me that it had been five years ago this very month that we had done so. I couldn't believe it had been that long and, in our reminiscing, I was reminded of the exercise where we had to write a letter to ourselves from five years in the future. Knowing how impactful the program and that particular exercise were for me, I decided that I would revisit the letter and write myself another one, all the while thinking how perfect the timing to do this was just as I was heading off to The Haven.

Dear Heidi,

It is five years ago now. I cannot believe how time has flown since then. Well, in a way it feels like it has flown, but, reflecting, it has gone at a moderate tempo, which has allowed you the time to absorb what you learned and to incorporate it into your now peaceful life. I recall vividly the moment you realized that you were in a place that you could not get yourself out of. You remember I am sure, that moment. It felt like you were in a black hole that was blacker and deeper than you could have ever imagined. How shocking to you that you were there given all the work you had done over the prior two years to address issues both within yourself and with other people in your life. How had it happened that you fell deeper into a place you were actively trying to get out of?

How proud I am of you for asking for help at that time. I know it took a great deal of courage to do so. I thought I would never understand from where that courage came but, as you are coming to learn, we all have a team of angels, guides, and loved ones working behind the scenes to help us and it is due to their support, guidance, love, and encouragement that you found what you needed at the time you needed it.

Asking for more help when you were already seeing My Guy was a tough one for you, I know, but I must tell you that the dialogue between the two of you during that extremely dark time, was inspiring. You were finally fully open about what was working and what was not working for you. Such urgency was put on the need to get you out of the blackness once and for all. While the decision to attend a program was delayed due to dad's cancer diagnosis and your desire to only focus on him, the chosen solution, after all that discussion and research, was life-changing for you.

While you found the resolve to ask for help and then find what you thought could be a solution, I wish you had been a bit braver to not have waited those many months before actually attending. I know you had your reasons for the delay, and, in the end, although I had doubts that you would, you did follow through and attend. Fear, while never fully addressed as one of the reasons, was the biggest factor for your delay. Please know how thrilled I was when your Breakthrough experience brought this to light, and you came to understand what a huge factor this had been in your life and how negatively impactful it was for your well-being.

Boy was that program intense; especially for you being an introverted person. Never a moment to breathe and always with others. Those days were filled with so many exercises, so many tears, and so much self-discovery and healing.

This is the fifth anniversary of your completing the program and while I realize that you are starting to turn your focus to your new life in North Carolina, I wanted to suggest that you take the time to review the letter you wrote during Breakthrough, the letter you wrote to yourself from five years in the future.

With Love and Gratitude – Me

$$* \quad * \quad *$$

Dear Me
   Well, thank you for that suggestion! How uplifting to refocus on that letter. It was like a peek back into that time and a reminder of where I was and what I wanted for myself. What is amazing is that that letter, almost exactly five years since the day I wrote it, was spot on. Virtually every bit of advice and the insights that I provided to myself have been fulfilled. Think about it. Fear is still on its never-ending vacation. I rarely frown and the thought of the weights holding that frown down for so many years is a foreign idea now. Sitting in the happy chair was new back then, but it is worn-in now, and I know I will never get rid of it. My relationships are now what I envisioned them being back then. It certainly was not easy to transform myself. Decisions to leave some people and some of my own behaviors back in my old ways were difficult, but it has gotten me to where I am now. As for work, that has been completely transformed, and I could never have imagined how great things could or would be. My Inner Critic does take long breaks, and while he still shows up periodically, his visits, thankfully, last for only brief periods. For his benefit, and mine, please continue to focus here and I am sure you will find a way to put him on the same never-ending vacation you put Fear on. I did as you suggested and focused a good deal of time on values and feelings, and it is amazing how helpful that has been to define me and the environment I wish to have along with what is not acceptable.
   As for the visual reminders of serenity, kudos for how I handled these. As they never did serve the purpose, they were intended to, great job gifting that lovely sign to a good friend as she embarked on her marriage with her long-time partner. They love it, and it looks and feels right in their backyard. As for the email address, a nice touch to just let that address go and establish a new one. Funny how I thought that having serenity in my email address would somehow make it so.

Such silliness I focused on then that I now know was not ever going to work.

Heidi, me, myself, and I want to take the time to thank you for being you. Thank you for putting us in the sunshine of life. You are now and will always be ... Mighty Heidi.

55
THE HAVEN

I PULLED INTO THE HAVEN AFTER A LONG SEVENTEEN-HOUR drive down from New York. I was too excited to stop for the night. I was home. The area where I would now live is quite different from the suburban area on Long Island, where I spent forty-seven of my first fifty-three years of life, and worlds different from New York City, where I worked for over sixteen years.

Now that I have arrived, my small town has 1,117 inhabitants, and, no, I am not making this number up. The day before I made an offer on the house, I looked up the population, and it was 1,116. As the current owners are staying in the same town and just moving to a larger house, it means that I add one to the population and, there I am, looking at my father's number yet again. Just an additional confirmation that I am where I was supposed to be.

I have always loved nature, especially the mountains. I love the smell of the trees. I love the crisp air. I love the gentleness of the wind through the leaves on the trees and I love the serenity of being away from the bustling world. I love the energy that I feel just being outside. I love how I feel renewed after spending time in nature.

* * *

I LIVE IN A NATIONAL FOREST. I AM SURROUNDED BY WILDLIFE and nature, and, as I have come to say, I live in the backyard of nature's home. With virtually all of the roads in my community only traveled by those who live here, it is quiet and serene with just the calming sounds of nature to keep you company. The lush, thick forest creates a natural buffer that dulls any human-generated sounds from my distant neighbors.

As I pull into my driveway, the only visible house across the street quickly disappears as I make my way down a somewhat steep incline that turns from blacktop to gravel about halfway down, lending to the rustic and natural feel of the property. There is a forty-five-degree turn to the left as the drive flattens out, and the thick forest, which makes up the front yard, envelopes me, hiding me and the house from view.

The Haven sits before me, and the wooden front porch is immediately calling me to come up and take a seat. A few wide wooden stairs lead up to the porch, which spans across half of the house and is adorned on either side by windows — one of which provides a glimpse of the hand-made wooden rails and banisters, the open floor plan on the main level, and the tall stone fireplace within. An oversized metal roof, which shields me from the rain, sun, and snow, is held up by four large wooden beams lined up across the front. There are similar beams that adorn the open ceiling. The wooden Adirondack style chairs, with a slight recline to the back and a seat lower to the ground than most, provide the perfect place to breathe and meditate to the sounds of nature.

 On the upper deck out back, there are two more Adirondack chairs but, unlike those on the front porch, they sit up much higher. I practically have to climb up to get into them. I call these my star-gazing chairs. At night, the view of the sky and the stars is magnificent, and these chairs provide a place for me to tilt my head back, take in the wonder above, and contemplate the worlds that exist within and beyond ours — all while being serenaded by katydids and small tree frogs, which loudly fill the night sky with their beautiful sounds. From the lower deck, which spans the entire length of the back of the house, I watch the beautiful sunrise come up over the mountain ridge.

The open area at the back of the house, that one might call a lawn, is mostly moss with tufts of thick green grass scattered about. In the spring, large areas are carpeted with small yellow flowers, which bloom above the shamrock plants' green leaves and the splendid blue, almost purple, wildflowers. It has a soft almost bouncy feel as I walk across it towards the creek, which runs the entire length of the backyard. While it is typically eight feet wide and ranges in places from eight to eighteen inches deep, a large rain can cause it to swell to a width of twenty feet and a depth of up to three feet. Making its way down from the local mountain, the water is clear and cool. Dragonflies dance along the top, and small fish and frogs inhabit the water itself. The creek is also home to a pair of beavers, and they build dams that, amazingly, virtually stop the water flow. Nature is wonderous.

There is an abundance and a great variety of tall trees surrounding my home, including oaks, white pines, and hemlocks, with some soaring above the house upwards of one hundred feet. There are wild rhododendrons, which grow almost fifteen feet high and sprawl outwards about ten feet, and they are filled with clusters of the most glorious soft purple flowers in the spring. Closer to the ground, the forest floor is filled with dog hobble, ferns, trillium flowers, and many other vines and plants. There are also beautiful tree stumps, softened over time, that grace the property and, those of us that are aware know these are home to the magical world of fairies and gnomes.

* * *

BEING IN AND SURROUNDED BY NATURE I WAS COMING TO KNOW was a spiritual experience itself, and I found myself still curious about the world of Spirit. On April 3, 2020, almost a year after my move to North Carolina, I had my next experience connecting with Spirit. This was the day that I began actively working on developing my mediumship and psychic abilities. It was just a few months later when I connected with my second animal — and this one was alive and still here on the earth plane. The experience, again, came courtesy of Winter Brook Ryan.

I was interested in connecting with one of my pets as they had some serious health issues, so I reached out to Winter for a bit of one-on-one mentorship. After she provided some instruction on how to communicate with a live animal, she had me jump right in and conduct an animal reading on one of her cats. Oh boy, I thought, as she held up her cat.

I connected with him immediately and began the communication. He showed me how he lays on the floor with all of his legs out to the side and that he likes to lay in the sun. We also talked about his favorite toy, which turned out not to be a toy at all, but his cat sibling. He showed me that, unlike my cats who use their carpeted perch for sleeping, they like to play on theirs. It was a surreal experience — especially when I asked the cat what she thought about the dog that also lives in their house. Magic, a large dog, is a Great Pyrenees. I laughed out loud when the cat answered, and I continued to giggle when I conveyed to Winter the answer, which was, "He thinks he's in charge because he's so big, but he's not." So fun and, just like the other experience, absolutely mind-blowing.

I am now building my spiritual business and focus my mediumship and psychic work not just on people but also on communicating with animals, those that are still here as well as those that are in Spirit. Such a privilege and a blessing to do this work.

* * *

As for animals, there is no shortage of them at The Haven. The wildlife that inhabits the property and surrounding forest include rabbits, chipmunks, flying squirrels, and birds of all varieties, including cardinals, blue jays, mourning doves, and hummingbirds. I watch them all in contented awe. One afternoon from up on the deck, I had the joy of watching a momma bear and her two cubs wander through the yard, stopping to eat the flowers off the azalea bush and sniff at the garbage can in hopes that there was something in it for them.

I have watched in amazement as the little fish in the creek took small pebbles into their mouths and dropped them in a central place to form a circular mound, which the females then used as a place to lay their eggs. The eggs, disappearing in between the small pebbles, were now hidden out of reach of hungry predators. Seeing a turtle digging in my backyard with its back legs one day, my curiosity was so piqued that I sat there enraptured for several hours. What a beautiful reward at the end when I just knew that she had laid her eggs as she covered up the deep hole and made her way back down to the creek.

As it gets almost ninety inches of rain each year, the forest I live in is considered a rain forest. I just love the rain and also love that it comes straight down and makes the most beautiful music as it hits the leaves of the trees and disrupts the surface of the creek. The smell of the air during and just after a rain is clean and fresh with a hint of soil. I love the time after a rain when, except for the rain dripping gently from the leaves of the trees onto the ground or the metal roof of the house, it is almost silent. This silence only lasts a brief moment before it is so beautifully interrupted by the birds beginning to sing again, but I find that time so peaceful. It is like the pause in between breaths, the time that most people do not even recognize or consider.

* * *

The animals and nature just outside have added so much to my life that it is not surprising that I have been slowly filling the inside with animals as well. Jennie, my oldest cat, has been with me since March 2013, and she has always made me feel loved. She has been through it all with me since then, including my moves. She has adjusted well each time, always seeming to find the good in the location change. One apartment offered a balcony where she could spend hours napping in a chair, while in another she was able to bask in the sunlight that shone in the window at dawn.

By the end of 2019, about seven months after our move, Lexi joined the family courtesy of my niece Lenore, who was visiting me and thought we should stop into the local cat café to just have a look. Peeps, as I have come to call Lexi due to her talkative nature, drew me in right away. Peeps was young at the time, maybe ten months, the rescue said, and, unlike Jennie, comes and lays on me in the quiet of the evening as I read or watch TV.

While it wasn't part of any plan, Harp arrived at the end of April, just four months later. I simply fell in love with him when Lenore, who was fostering him, put his picture on Facebook. A senior Brittany of thirteen years, he was recovering from recent surgery and also had a litany of health issues. Given all this and the fact that I had not had a dog since I was fourteen, some forty years prior, I understood why my niece cautioned me about the adoption, but I also knew he needed to come home. The day I met Harp, I promised him that every day would be a good dog day. What I didn't understand then was just how good my days would be with him. Harp was with me for eight months and five days before he ran over that rainbow bridge to play in the beautiful meadow where all dogs eventually go. It was never going to be long enough, but I would not trade one moment of any of my time with him.

Harp's passing was devastating and, while it took a few months, I knew I wanted to adopt another dog. I wanted a rescue who was at least eight years old that could hike with me and wouldn't mind spending all or part of the day sleeping on those days when I was working. Mr. Marty Funkman, named by Jordan and Patrick, his beautiful and loving foster parents, joined me in April 2021. Marty was found on the streets and thought to be around ten-years-old. He is the sweetest dog who wags his tail virtually every moment of the day. His only want is to be near his human, and I am happy that the life I have built for myself allows for that to be the case virtually every moment of every day. My home is filled with more love and joy than I could have ever imagined.

Living with my beautiful animals in the mountains, immersed in nature, is quite different from what and how I have lived previously. While so significantly different, my transition to this new location and way of life was effortless. It took me many years to prepare for this part of my journey, with most of those years filled with anger, sadness, loneliness, distrust, chaos, fear, negativity, despair, and no hope of anything changing. All of that did, thankfully, change. I changed. It was hard-fought and hard-won, as they say, as the change in me did not come easy. All that matters, though, is that I have changed.

I certainly did not get here all on my own, and I am grateful for each person who has helped me along the way. I am in a different place or, maybe more accurately put, I live my life from a different place or perspective. While I am the same, I am different now. It is the different that I needed me to be and has much to do with why I named my home The Haven. By definition, a haven is a place offering favorable conditions or opportunities — and that is just what the Universe had in store for me when it led me to this serene and energetic place to continue on in my journey, and to finalize my transition from a broken, sad, and lonely existence to the new human I know I have become.

I now live in a place of peace. This is the peace that I was so desperately looking for when I arrived in the office of My Guy in September of 2010. I know now that this peace, *my peace*, was within me all the time. I just needed to find the courage to uncover it and to also recognize that I was worthy of having such a life.

...... **My Journey Continues**

AFTERWORD

The healing and other gifts that I received by completing this book are larger and more complex than I ever could have imagined.

One gift I received was through the actual process of writing the individual stories then weaving them together. These actions allowed me to see people, situations, and memories with an insight that I had not previously realized or focused on. I was also able to step back from these same things to see the interconnectedness and how my life, over time and through experiences and circumstances, came to be what it is.

So many things may stand in the way of us living a kind, peaceful, and more joyful life. Feelings such as pain, anger, guilt, worthlessness, shame, and remorse can hold us back while impacting our own actions as well as the actions of others. We carry negative and destructive thoughts and perceptions forward from the past, and they weigh us down, affecting who we are and how we act. We must recognize this, then find a way to overcome them to truly leave them where they belong ... in the past. We can only live differently when we find a way to accept, forgive, and move on and beyond those things that do not allow us to be the best version of ourselves.

The process of publishing this book has also brought me forgiveness and closure. I arrived at a place of compassion by understanding that my story is filled with imperfect humans, myself included, who did the best that we could in any given moment, beginning in childhood, through our relationships and experiences.

This journey has enabled me to see a much clearer picture of my life, allowing me to piece some bits of the puzzle together, some very loosely, while discovering details I hadn't even known existed. This has brought a deeper and more profound sense of awareness and context regarding my life and experiences.

Take my father, for instance. He did many things that simply baffled me that I can't justify or explain. Through my writing, I was able to see how our relationship developed over time and how it was that I loved him so dearly. My father was an only child and didn't have any cousins. Perhaps these two facts alone impacted him and how he behaved with my brothers and me, as he had no direct experiences from his childhood to show him how to interact. Perhaps, it is also possible that his parents didn't show him how a loving family could or should act. My father's father was physically unavailable to him. He spent twelve hours each day at work and then another four hours each evening isolating himself in the attic monitoring his ham radio. From here, it is not a stretch to think that my grandfather was also emotionally unavailable to my father. If we accept this, then we must also accept that he was unavailable to his wife, which may have, in turn, impacted how she interacted with my father. Perhaps this was part of the undercurrent of their relationship that made it acceptable for my father to have a falling out with her just before I was born, then never speak with her again. These facts and possibilities from my father's childhood may have also impacted how he treated his wives and children. Perhaps my dad did the best that he knew how based on his own experience.

As for my mother, I don't know much about her, but I have been told she was an alcoholic. While my mother was an alcoholic, I have heard that *her* mother was a raging alcoholic. Perhaps this insight, coupled with the loss of her father just a year before her marriage, provides some understanding of why my mother behaved the way she did. I also imagine that her behavior was impacted by the fact that she moved seven hours away from her small hometown and all of her family when she married my father. She then, within three years, gave birth to four children. Perhaps, like my father, she did the best that she knew how.

I have yet to fully comprehend all I have gained from and by this experience but do know that my new vantage point has helped me reconcile a number of things and obtain much-needed healing. Healing from the wounds inflicted upon me by others, those that have been self-inflicted, and, much to my regret, those I have inflicted upon others. I ask forgiveness and understanding for the things that I have done or said that have hurt or negatively impacted others. I always tried to do the best that I knew how. I am thankful that I now know much better.

JOIN THE
CONVERSATION

Thank you for taking the time to read my story. Have you gained something from what you read? Has it helped you to sort through your own life and view it, or certain circumstances, differently? Do you have insights to share with others about how this book has helped you live your life more positively and peacefully?

For the benefit of others still searching for their peace, I invite you to share your own experiences and your inspiring progress on how you found peace by joining the conversation on Instagram using the hashtag #findingmypeace and tagging @findingmypeacebook.

* * *

Follow *Finding My Peace* on Instagram
@findingmypeacebook

JOIN THE CONVERSATION

"When you feel a peaceful joy, that's when you are near truth."

—— *Rumi*

ABOUT THE AUTHOR

Heidi Hayden joined the military right out of high school and served four years in the U.S. Marine Corps. She then began a career in human resources and spent more than thirty years working for various organizations in that field. She loved the work and successfully held top executive positions at Nikon, two prominent New York City-based law firms, and the National September 11 Memorial & Museum. Heidi spent fifteen years teaching human resources and also taught leadership and business courses at the graduate level as an adjunct professor.

In 2017, unexpectedly, Heidi found herself successfully self-employed as a human resources consultant. During this time, through a growing curiosity, she began to awaken spiritually. Fully embracing this new journey, Heidi is now a professional psychic and medium (SpiritualWhisperingsbyHeidi.com). She also teaches mediumship, showing others how to access and use these gifts we all possess. Through this work, Heidi enjoys connecting with people, those here as well as those who have crossed over. She also has a unique passion for and a powerful gift for animal communication. Heidi also continues her human resources consulting work.

Heidi found the peace she was looking for and is now living a beautiful and calm life. Heidi enjoys hiking in the mountains of western North Carolina, where she lives surrounded by nature.

Made in United States
North Haven, CT
23 April 2022

18517348R00176